What people are saying about …

FINDING TRUTH

"Nancy Pearcey invites her readers to 'test everything,' as her journey of searching for answers (like my own) revealed that the deepest questions of the heart and mind do not go away and must be addressed. Whether religious or irreligious, everyone has a worldview. *Finding Truth* illustrates how competing systems of thought borrow from Christianity even while rejecting it and provides helpful tools to critically assess the coherency and livability of one's worldview. This is an immensely practical and insightful resource."

Ravi Zacharias, author and speaker

"Nancy Pearcey has done it again. She's written yet another important resource examining the importance of worldview presuppositions. I wish I'd had Nancy as part of my investigative team as a detective. She gets it; she understands how important our foundational beliefs are to any investigation. Principle #5, for example, describes my life as an atheist perfectly. If I'd read this book as a young man, I think I would have been challenged to re-examine my views much earlier. Nancy's work has been important to my growth as a Christian, and her latest book will help seekers understand the importance of worldview, even as it helps believers grow in their confidence."

J. Warner Wallace, author of *Cold-Case Christianity: A Homicide Detective Investigates the Claims of the Gospels*

"Nancy Pearcey intellectually dismantles humanism, atheism, reductionism, and every other ism that sets itself up against the knowledge of our Lord. The most glaring flaw of all the isms that Nancy addresses is that they offer no hope. Her arguments combined with the gospel of Jesus leave all other worldviews outside of Christianity without a leg to stand on."

Phil Robertson, *Duck Dynasty*

"Nancy Pearcey at her very best—totally profound, persuasive, and yet practical. Read it with your highlighter handy!"

Lee Strobel, *New York Times* bestselling author

"Wonderful book ... Secular worldviews have become the intellectual fast food of our day—nice taste, no nourishment. Nancy Pearcey shines a bright light on worldviews that compete with Christianity, and she tells us what is wrong with them—almost everything. They create false idols. They lead to despair, despotism, and absurdity. They rub out God and reduce man to a sack of proteins. They don't fit our experience of what it means to be a human being. Pearcey's book ought to be in the survival kit of every student heading to college. I wish I'd had it in 1962."

John R. Erickson, rancher, author of the Hank the Cowdog series

"This book is fantastic! We live in a culture beset by the twin dragons of modernism and postmodernism. Under the inspiration of Romans 1,

Nancy Pearcey draws a sword and cuts their heads off. I found the apologetics work top-notch, yet totally readable for everyman."

Doug TenNapel, author of *Tommysaurus Rex,* creator of *Earthworm Jim*

"Truly a great book.... For several decades, Nancy Pearcey has been to the church what Francis Schaeffer was to the believers of his day: a cultural intellectual who provides careful, thoughtful, well-researched critiques of and interactions with the various worldview ideologies competing with Christianity. *Finding Truth* may well be Pearcey's best offering to date. It is very clearly written and wide in its coverage. Aiming to aid Christians to think critically about the specific theories they encounter in Western culture, Pearcey surfaces five principles from Romans 1 that she uses to analyze various extant worldviews. My favorite principle was 'Identify the Idol's Reductionism.' Anyone who knows about contemporary worldviews will acknowledge that reductionism is at the very heart of Christianity's rivals. I highly recommend this delightful book and wish it widespread circulation."

J. P. Moreland, distinguished professor of philosophy at Biola University

"Nancy Pearcey has produced another winner. Here again we find what we have come to expect from her: readability, clear thought, a nose for remarkable quotations, a high regard for biblical authority, and a passion for Christian cultural engagement."

Albert M. Wolters, author of *Creation Regained*

"Pearcey has done it again. When a third of young people are leaving church because of intellectual doubts, Pearcey shows how biblical truth is more *convincing* than competing worldviews, and also more *appealing*. The gospel is the highest love for human beings. The gospel is the key that fits the lock of the universe."

Kelly Monroe Kullberg, author of *Finding God Beyond Harvard,* founder of The Veritas Forum, founder and president of The America Conservancy

"Nancy Pearcey shows us that apologetics can be profound *and* practical. She demonstrates that resistance to Christ traces to a single source, a cognitive idolatry that divinizes creation and absolutizes the works of the human mind. The result is a variety of reductionist schemes that falsify the facts, contradict themselves, and promote doublethink. Pearcey offers not only diagnosis but a cure: a fair, respectful, and *universally applicable* strategy to help unbelievers see the advantages of a biblical worldview. Everyone concerned about effective apologetics and evangelism should read this book."

Angus Menuge, PhD, president of the Evangelical Philosophical Society, professor of philosophy at Concordia University Wisconsin

"Nancy Pearcey is a wonderful philosophical guide for our students, so they can bring the Biblical message into the world rather than being captivated by the mental idols of the world. As she notes so well, our neighbors live on the basis of truths they learn from God's general revelation even if they totally deny God. Because of their conflict with God, people are incurably religious, even if they make a God-substitute from some dimension of God's good creation. This internal conflict of the unbelieving heart and mind provides the starting point for both a serious critique of non-Christian worldviews an open door for presenting the compelling power of Christian truth claims."

Thomas K. Johnson, senior advisor at the Theological Commission of the World Evangelical Alliance

"Professor Pearcey astutely applies the philosophical wisdom of Romans 1 in order to refute a variety of non-Christian philosophies and religions. For those seeking rational grounding for their Christian worldview, this book is a godsend."

Douglas Groothuis, professor of philosophy at Denver Seminary, author of *Christian Apologetics: A Comprehensive Case for Biblical Faith*

"This wonderfully insightful book helps readers avoid becoming 'intoxicated' with idols and false ideas. Readers of this work will be 'lion-tamers' of many ideas and *reductionism* is one of them. If hastiness and superficiality were chief maladies of the twentieth century, as Solzhenitsyn said, then perhaps *reductionism* is a chief one in the twenty-first. In this volume, people are duly warned about the devastatingly reductionistic consequences of idolatry. Intellectual teetotalers need not apply."

David K. Naugle, distinguished professor at Dallas Baptist University, author of *Worldview: The History of a Concept*

"Pearcey's book is a valuable tool in exposing the many idols that masquerade as truth. She gives readers the eyes to see non-Christian worldviews from within, demonstrating that their strongest defenders cannot live with the implications of the ideas they put forward—at least not without denying life as it is lived. Pearcey's vast intellect and her clear and cogent writing style make this book an invaluable decoder for the times in which we live."

Bill Wichterman, special assistant to the president under George W. Bush

"A fine book … Nancy Pearcey's book reminds us that worldviews are, at root, heart commitments; thus, false worldviews or philosophies of life are exercises in idolatry. Pearcey deftly exposes both the inconsistencies and the failures of a host of modern idols, and she astutely points us to the light and truth of Jesus Christ, 'in whom are hidden all the treasures of wisdom and knowledge.'"

Paul Copan, professor and Pledger Family Chair of philosophy and ethics at Palm Beach Atlantic University

"Wonderful … Nancy Pearcey has the unique ability of getting to the heart of things in the cultural conversation. Pearcey's penetrating critique of the worldview 'idols' of our age is chock-full of gems. Better, it equips us with an easy-to-follow game plan for assessing any worldview. This is one of those books that not only challenges the critics; it also gives a huge dose of confidence to the Christian who will catch himself walking away from its pages saying, 'Gosh, this stuff really *is* true.'"

Gregory Koukl, president of Stand to Reason, author of *Tactics: A Game Plan for Discussing Your Christian Convictions*, and *Relativism: Feet Firmly Planted in Mid-Air*

"Fantastic! ... Pearcey has done it again. *Finding Truth* is one of the most insightful apologetics books I have read in a while. It provides a sharp critique of secular culture and a helpful guide for correcting it."

Sean McDowell, author, speaker, and assistant professor of Christian apologetics at Biola University

"As Pearcey (author of the 2005 classic *Total Truth*) so ably points out, both explicitly and through poignant real-life stories, 'finding truth' is not a dry intellectual exercise.... [She] leads the reader step-by-step through these principles in an accessible way ... providing concrete examples.... This book would make a fantastic graduation gift for high school seniors, especially those on their way to college ... I hope that Christians might pass on copies of *Finding Truth* to non-Christians, who might find Pearcey's analysis of secular worldviews convincing and her presentation of Christianity appealing."

Richard Weikart, *Christianity Today*

"Scholarly, but fully accessible.... Pearcey surveys the various idols upon which the various schools of modernism and postmodernism have built their systems: reason, imagination, economics, matter.... Just as Paul warns that those who serve idols will exchange the glory of the immortal God for the images of animals, so Pearcey warns that worldviews that begin with a false starting point inevitably end up reducing man from a free individual made in God's image to a determined and dehumanized unit in nature.... A full, carefully-nuanced exposé of the bankrupt, dead-end nature of materialism.... A splendid coup d'état."

Hope's Reason: A Journal of Apologetics

"In *Finding Truth*, Pearcey provides her readers another great tool for evaluating competing worldviews.... Sure to facilitate powerful discussion, the study questions at the end will develop critical thinking skills ... Pearcey's wonderfully readable style makes it a resource for anyone serious about discovering truth ... Stories ... make the book fascinating and real."

Marilyn Stewart, Defendmag.com

"Pearcey promises that the principles she lays out will 'provide you with the tools to recognize what's right and [what's] wrong with any worldview—and then to craft a biblically informed perspective that is both true and humane.' She makes the promise and she delivers on it. *Finding Truth* is, all-in-all, a worthy successor to *Total Truth*."

Challies.com

FINDING TRUTH

5 PRINCIPLES *for* UNMASKING ATHEISM, SECULARISM, *and* OTHER GOD SUBSTITUTES

NANCY PEARCEY

transforming lives together

FINDING TRUTH
Published by David C Cook
4050 Lee Vance Drive
Colorado Springs, CO 80918 U.S.A.

Integrity Music Limited, a Division of David C Cook
Brighton, East Sussex BN1 2RE, England

The graphic circle C logo is a registered trademark of David C Cook.

All rights reserved. Except for brief excerpts for review purposes,
no part of this book may be reproduced or used in any form
without written permission from the publisher.

The website addresses recommended throughout this book are offered as a resource to you. These websites are not intended in any way to be or imply an endorsement on the part of David C Cook, nor do we vouch for their content.

Unless otherwise noted, all Scripture quotations are taken from The Holy Bible, English Standard Version® (ESV®), copyright © 2001 by Crossway, a publishing ministry of Good News Publishers. Used by permission. All rights reserved. Scripture quotations marked KJV are taken from the King James Version of the Bible. (Public Domain); NIV are taken from the Holy Bible, New International Version®, NIV®. Copyright © 1973, 2011 by Biblica, Inc.™ Used by permission of Zondervan. All rights reserved worldwide. www.zondervan.com; and NLT are taken from the *Holy Bible*, New Living Translation, copyright © 1996, 2007 by Tyndale House Foundation. Used by permission of Tyndale House Publishers, Inc., Carol Stream, Illinois 60188. All rights reserved.
The author has added italics to Scripture quotations for emphasis.

Library of Congress Control Number 2014957657
ISBN 978-0-7814-1308-4
eISBN 978-0-7814-1328-2

© 2015 Nancy Pearcey

The Team: Tim Peterson, Carly Razo, Amy Konyndyk,
Jack Campbell, Helen Macdonald, Karen Athen
Cover Design: Nick Lee
Cover Images: *Poppy Field* © Corbis; Lionel Pincus and Princess
Firyal Map Division, New York Public Library (map)

Printed in the United States of America
First Edition 2015

5 6 7 8 9 10 11 12 13 14

CONTENTS

FOREWORD by J. Richard Pearcey   13

PART ONE
   "I Lost My Faith at an Evangelical College"   21

PART TWO
   PRINCIPLE #1—Twilight of the Gods   55
   PRINCIPLE #2—How Nietzsche Wins   93
   PRINCIPLE #3—Secular Leaps of Faith   141
   PRINCIPLE #4—Why Worldviews Commit Suicide   177
   PRINCIPLE #5—Free-Loading Atheists   219

PART THREE
   How Critical Thinking Saves Faith   253

NOTES   277
APPENDIX—Romans 1:1–2:16   323
ACKNOWLEDGMENTS   327
STUDY GUIDE   331
INDEX   375

*"Nearly all that we call human history …
[is] the long terrible story of man trying to find
something other than God
which will make him happy."*
C. S. Lewis, *Mere Christianity*

FOREWORD

It's not every day that an avowed atheist and devout hymn writer agree.

First, from famed atheist Richard Dawkins: "Faith is the great cop-out, the great excuse to evade the need to think and evaluate evidence. Faith is belief in spite of, even perhaps because of, the lack of evidence."

Second, these words from the composer of a beloved hymn: "You ask me how I know he lives? He lives within my heart." Pastor and musician Alfred Ackley wrote the hymn "He Lives" when challenged by the question "Why should I worship a dead Jew?" His answer is that Jesus is not dead but is the resurrected Messiah. How does Ackley know? "He lives within my heart."

What Dawkins condemns, Ackley approves. But note: both atheist and hymnist declare that "faith" is a matter of internal realities.

In contrast to this internalized definition of faith is the liberating call to "test everything" that infuses the Christian worldview and animates *Finding Truth*. In this vibrant mind-set, people are expected to think for themselves, question authority, examine evidence, and push for answers that make sense of our world.

The phrase "test everything" is in Paul's letter to the young church in the cosmopolitan seaport city of Thessalonica in ancient Greece (1 Thess. 5:21). Paul is urging Christians to maintain a critical distance against claims to speak prophetically for God. After all, anybody can proclaim, "God gave me a vision," but that doesn't make it so.

The humane position, and the biblical position, is that individuals are under no obligation to affirm as true something they have not adequately examined. Moreover, if after careful examination, a claim is falsified by the evidence, it should be rejected.

There are no privileged truth claims under this theistic mobilization of mind, and that includes an affirmation as central to Christianity as the space-time resurrection of Jesus of Nazareth. "If Christ has not been raised, your faith is futile," states 1 Corinthians 15:17. Some people may balk at the linkage of fact to commitment, but the dynamic worldview set forth in the biblical data welcomes the connection.

For example, when the skeptical disciple Thomas refused to conclude, apart from empirical evidence, that Jesus had risen physically from the dead, precisely that kind of information was presented to him (John 20:24–28). Thomas was not persuaded by looking inward to his heart, but by evaluating evidence in the external world. He then made a commitment on the basis of relevant facts, not because of a lack of facts and certainly not against them.

The same tough-minded realism is evident throughout the scriptural record. The Old Testament reports, for example, that in the exodus of the Hebrew people from Egypt, they were led by a "pillar of cloud" during the day and by a "pillar of fire" during the night (Exod. 13:21–22). These were public phenomena visible to the naked eye.

When the Hebrews reached the Red Sea, they crossed at a specific geographical point on dry land that just moments before was deep under water. This was a miraculous event that all the people of Israel observed and participated in. The return of the water, wiping out the pursuing Egyptian troops, was likewise an event open to observation (Exod. 14).

At Mount Sinai, the people of Israel saw the flashes of lightning and heard the clashes of thunder. They saw fire and heard its crackle; they saw smoke and smelled it too. They felt the trembling of the mountain, a trembling that could have been measured by a modern seismograph. This is the empirical context in which the Hebrews listened to the audible voice of God as he communicated the Ten Commandments to Moses (Exod. 19; Deut. 4:9–13).

As we turn to the New Testament record, the shepherds of Bethlehem were able to check out for themselves the real-world truth of what angels said about the birth of a baby not far away—not merely a subjective vision but a flesh-and-blood infant in a real manger. "Let us go over to Bethlehem and see this thing," they said. Later, the shepherds returned to their fields "glorifying and praising God." Why? Because what they found was just "as it had been told them" (Luke 2:15–20).

When John the Baptist was in prison and facing capital punishment, he sent followers to ask if Jesus really was the Messiah.

Jesus's response was to adduce publicly observable miracles that lined up with previously given biblical indicators on how to identify the coming Messiah. "Tell John what you hear and see," Jesus said. "The blind receive their sight and the lame walk, lepers are cleansed and the deaf hear, and the dead are raised up, and the poor have good news preached to them" (Matt. 11:2–5). Because these events were public, their status as facts could be confirmed by friend and foe alike.

When the Jewish religious leaders were outraged over Jesus's claim to forgive sins, he did not appeal to the "heart" or make a bare claim to divinity. Instead he provided physical evidence: "'That you may know that the Son of Man has the authority on earth to forgive sins'—he said to the paralytic—'I say to you, rise, pick up your bed, and go home.' And he rose and immediately picked up his bed" (Mark 2:10–12).

These robust responses are typical of Jesus. His ministry was a public work of question and answer and give and take. He set forth propositions that can be considered and discussed, and he invited people to observe public miracles that confirmed his claims in the here and now.

It is true that not every person in Jesus's own day would have observed every miracle he performed, heard every sermon he delivered, or encountered the physically raised Jesus of Nazareth. Nevertheless, whether in his day or ours, the total body of his actions and communications evinces an attitude of openness to examination so that inquisitive people are welcomed to explore and investigate.

It is against this historical backdrop that Paul argued that the events grounding the Christian worldview were not "done in a corner" (Acts 26:25–26). Shepherds, kings, doctors, and tax collectors could all check out the facts that are central to the Christian message. What is being communicated is an accurate description of reality, not a belief system about it.

This reality orientation is the positive intellectual climate in which the core propositions and events of the gospel live and breathe. It is a mentality in which people are liberated by verifiable truth to challenge tradition, question power, and fight for life and healing against death and decay.

Despite this auspicious heritage, many of our contemporaries find solace in what Francis Schaeffer describes as an "escape from reason." They accept polite society's dumbed-down redefinition of faith as something totally privatized—that is, a commitment so private and so personal that evaluation and evidence are irrelevant.

This is a far cry from the holistic respect for information that characterizes a biblical worldview. Scripture nowhere encourages the notion that "faith" equals commitment quarantined from evidence or isolated from the mind—the "will to avoid knowing what is true," as Friedrich Nietzsche put it in his work *The Antichrist*.

To accurately reflect the biblical emphasis, we must acknowledge that a falsified "faith" is quite properly a discarded faith. It is a futile faith and therefore not worth keeping. But this sharp challenge cuts in a positive way as well.

For we must also say that a confirmed faith, or better, a well-grounded *trust*, is well worth embracing by the whole person. In fact, the word "trust," rather than the now-privatized words "faith" or "belief," better captures the understanding of commitment set forth in the Bible. The New Testament Greek word often translated as "believe" is more accurately rendered as "trust" (from the word *pistis*, "trust" or "believe," rooted in the word *peitho*, "I persuade"). The biblical attitude is one of persuasion, a will to verify and know what is true and to respond accordingly.

Mark Twain once described faith as "believing what you know ain't so." But *that* definition of faith "ain't so," at least among those who operate on the biblical insistence to live an examined life. This approach expresses a profound respect for the human being as a person made in the image of a knowable God who affirms the mind as good and who embraces this world as a rightful arena in which to evaluate truth claims.

Into this setting *Finding Truth* arrives, a timely, strategic, and principled call to transcend mere belief and privatized "faith" in order to identify truth that merits trust. You may be a student or a worker, a professor or an officeholder, an artist or a scientist—all who engage this book will find encouragement to think humanely and critically about possible answers to ultimate questions. You will be invited to consider how verifiable historic Christianity incisively and rightly answers the great questions of life, "outperforms all competing worldviews," and "fulfills humanity's highest hopes and ideals," as Nancy Pearcey states in this book.

Finding Truth articulates a set of key strategic principles by which to evaluate the authenticity of any worldview, whether encountered in the classroom, at the office, in the news, or on the street. In this book you will be equipped to critically examine secularism and other idols of our day as they are advanced in the garb of politics, science, entertainment, or religion.

You will also see doctrines of atheism and materialism put to the test, to assess whether they stand up under critical thinking. And you will explore faiths such as relativism and postmodernism, to consider whether they merit the informed trust of the human being.

People's lives hang in the balance. *Finding Truth* argues that no secular worldview adequately accounts for the phenomena of man and the cosmos—what we know of human nature and physical nature. For these worldviews see only a slice of reality and then try to direct human beings into measuring themselves by that narrow slice and living accordingly. Materialists thereby deny the reality of mind (while they use their minds to advance materialism), determinists deny the reality of human choice (while they choose determinism), and relativists deny the fact of right and wrong (while they judge you if you disagree).

These unfortunate theories do more harm than good. They undercut mind and reasoning, choice and freedom, truth and moral ideals. Inevitably, then, people who place their trust in such solutions begin to order their lives in ways that are less than humane. Likewise, cultures in the grip of inadequate worldviews begin to actualize societies that are less than humane. Ideologues may advance their idols under politically correct banners of tolerance, diversity, and fairness, but the actual impact is regress, not progress, fragmentation, not wholeness. People are crushed. The human being necessarily revolts against gods that fail.

For many journeying through the twenty-first century, losing "faith" and saying good-bye to empty answers may be key to finding livable solutions to the great questions of life. *Finding Truth* articulates a rationale and a strategy to critically evaluate the possible answers to the big questions of life and to seek solutions that reconnect our deepest longings with our highest aspirations. Offered here is a humanizing unity of fact and meaning that open-minded people can consider and discuss, test and examine, and then actualize with integrity across the whole of life. This is good-bye to privatized religion and hello to a knowable and verifiable God. It is holistic trust grounded in the facts of life.

A wise traveler who goes off course retraces his steps to get back on track. So let there be no doubt among atheists, hymnists, and others on the journey of life: To be human is to write, to compose, to create, and to dream. So is to think, to test, and to know why. Now in *Finding Truth* you have a guide to help show the way.

—J. RICHARD PEARCEY
Editor and Publisher
The Pearcey Report
www.pearceyreport.com

PART ONE

·····
"I LOST MY FAITH AT AN EVANGELICAL COLLEGE"

I was once invited to give a presentation on Capitol Hill on the application of Christian worldview principles in the public arena. During the question period, the audience hushed in surprise as a congressional chief of staff stood up and announced, "I lost my faith at an evangelical college."

Not at a secular university, not in political battles on Capitol Hill—but at a respected evangelical college.

How did it happen? Afterward, I sought out the chief of staff to hear his story. Bill Wichterman explained that the professors at his college had taught the prevailing theories in their discipline—most of which were secular and sometimes explicitly anti-Christian. Yet they did little to offer a biblical perspective on the subject.

Bill met with several of his professors outside of class, always asking the same question: "How do you relate your faith to your academic discipline—to what you teach in the classroom?" Tragically, not one could give him an answer.

Eventually Bill concluded that Christianity did not *have* any answers, and he decided to abandon it. "I was sorry to give up my Christian faith," he told me. "But it seemed to have no intellectual foundation."

Bill's story reflects an all-too-common pattern today. When young people leave home, they often leave behind their religious upbringing as well. In the past, many returned to Christianity after they married and had children. But today, a growing number are staying away for good.[1]

Is there hope? Can a biblical worldview equip us with the resources to meet the challenge, reverse the pattern, and confidently set forth our case in the public arena?

The answer is a resounding yes. *Finding Truth* offers a fresh and original strategy to answer the questions raised by young people—and seekers of all ages. It unpacks five powerful principles from Scripture that cut to the heart of any competing worldview or religion. It highlights the life-giving truths that everyone wants but only Christianity can give.

Study Your Way Back to God

How does Bill's story end? After graduating from college, he discovered there is a field called apologetics that supports Christian claims with logic and reasons. He read books by C. S. Lewis, Francis Schaeffer, Alvin Plantinga, William Lane Craig, and many others. Eventually he was persuaded that Christianity has the intellectual resources to respond successfully to competing worldviews after all.

He told me, "I studied my way back to God."

My personal history is similar to Bill's. Though raised in a Lutheran family, I could not get answers to the questions that bubbled up in my mind as a teenager. Midway through high school, I abandoned my religious upbringing altogether. Years later, in a ministry called L'Abri hidden away in a tiny village in the Swiss Alps, I finally met people who could answer my questions. (I tell my story in Principle #5.)

My own years of searching and struggling as an agnostic left me with an intense conviction that Christians need to take questions seriously. They need to be prepared to help people "study their way back to God."

The task can seem daunting. At every turn—from the classroom to the workplace to the Internet—ideas contrary to Christianity are clamoring for our allegiance. Learning how to respond thoughtfully to every competing worldview would take a lifetime of study. And what happens when we encounter a *new* idea? Do we have to come up with a new argument every time?

Or is it possible to find a single line of inquiry that we can apply universally to all ideas?

That was a question I wrestled with for years after I became a Christian. What I have discovered is that the Bible itself offers a powerful strategy for critical thinking—five principles that cut to the heart of any worldview. By mastering these principles, you will be equipped to answer any challenge—while making a compelling and attractive case for Christianity.

Give Me Evidence

The key passage is the first chapter of Romans. Because the apostle Paul was writing to a congregation that had not heard him speak before, he presents the Christian message in a comprehensive way suitable for an audience hearing it for the first time. In fact, we can think of Romans 1 as Paul's apologetics training manual. It describes the dramatic interaction between God and humanity that is the source of all worldviews, from ancient times to our own. (If you are not familiar with Romans 1, you may want to flip forward to the appendix and read it first.)

Where does Paul begin his training manual? His first major point is that all people—everywhere and at all times—have access to evidence for God's existence. How? Through the created order: "the things that have been made." This is called *general* revelation because it is evidence for God that is accessible to anyone, including those who do not have the written Scripture (which is called *special* revelation). As the psalmist writes, "The heavens declare the glory of God, and the sky above proclaims his handiwork. Day to day pours out speech, and night to night reveals knowledge" (Ps. 19:1–2). Let's begin with the verses where Paul explains the concept of general revelation:

We all have access to evidence for God through creation.

Romans 1:19—What can be known about God is plain to them, because God has shown it to them.

Romans 1:20—His invisible attributes, namely, his eternal power and divine nature, have been clearly perceived, ever since the creation of the world, in the things that have been made.

Paul's claim is that both physical nature and human nature give evidence for the Creator. "The whole creation of God preaches," as Jonathan Edwards put it.[2] How does physical nature give evidence for God? Because the existence of the universe cannot be explained as a product of natural causes alone. This is as true for us as it was for Paul's first-century readers. Let's run through a quick survey of some of the most relevant areas of scientific research: the origin of the universe and the origin of life.

The origin of the universe has given rise to a puzzle known as the fine-tuning problem. The fundamental physical constants of the universe are exquisitely balanced, as though on a knife's edge, to sustain life. Things like the force of gravity, the strong nuclear force, the weak nuclear force, the electromagnetic force, the ratio of the mass of the proton and the electron, and many other factors have just the right value needed to make life possible. If any of these critical numbers were changed even slightly, the universe could not sustain any form of life. For example, if the strength of gravity were smaller or larger than its current value by only one part in 10^{60} (1 followed by 60 zeros), the universe would be uninhabitable.[3]

Cosmologists call this the Goldilocks dilemma: Why are these numerical values so precisely calibrated that they are not too high, not too low, but just right to support life? A *New York Times* article says, "These mysterious numbers ... are like the knobs on God's control console, and they seem almost miraculously tuned to allow life."[4]

What makes the fine-tuning problem so puzzling is that there is no *physical* cause to explain it. "Nothing in all of physics explains why its fundamental principles should conform themselves so precisely to life's requirement," says astronomer George Greenstein. Indeed, they interact in an intricately coordinated way to fulfill a goal or purpose—which is the hallmark of design. As physicist Paul Davies says, "It's almost as if a Grand Designer had it all figured out."[5]

Evidence from Life

The origin of life is equally difficult to explain by any naturalistic scenario. Every cell in our bodies contains a complex coded message. Today the origin of life has been reframed as the origin of biological information.

The central role of information explains why scientists have failed "to cook up life in the chemistry lab," says Davies. "Chemistry is about substances and how they react, whereas biology appeals to concepts such as information"—which is clearly *not* chemical. Genetic information can be described only by using terminology borrowed from the mental world of language and communication: DNA is "a genetic 'database,' containing 'instructions' on how to build an organism. The genetic 'code' has to be 'transcribed' and 'translated' before it can act."

Biologists' favorite analogy for DNA is a computer: The molecule itself (the physical chain of chemicals linked together) is the hardware. The encoded information is the software. In origin-of-life research, the focus is on building the hardware. "Attempts at chemical synthesis focus exclusively on the hardware—the chemical substrate of life," Davies writes; they "ignore the software—the informational aspect."[6] Yet any twelve-year-old kid with a laptop knows that building an electronic device out of copper, plastic, and silicone has nothing to do with writing code to create a software program.

The surprising implication is that even if scientists succeeded in coaxing all the right chemicals to link up and form a DNA molecule in a test tube, *that would do nothing to explain where the encoded genetic information came from.*

In all of human experience (and science is supposed to be based on experience), the source of encoded information is an intelligent agent. Therefore, it is reasonable to infer that an intelligent agent was necessary at the origin of life.[7]

Yet we don't really need the latest findings from science to recognize that a mind is needed to explain the universe. In every age, people have realized that an *intelligible* universe must be the product of *intelligence*. In ancient Rome, the Stoic philosophers offered an argument from design that sounds very familiar to modern ears. In the century before Christ, the great Roman orator Cicero wrote, "When we see something moved by machinery, like an orrery [model of the planetary system] or clock or many other such things, we do not doubt that these contrivances are the work of reason." He then drew the logical conclusion: "When therefore we behold the whole compass of the heaven moving with revolutions of marvelous velocity and ... perfect regularity ..., how can we doubt that all this is effected not merely by reason, but by a reason that is transcendent and divine?"

Sounding almost biblical in his language, Cicero wrote, "You see not the Deity, yet ... by the contemplation of his works you are led to acknowledge a God."[8]

Clearly, people in the ancient world were capable of "reading" the message of general revelation in nature. The opening theme in Romans 1 is that anyone can conclude that the created order is the product of an intelligent being. Created things speak of God: "Their voice goes out through all the earth, and their words to the end of the world" (Ps. 19:4).

Evidence from Personhood

In speaking of evidence from creation, however, Paul does not mean only physical nature. He also means human nature. Human beings are among the things "that have been made" (Rom. 1:20). Because I have written about the evidence for God in physical nature in earlier books,[9] in the rest of this book I will focus on human nature.

How do humans constitute evidence for God? Because they are personal agents. In philosophical terminology, *personal* does not mean warm and friendly. A personal being is a conscious agent with the capacity to think, feel, choose, and act—in contrast to an unconscious principle or substance that operates by blind, automatic forces (such as the forces of nature).[10] The existence of personal beings constitutes evidence that they were created by a personal God, not by any non-personal cause.

We'll discuss the details of this argument in later chapters, but the gist is clear: Because humans are capable of knowing, the first cause that produced them must have a mind. Because humans are capable of choosing, the first cause must have a will. And so on. Philosopher Étienne Gilson captures the argument neatly: because a human is a *someone* and not a *something*, the source of human life must be also a *Someone*.[11]

Many Bible writers use the same reasoning when they speak against idolatry. Their implied argument is that despite external appearances, an idol is a *something*, not a *someone*. "They have mouths, but do not speak; eyes, but do not see. They have ears, but do not hear" (Ps. 115:5–6). Therefore idols cannot be the origin of beings who *do* speak and see and hear. The prophet Jeremiah says mockingly, They "say to a tree, 'You are my father,' and to a stone, 'You gave me birth'" (Jer. 2:27). It is the height of illogic to think that humans originated from anything with lower functionality than themselves—from a something instead of a Someone.

It is sometimes said that a mind capable of forming an argument *against* God's existence constitutes evidence *for* his existence. That is, a conscious being with the ability to reason, weigh evidence, and argue logically must come from a source that has at least the same level of cognitive ability. "He who planted the ear, does he not hear? He who formed the eye, does he not see?" (Ps. 94:9). The cause must be capable of producing the effect. Water does not rise above its source.

Atheists' Children and Their God

General revelation falls under the category of *common grace*, the blessings God bestows on all people regardless of their spiritual condition (in contrast to *special grace*, the blessings of salvation). The concept of common grace is derived from Jesus's saying that God "makes his sun rise on the evil and on the good, and sends rain on the just and on the unjust" (Matt. 5:45). Common grace functions as a constant testimony to God's goodness. When Paul preached to a Gentile audience in an area that is now Turkey, he used an argument from common grace: God "did not leave himself without witness, for he did good by giving you rains from heaven and fruitful seasons, satisfying your hearts with food and gladness" (Acts 14:17). The regularity of the natural order allows humans to grow food, raise families, invent technology, and maintain some level of cultural and civic order. All human endeavors depend on God's common grace.

The upshot is that humans are surrounded by evidence for God simply because we are all made in the image of God, live in

God's universe, and are upheld by God's common grace. "For from him and through him and to him are all things" (Rom. 11:36).

This may explain why young children in every culture have a concept of God. Psychologist Paul Bloom at Yale University reports that "when children are directly asked about the origin of animals and people, they tend to prefer explanations that involve an intentional creator, even if the adults who raised them do not."[12] In other words, children tend to hold a concept of God even if their parents are atheists.

Psychologist Justin Barrett at Oxford University reports similar findings. Scientific evidence has shown that "built into the natural development of children's minds [is] a predisposition to see the natural world as designed and purposeful and that some kind of intelligent being is behind that purpose." Even if a group of children were put "on an island and they raised themselves," Barrett adds, "I think they would believe in God."[13] It appears that we have to be educated out of the knowledge of God by secular schools and media.

Suppressing the Evidence

These findings from psychology may cast new light on what Jesus meant when he urged his followers to "become like children" to enter the kingdom of God (Matt. 18:3). Calvin taught that all people have an innate sense of the divine (*sensus divinitatis*). Yet if general revelation impinges on all human consciousness, why don't all people acknowledge God? What is Paul's answer? He says we "suppress the truth" taught by general revelation. Let's pull out the verses that describe the next stage in the cosmic drama:

We all suppress the evidence for God from creation.

Romans 1:18—[They] suppress the truth.
Romans 1:21—Although they knew God, they did not honor him as God or give thanks to him.
Romans 1:28—They did not see fit to acknowledge God.

Why do people suppress the evidence for God? The God described in the Bible goes against the grain of today's popular notions of spirituality. Many people may be receptive to the idea of a non-personal spiritual force that they can tap into. They might be willing to consider a great pantheistic pool of spirituality of which they are a part. But they are far less comfortable with the concept of a living, active, personal God who knows them, wants to interact with them, and has his own views about what they are doing with their lives.

Encountering *this* God can be like stumbling in the dark against something warm and lumpy, only to discover that you've bumped into another person you didn't know was there. You may be startled, and perhaps a little frightened. C. S. Lewis puts it colorfully. "There comes a moment when the children who have been playing at burglars hush suddenly: was that a real footstep in the hall? There comes a moment when people who have been dabbling in religion ('Man's search for God'!) suddenly draw back. Supposing we really found Him? ... Worse still, supposing He had found us?"[14]

Suppose what you thought was a non-personal spiritual force, which could safely be treated as an inanimate object, turns out instead to be a transcendent Person—with a legitimate moral claim on your life? What do people do when they hear the footstep of the real God?

Their first reaction, Paul says, is fear and denial. They "suppress the truth" (Rom. 1:18).

The concept of denial or suppression is said to be one of the most distinctive discoveries of modern psychology. Research has found that humans tend to suppress thoughts that are painful, disturbing, or traumatic. Today we casually use the pop psychology phrase "You're in denial" to mean someone is refusing to admit a problem or face an unpleasant fact.[15]

Yet the idea that people often stifle or suppress what they know is nothing new. The Bible taught it long before the rise of modern psychology. Romans 1 says that fallen, sinful humans have a strong tendency to deny what we know about God—or what we should know.

Tug of War

It may sound unusual to say there are things about God that we "should" know, as though it were a moral requirement. Yet in many situations we are morally responsible for what we know. If you are a witness in a court of law, you must solemnly swear to tell everything you know—"the whole truth"—about the crime. If you hold anything back, you may be charged with a crime yourself (obstruction of justice).[16] Or if you are arrested, you cannot argue that you did not know the law. Courts operate by the principle that ignorance of the law is no excuse. If you try to avoid liability by closing your eyes to the facts, you may be charged with "willful blindness." For example, people arrested for transporting illegal drugs have claimed that they did not know what was in the package. Courts have ruled that the defendant *should* have known and was responsible for finding out.[17]

We apply the same principle outside the courtroom. If a student says he didn't know his homework was due on Thursday, that is no excuse. It was his responsibility to know the due date.

The branch of philosophy that focuses on the nature of knowledge is called epistemology. We have an epistemic duty to acknowledge what we know and conform our lives to it. When we fail in that duty, we commit an "epistemological sin."

These examples clarify what Paul says in Romans 1. At the heart of the human condition, we might say, is an epistemological sin—the refusal to acknowledge what can be known about God and then to respond appropriately: "Although they knew God, they did not honor him as God or give thanks to him" (Rom. 1:21). They engage in willful blindness.

The great drama of history is the tug of war between God and humanity. On one hand, God reaches out to humanity to make himself known. On the other hand, humans desperately seek to avoid knowing him. In the words of theologian Thomas K. Johnson, we "can take the account of Adam and Eve hiding from God behind a bush or tree as a metaphor for the history of the human race."[18]

How Humans Hide

How do humans try to hide from God? What is the next point in Paul's dissection of human motivations? They avoid God by creating idols. Those who reject the Creator try to find a God substitute in creation. Paul highlights the underlying dynamic by using the word *exchanged*:

> **We all create idols to take the place of God.**

> *Romans 1:23—[They] exchanged the glory of the immortal God for images resembling mortal man and birds and animals and creeping things.*
> *Romans 1:25—They exchanged the truth about God for a lie and worshiped and served the creature rather than the Creator.*

The most fundamental decision we all face over the course of our lives is what we will recognize as the ultimate reality, the uncaused source and cause of our existence. Everything else in our worldview depends on that initial decision. The Bible speaks of this foundational choice in terms of who or what we worship. We must all answer the challenge Joshua issued to the Israelites as they were poised to enter the Promised Land: "Choose this day whom you will serve" (Josh. 24:15).

The Ten Commandments likewise begin by addressing the question of worship: "You shall have no other gods before me" (Exod. 20:3). Why does this commandment come first? Because all the other commandments hinge on it. They explicate what it *means* to worship the biblical God, living out his truth across the whole of life. The commandments spell out the kind of people we become when we are in relationship with God.

An atheist professor once told me that the Bible teaches polytheism because the first commandment speaks of "other gods." He said the biblical God just wanted to be the top god over a panoply of other deities. But the Hebrew phrase *before me* actually means *in my presence* or *in my sight*. God is saying, Get your idols out of my sight! Do not bring your phony gods into my presence!

The first commandment may seem outdated if we think of idols as statues of wood or stone. But Scripture treats the topic of idolatry far more subtly. An idol is anything we want more than God, anything we rely on more than God, anything we look to for greater fulfillment than God. Idolatry is thus the hidden sin driving all other sins.

For example, why do we lie? Because we fear the disapproval of people more than we want the approval of God. Or because we value our reputation more than we value our relationship with God. Or we are trying to manipulate someone into giving us something we think we need more than we need God. The more visible sin (lying) is driven by an invisible turn of our hearts toward something other than God as the ultimate source of security and happiness.

This explains why, as psychologist David Powlison says, "idolatry is by far the most frequently discussed problem in the Scriptures."[19] In the Old Testament, the prophet Habakkuk describes people whose idol is their military power: "whose own might is their god." Painting a vivid word picture of the enemy's military as a "dragnet" for sweeping up whole societies, Habakkuk says "he sacrifices to his net and makes offerings to his dragnet" (Hab. 1:11, 16).

In the New Testament, Paul treats idolatry with the same penetrating psychological insight. Writing to members of the church in Ephesus, he urges them not to be sexually immoral, impure, or covetous—then adds what may seem a surprising twist: For that "person is an idolater, worshiping the things of this world" (Eph. 5:5 NLT). The hidden sin beneath the others is the tendency to make an idol of "the things of this world." We sin because we want something in the created world more than we want the Creator.[20]

When Good Gifts Are False Gods

We tend to equate idols with things that are forbidden or intrinsically evil. But things that are intrinsically good can also become idols—*if* we allow them to take over any of God's functions in our lives. "The trust and faith of the heart alone make both God and an idol," writes Martin Luther. "That to which your heart clings and entrusts itself is, I say, really your God."[21]

I was once invited to give a presentation to a group of Christian artists on how the arts have often functioned as a substitute religion.

The nineteenth-century poet Arthur Symons observed that literature became "itself a kind of religion, with all the duties and responsibilities of the sacred ritual."[22] The arts are a good gift from God, but like any other good thing, they can be used as a substitute for God.

The artists at the conference then began to disclose their personal idols. One said, "I came to see that my family was my idol. We always told one another, 'Family is everything.'" Another said, "For me, it was my marriage; my relationship with my husband had become the most important thing in my life." Marriage and family are good; they are part of God's original creation. But they are too limited to provide the ultimate meaning and purpose of our lives.

For some people, the greatest source of security and self-worth may come from professional achievements, sexual attractiveness, or physical pleasure. Writing to the Philippian church, Paul describes people whose minds are "set on earthly things," whose "god is their belly" (Phil. 3:19). They are driven by sheer physical appetite, even if they cover their cravings under a veneer of sophistication.

John Calvin defines idolatry as worshipping "the gifts in place of the giver himself."[23] The way to uncover idols in your life is to ask whether any gift has become more important to you than the Giver.

Idols Have Consequences

So here is Paul's diagnosis of the human condition so far: God is constantly reaching out to people with evidence of his existence through general revelation. But humans are constantly suppressing those truths by creating idols.

This pattern of suppression creates an acute internal tension. On one hand, people are aware of the evidence for the biblical God from general revelation. On the other hand, they keep creating surrogate gods in a desperate attempt to suppress that evidence. To borrow a term from psychology, humans are trapped in cognitive dissonance, the mental stress of harboring concepts that contradict one another.

How does God break us out of the trap? He responds in a way we might not expect: He ratchets up the tension. He allows us to live out the consequences of our idols in order to intensify the cognitive dissonance—and ultimately to press us to the point of making a decision. In Paul's words, God "gives people up" to experience the consequences of their choices:

God gives us up to the consequences of our idols—to a "debased" mind.

> *Romans 1:21—Although they knew God, they did not honor him as God or give thanks to him, but they became futile in their thinking.*
>
> *Romans 1:28—Since they did not see fit to acknowledge God, God gave them up to a debased mind.*

What *are* the consequences of serving idols? Paul's answer starts with the inner life: "They became futile in their thinking." "God gave them up to a debased mind" (Rom. 1:21, 28). The Greek word for mind is *nous*, but it has a much richer meaning than the English word. It can be translated reason, understanding, or intellectual intuition. (The same word is at the root of the Greek term for repentance, *metanoia*, which means to change one's *nous*—not just the mind but a whole-person transformation.) The church fathers often translated *nous* as the faculty for evaluating and directing the course of one's life: "the eye of the soul." So it is no great stretch to translate the word as worldview, the convictions by which we direct our lives.

Today the word *debased* has a primarily moral connotation, meaning wicked or degenerate. But in the original Greek, the word meant counterfeit money. So a debased worldview is one that offers a counterfeit god. It makes false promises. It gives misleading answers to the questions of life.[24]

In the original language, this verse (Rom. 1:28) contains a fascinating wordplay. The word *worthwhile* in the first clause has the same root as *debased*. The parallel can be expressed like this: Just as people did not think it worthwhile to acknowledge God, so God gave them up to a worthless worldview. And a worldview shapes not only their thought life but also their actions. "They followed worthless idols and became worthless themselves" (Jer. 2:5 NIV). Here's how Paul expresses the connection:

God gives us up to the consequences of our idols—to "dishonorable" behavior.

> *Romans 1:24—God gave them up in the lusts of their hearts to impurity, to the dishonoring of their bodies among themselves.*

> *Romans 1:26—God gave them up to dishonorable passions.*
> *Romans 1:28—God gave them up to a debased mind to do what ought not to be done.*

Once again the connection is captured by the word *exchanged*. First Paul says people "exchanged the glory of the immortal God for images" of created things (Rom. 1:23; see also Rom. 1:25).[25] Next Paul shows what this trade-off does to human behavior: "Women exchanged natural relations for those that are contrary to nature," and men did the same (Rom. 1:26–27). At the time Paul was writing, in both Greco-Roman culture and Hellenistic Jewish culture, "contrary to nature" was a standard phrase referring to homosexual behavior.[26]

At the time, the term *nature* was not used the way people use it today, to mean behavior observed in the natural world. Instead *nature* meant behavior that is normative for *human nature*: behavior that fits the way humans were originally created, that accords with God's purpose for humanity, that matches the ideal standard of what it means to be fully human.

In this sense of the term, all sin is contrary to human nature, and Paul goes on to itemize a representative sampling: "They were filled with all manner of unrighteousness, evil, covetousness, malice. They are full of envy, murder, strife, deceit, maliciousness. They are gossips, slanderers, haters of God, insolent, haughty, boastful, inventors of evil, disobedient to parents, foolish, faithless, heartless, ruthless" (Rom. 1:29–31). All these behaviors—and more—are contrary to what it means to be fully human.

In this chapter Paul has unfolded a highly sensitive analysis of the link between mind and behavior. He outlines a clear and calamitous progression: First, "they did not *honor* him as God" (Rom. 1:21). "Therefore God gave them up ... to the *dishonoring* of their bodies" (Rom. 1:24). "God gave them up to *dishonorable* passions" (Rom. 1:26). The principle is that those who dishonor God inevitably dishonor themselves and others. To adapt a phrase, idols have consequences.

Five Strategic Principles

In Romans 1, Paul has unfolded a series of actions—a drama of divine-human interaction—whose plot line provides the underlying rationale for a biblical apologetic. From it we can extract five strategic principles. Translated into modern terms, these principles enable us to identify the key elements in any worldview—including the cutting-edge ideas of our day—and then to craft a compelling positive case for Christianity. Let's briefly get acquainted with the five principles. Then we will explore them more deeply through the rest of the book.

Principle #1
Identify the Idol

Since everyone who rejects God sets up an idol, this is the strategic place to begin. An idol is anything in the created order that is put in the place of God. This definition not only gives us tools to identify our personal idols, it also gives insight into the world of ideas. Philosophies and worldviews can also function as counterfeit gods.

Think of it this way: As a matter of sheer logic, any explanation of life must have a starting point. It must trace the universe back to something that functions as the primal reality, the self-existent cause of everything else. As Paul says in Romans, if you reject the biblical God, you will deify something within the created order. Those who do not honor the transcendent God *beyond* the cosmos must make a divinity out of some power or principle immanent *within* the cosmos.

What about matter? Is matter part of the created order? Sure it is. Thus the philosophy of material*ism* qualifies as an idol. It claims that matter is the ultimate reality—the uncreated first cause of everything else. It denies the existence of anything beyond the material world, such as soul, spirit, mind, or God. It urges us to set our minds "on things that are on earth," not on things above (Col. 3:2). New Atheists like to think of themselves as nonbelievers, but they believe devoutly in matter (or nature) as their substitute religion.

What about reason? Can it be an idol? Certainly. The philosophy of rationalism puts human reason in the place of God as the source and standard of all truth. Albert Einstein once described himself as "a believing rationalist." He summarized his creed by saying, "I believe in Spinoza's God," referring to a philosopher who used *God* to mean merely the principle of rational order within the universe.[27] Rationalism refuses to accept any source of truth *beyond* human reason, such as information communicated by the Creator. It is dogmatic in worshipping the idol of "unaided" or "autonomous" human reason.

This explains why the Bible does not contrast Christianity with atheism but with idolatry. The "Bible writers always address their readers as though they (the readers) already believe in God or some God surrogate," notes philosopher Roy Clouser.[28] Humans have a tendency to look to some power or principle or person to make sense of life and give it meaning. And *that* constitutes their de facto religion, whether they use theological language or not.

Principle #2
Identify the Idol's Reductionism

Romans 1 tells us that idolatry leads to a "debased" worldview, which opens the door to oppression, injustice, and all the other evils listed at the end of the chapter. What is the connection between idols and immoral behavior? The link is that idols always lead to a lower view of human life. The Bible teaches that humans are made in the image of God. When a worldview exchanges the Creator for something in creation, it will also exchange a high view of humans made in God's image for a lower view of humans made in the image of something in creation.

We could say that every concept of humanity is created in the image of *some* god.

To translate Paul's argument into modern language, we need to master one philosophical term: *reductionism*. It means *reducing* a phenomenon from a higher or more complex level of reality to a lower, simpler, less complex level—usually in order to debunk or discredit it.

For example, you have probably heard people say that Christianity is nothing but an emotional crutch. Or that ideas are nothing but products of chemicals reacting in our brains. Or that living things can be explained solely by physics and chemistry.[29]

These are all forms of reductionism.

To say that idols always lead to reductionism, then, is another way of saying that they lead to a low view of human life. You might picture reductionism as someone trying to stuff the entire universe into a box. When some part of creation is absolutized, then everything is redefined in its terms. Humans are recast in its image.[30]

Recall that in materialism, the idol is matter. Everything else is reduced to material objects produced by material forces. Anything that does not fit in the materialist box is dismissed as an illusion, including spirit, soul, will, mind, and consciousness. Reductionism is a strategy for suppressing the truth: For if we can *reduce* humans to machines operating by natural forces, then we can explain their *origin* by purely natural forces.

By contrast, a biblical worldview begins with a transcendent God, so it is not reductionistic. It does not try to stuff everything into a box defined by one part of creation. Instead Christianity offers a high view of the human person, created in the image of a transcendent Person. It affirms all the features that make us fully human.

Principle #3
Test the Idol: Does It Contradict What We Know about the World?

Once we have identified the idol and its reductionism, we are ready to ask the most important question: Is this worldview true? Does it fit what we know about the world?

Romans 1 teaches that some things are knowable by everyone—the truths of general revelation. It follows that any truth claim must match up with general revelation. We could say that the purpose of a *worldview* is to explain what we know about the *world*. If it contradicts what we know about the world through general revelation, then it fails.

And we can be confident that every idol-based worldview *will* fail. Why? Precisely because it leads to reductionism. If reductionism is like trying to stuff the entire universe into a box, we could say that inevitably something will stick out of the box. A box that deifies a *part* of creation will always be too limited to explain the *whole*. Whatever does not fit into the box will be denigrated, devalued, or dismissed as unreal.

Think again of the example of materialism, since it is the dominant view in academia today. When it reduces humans to complex biochemical machines, what sticks out of the box? Free will. The power of choice. The ability to make decisions. These are dismissed as illusions. Yet in practice, we cannot live without making choices from the moment we wake up every morning. Free will is part of undeniable, inescapable human experience—which means it is part of general revelation. Therefore the materialist view of humanity does not fit reality as we experience it.

Materialists themselves sometimes recognize the problem. Writing in the *New York Times*, science journalist John Horgan reports that many neuroscientists reject concepts such as *free will* as myths. But surprisingly Horgan concludes, almost defiantly, "No matter what my intellect decides, I'm compelled to believe in free will."[31]

No matter what anyone's worldview says, we are all "compelled to believe" the truths of general revelation.

Another example is philosopher John Searle, who embraces materialism yet admits that we cannot live by its principles. In an interview, he explains that materialism pictures the universe as a vast machine, where all human action is determined; yet experience shows that we are agents capable of making decisions. "We can *say*, OK, I believe in determinism," Searle says, but "the conviction of freedom is built into our experiences; we can't just give it up. If we tried to, we *couldn't live with it.*" He concludes, "We *can't give up* our conviction of our own freedom, even though there's no ground for it."[32]

No ground, that is, within Searle's own materialist philosophy. He is acknowledging that his worldview box is too small to account for reality as *he himself* experiences it. He "can't give up" his conviction of freedom. He "can't live with" his own philosophy.

Searle is trapped in cognitive dissonance—what his worldview tells him contradicts what he knows from general revelation.

What do materialists do when they realize that their worldview box is too small to fit the evidence? They suppress the evidence, just as Paul says in Romans 1. They cannot deny that the concept of free will is hardwired into human thinking. What they *can* do, however, is reduce that concept to an illusion. A useful fiction.

You might think of reductionism as a strategy of suppression. If a materialist were to acknowledge the reality of free will, that would give evidence that humans are personal beings whose origin must be a personal Being. Therefore materialists have to suppress the evidence from general revelation. Otherwise it would falsify their worldview.

At some point, every idol-based worldview contradicts reality. This creates an opportunity to make a positive case for Christianity. Because it is not reductionistic, it does not dismiss important parts of human experience as illusions. It does not contradict what we know from general revelation, or lead to cognitive dissonance. Instead Christianity is total truth—consistent, coherent, and comprehensive. It can be lived out in the real worldview without contradicting our most basic human experience.

Principle #4
Test the Idol: Does It Contradict Itself?

Idol-centered worldviews not only fail to match the external world, they also collapse internally. They are self-refuting. The technical term is that they are self-referentially absurd, which means they propose a standard for truth that they themselves fail to meet.

For example, a person may propose cultural relativism, which claims that there is no universal truth. But that statement itself makes a universal claim. Thus it contradicts itself.

The argument from self-referential absurdity is a standard tool in every apologist's toolbox. But *why* does it work? Again the key is reductionism. A reductionistic worldview leads to a lower view of humanity—and thus of the human mind. It reduces human reason to something less than reason. Yet the only way any worldview can argue its *own* case is by using reason. By discrediting reason, it undermines its own case. It is self-defeating.

To illustrate how the argument works, let's use the example of materialism once more. Materialism reduces thinking to biochemical processes in the brain, akin to the chemical reactions in digestion. But digestion is not something that can be true or false. It is just a biological fact. If thinking is reduced to brain processes, then our ideas are not true or false either. But in that case, how can the materialist know that *materialism* is true? The philosophy is self-refuting.

Once again, Christianity offers a better answer. Because humans are made in God's image, human reason has the high dignity of reflecting the divine reason. Christianity thus affirms the reliability of human cognitive capacities (without becoming rationalistic, turning reason into a god). It is not self-refuting.

Ironically, then, adherents of reductionist worldviews have to disregard their own reductionism—at least while arguing their case. They have to borrow Christianity's high view of reason in order to give reasons for their own view.

Principle #5
Replace the Idol: Make the Case for Christianity

The final step is to propose a biblical alternative to secular and pagan worldviews. To craft an approach that is most relevant to our own day, we should take our cues from precisely those points where other worldviews fail. Think back to Principle #3 where we met materialists who openly acknowledge that "they cannot live" with the consequences of their own worldview, that they are "compelled to believe" in free will. Think of Principle #4 where we learned that adherents of reductionistic worldviews cannot even affirm their own claims unless they borrow Christianity's high view of the human mind.

What a powerful image of people caught in cognitive dissonance, reaching out to grab on to truths that their own worldviews deny—truths that only a biblical worldview logically supports.

In Principle #5 we will explore several real-world examples of secular thinkers who are "free-loading" what they like best from Christianity. They find a biblical worldview so appealing that they keep borrowing from it (whether consciously or unconsciously). In admitting that they cannot live within their own worldview, they are showing that they are hungry for more fulfilling answers than their idols give them. And by free-loading from Christianity, they are showing that they need what only Christianity can offer.

The five principles derived from Romans 1 build a powerful case to show that idol-based worldviews fail to give adequate answers to the basic questions all people must answer. At the same time, the five principles demonstrate that Christianity provides better answers—answers that fit the real world and are internally coherent. Because a biblical worldview starts with a transcendent Creator, it does not deify anything in creation. Therefore it does not need to ramrod everything into a limited set of categories derived from one part of the cosmic order. Christianity liberates us from any life-denying reductionism that dishonors and debases humanity. It affirms the high dignity of humans as full persons made in the image of a personal God.

No wonder Paul proclaims that he is "not ashamed" of the gospel (Rom. 1:16). Christianity has greater explanatory power than any other worldview or religion. It fits the data of general revelation better. And it leads to a more humane and liberating view of the human person.

At School, At Work

The five principles of Paul's apologetics training manual can be applied in the classroom, in the workplace, or in conversations with neighbors over the backyard fence. To give you practice, in the rest of *Finding Truth* we will apply the principles to today's most widespread philosophies. For example, materialism is not so much a single philosophy as a family of interrelated theories. Consider how it permeates just one field: psychology. Leading thinkers such as Ivan Pavlov, Sigmund Freud, B. F. Skinner, Erich Fromm, and Albert Ellis proposed quite different theories. Yet they were all committed to materialism and atheism. Thus when you reveal the flaws in materialism, you discredit not just one philosophy but an entire family of materialist theories.

Because philosophies cluster in families, learning to analyze them is easier than you might have thought before you picked up *Finding Truth*.

Some families are so widespread we will examine them more than once. At first sight, this may appear repetitive. Each time, however, we will be advancing to a new strategic principle. As one of my students said, "This book is different from any other apologetics book I've read. Most books teach *about* worldviews, going through them one by one. This book teaches us how to *do* apologetics," using elements from worldviews merely to illustrate each stage.

Liberated Minds

Learning critical thinking is important not only for speaking to people *outside* the church but also for educating people on the *inside*. They often absorb ideas from the cultural atmosphere and thus need help liberating their minds from secular assumptions.

In the hallway of a Christian college where I was teaching, I noticed a student reading a book on postmodernism. "What are you learning?" I asked.

"It's showing me myself!" the student said. "I finally understand why I think the way I do."[33] He had absorbed elements of postmodernism without knowing it.

A woman once sent me an email saying she was raised in a home where the rule was that Christians should never expose themselves to nonbiblical ways of thinking. "But when I read your book *Total*

Truth," she wrote, "I discovered that I had unconsciously absorbed ideas from secular thinkers like Rousseau and Kant." Because she had never studied their ideas, she had no critical grid to recognize and reject them.

The lesson is that Christians must never treat idol analysis as a matter of addressing only how *other people* think. Scripture does not allow us that luxury. In the original Greek, there are no chapter breaks; the first chapter of Romans flows immediately into the second chapter, where Paul turns to the reader—the person who has God's written revelation—and says, "Therefore you have no excuse, O man, every one of you who judges. For in passing judgment on another you condemn yourself, because you, the judge, practice the very same things" (Rom. 2:1).

All through Romans 1, it appeared that Paul was directing his teaching to pagan idol worshippers. But now, in a surprise move, he places his readers on the same level as pagans. He even repeats the same phrase as in 1:20, "without excuse."

By that verbal link, Paul implicates everyone in the charge of suppressing the truth and creating counterfeit gods. Christians are not immune. Scripture is addressing Christians in verses like "flee from idolatry" and "keep yourselves from idols" (1 Cor. 10:14; 1 John 5:21). We must be committed to turning away from idols and toward God as the ultimate source of truth in every area of life. To avoid being "conformed to this world," we must "be transformed by the renewal of your mind" (Rom. 12:2).

The ultimate goal of learning a biblical apologetics strategy is to love God "with all your mind" (Luke 10:27). Whether you are a Christian already or just beginning to learn about God, you may be surprised by joy when you discover that biblical truth is bright and resilient enough to be "a lamp to my feet and a light to my path" (Ps. 119:105), illuminating every area of life.

Let's get started honing our skills to identify the idols of our age. How can we learn to recognize false gods, especially when they are hidden under secular labels and taught through the secular education system?

PART TWO

PRINCIPLE #1

.....

TWILIGHT OF THE GODS

Dylan was not your stereotypical intellectual. In high school he was an athlete. Football, basketball, track—you name the sport, Dylan was in the thick of it. As captain of his football team, he won the Most Valuable Player Award and was courted by top colleges. Witty and outgoing, he was a natural leader.

Then, in his senior year of high school, Dylan's life took an unexpected turn. His achievements began to seem empty, and he wondered if there wasn't more to life. Through a Young Life group and a local church, he heard the gospel and became a Christian. Immediately he knew that he wanted to live a life completely sold out to God.

But when he started college the next year, Dylan suddenly found himself in a fierce battle with doubts and disappointments.

In his science classes, Darwinian naturalism was assumed as unquestioned dogma. In his psychology classes, most of the theories—from Freud's psychoanalysis to Skinner's behaviorism—promoted negative views of Christianity. In a humanities class, the professor told him that Christianity was just a "values choice"—something that might be meaningful to him personally but was not objectively true.

Dylan's church had taught him the basic gospel message, but it had not equipped him to meet the challenges he now faced in the classroom. It had not taught him how to "destroy arguments and every lofty opinion raised against the knowledge of God" (2 Cor. 10:5).

Dylan joined an evangelical campus group, but when he raised questions there, the leaders essentially said, "You've got the Bible; why do you have any questions?" They urged him to redouble his devotional efforts—pray more, evangelize more, memorize more Scripture. Yet Dylan was already active in the group's intensive discipleship-training program, even living and working with other group members. When his questions refused to be silenced, the group leaders accused him of being proud, of thinking too much, of being too intellectual.

"Having been an athlete all my life, it was the first time anyone had accused me of being an intellectual," Dylan later recalled with bemusement. Frustrated that he could not find answers, he finally decided the intellectually honest course was to start over and reconsider the case for Christianity from square one. He embarked on a serious investigation of philosophy, theology, science, and biblical criticism.

Midway through college, Dylan traveled to Europe to visit the country where he was born, and decided to take a detour to L'Abri in Switzerland. The "detour" turned into an extended visit.

There, for the first time, Dylan met people who were not afraid of questions. He heard a case for Christianity that was both intellectually persuasive and practically viable. After nearly a year of study and discussions with Francis Schaeffer and the other L'Abri staff, he was finally convinced that a Christian worldview does provide livable answers to the questions of life.

Instead of an escapist attitude of *avoiding* the world by retreating into purely devotional activities, Dylan found he could now *engage* the world with confidence.

Does Devotion Defeat Doubt?

It is a serious mistake for Christian parents, teachers, or churches to dismiss young people's doubts and questions, or to think they can be overridden merely by cultivating a more intense devotional life. Because we are created in God's image, we are all endowed with a mind and a natural urge to make sense of life.

My own experience as a teenager was as discouraging as Dylan's. I found it all but impossible to find adults in the church who would take my questions seriously. It may not have helped that I had long, blonde Alice-in-Wonderland hair. People were constantly asking if I was a cheerleader.

Stereotypes like these have done enormous damage, robbing young people of opportunities to find answers to their questions. Athletes and cheerleaders are just as intellectually curious as anyone else. And they need facts and reasons just as much. All Christians are invited to "have the mind of Christ" (1 Cor. 2:16).

Because we are created in God's image as rational and responsible beings, we all have a philosophy—not necessarily one learned out of a textbook, but an overall view of life by which we make sense of the world. The biblical view of human nature implies that we are "incapable of holding purely arbitrary opinions or making entirely unprincipled decisions," writes Albert Wolters. "We need some creed to live by, some map by which to chart our course."[1]

If we take the Bible's view of the human person seriously, we need to take questions seriously.

Leaving Teens Vulnerable

Recent research underscores how important teenagers' questions are. In one sociological study, teens were asked why they fell away from the religion in which they were raised. Researchers expected to hear about emotional or relationship issues. To their surprise, the answer given most frequently was that teens had unanswered doubts and questions. They told researchers, "It didn't make any sense anymore." "Some stuff is too far-fetched for me to believe." "I think scientifically, and there is no real proof." "Too many questions that can't be answered."[2]

A Barna study turned up similar results. In *You Lost Me: Why Young Christians Are Leaving Church ... and Rethinking Faith*, David Kinnaman reports that 36 percent of young adults felt they could not ask "life's most pressing questions in church." As a result, 23 percent said they had "significant intellectual doubts" about Christian teachings."[3]

In today's pluralistic, multicultural society, teens have to navigate their way through a complex web of competing worldview claims. One study found that the age at which most people leave the church is in the high school and college years.[4] Yet church youth groups rarely teach apologetics, majoring instead on games and goodies. The goal seems to be to engineer events that ratchet up emotional commitment, as though sheer intensity of experience will compensate for intellectual doubts. But emotional intensity is not enough to block out teens' questions. If anything, it leads them to redefine Christianity in purely emotional terms—which leaves them even more vulnerable when they finally face their questions.[5]

If my own students are at all representative, teens regard emotional tactics as manipulative anyway. They know it's easy to manufacture an artificial sense of belonging with loud music, water-balloon fights, and Ultimate Frisbee games. But they also know that those feelings burn out quickly. As one student told me, "What I hear at my church are mostly 'feel good' messages. But I don't want to feel good. I want to wrestle with difficult questions."

No wonder *Christianity Today* announced, "Apologetics Makes a Comeback among Youth."[6]

Parents are rightly concerned about the risk involved in exposing their children to nonbiblical perspectives. But there is also a risk in raising children who think the only way they can test their mettle is by breaking away from their family and church. Competing worldviews often appear more attractive when they acquire the allure of the forbidden. The only way teens become truly "prepared to make a defense to anyone who asks" (1 Pet. 3:15) is by struggling personally with the questions.

The danger was brought home to me when I talked with a Christian mother who told me, "All the answers we need are in the Bible. We should not have to read anything else." In the next breath, she confided that her son had recently gone off to college where he promptly joined a New Atheist group and vehemently rejected his Christian upbringing. This mother thought she was protecting her son by avoiding discussions of doubts and difficulties. Instead she had left him defenseless. Paul warns that Christians can be "outwitted by Satan" if they are "ignorant of his designs" (2 Cor. 2:11).

It is far better for young people to explore the fascinating world of ideas with parents, teachers, and church leaders as guides who can give them the tools to think critically and think well. As one of my students put it, "Exposing the mind to ideas is like exposing the body to germs. It's the way to build immunity."

No age is too young to get started. A friend's eight-year-old son asked him, "Dad, people with other religions believe they're right about their gods, and we believe we're right about our God. How do we know who's *really* right?" Even second-graders' questions need to be taken seriously.

Principle #1
Identify the Idol

Where do we begin? According to Romans 1, those who reject the Creator will create an idol. They will absolutize some power or element immanent within the cosmos, elevating it into an all-defining principle—a false absolute.[7] When evaluating a worldview, then, the first step is to identify its idol. What does it set up as a God substitute?

Despite the vast diversity of religions and philosophies, they all start by putting something created in the place of God. In *Culture and the Death of God*, literary critic Terry Eagleton lists several idols of the modern age: Enlightenment rationalists made a god of reason; Romantics deified the imagination; nationalists idealize the nation; Marxists offer an economic version of sin and salvation.

"Not believing in God is a far more arduous affair than is generally imagined," Eagleton concludes. God cannot be rejected without putting something else in his place. The history of philosophy is largely a history of setting up God surrogates.[8]

It is a history of idol-making.

One of the most effective ways to understand history, then, is to identify the prevailing idols. As Timothy Keller writes, "Every human personality, community, thought-form, and culture will be based on some ultimate concern or some ultimate allegiance—either to God or to some God substitute." Thus, "The best way to analyze cultures is by identifying their corporate idols."[9]

In its teaching on idols, Scripture has given us the key to unlock all of history.

This is an exciting insight because it means Scripture provides conceptual tools not only for ideas that are normally labeled "religious" but also for ideas that are labeled "secular." In the Old Testament, Ezekiel calls them idols of the heart (Ezek. 14:3). Today when we speak of the heart, we mean the emotions. But in Hebrew the word means your innermost self, including the will, mind, moral character, and spiritual commitment. "Man looks on the outward appearance, but the LORD looks on the heart" (1 Sam. 16:7).

In the New Testament, the Greek word for heart (*kardia*) likewise means the center or core of a person's being.[10] Thus idols of the heart are the convictions that engage us most deeply and drive our behavior.

We often contrast "believers" to "nonbelievers," but that can be misleading. Everyone believes something, in the sense that they must assume some principle as fundamentally true. Atheists often fail to recognize that they are in the same boat as everyone else. A common mantra on atheist websites goes like this: "Atheism is not a belief. Atheism is merely the lack of a belief in God or gods." But it is impossible to think without some starting point. If you do not start with God, you must start somewhere else. You must propose something else as the ultimate, eternal, uncreated reality that is the cause and source of everything else. The important question is not which starting points are religious or secular, but which claims stand up to testing.

The advantage of using the biblical term *idol* is that it levels the playing field. Secular people often accuse Christians of having "faith," while claiming that they themselves base their convictions purely on facts and reason. Not so. If you press any set of ideas back far enough, eventually you reach an ultimate starting point—something that is taken as the self-existent reality on which everything depends. This starting assumption cannot be based on prior reasoning, because if it were, you could ask where *that* reasoning starts—and so on, in an infinite regress. At some point, every system of thought has to say, This is my starting point. There is no reason for it to exist. It just "is."

If starting premises do not rest on reasons, how can they be tested? Although you cannot argue *backward* to their prior reasons, you can argue *forward* by spelling out their implications, then testing those implications using both logic and experience. This is the strategy we will follow throughout the rest of *Finding Truth*. It will prove remarkably effective, demonstrating that Christianity outperforms all competing worldviews.

Religion without God

Another advantage of using the term *idol* is that it avoids a kind of dry intellectualism, as though people choose a life philosophy the way they solve a logical puzzle. When people commit themselves to a certain vision of reality, it becomes their ultimate explainer. It serves to interpret the universe for them, to guide their moral decisions, to give meaning and purpose to life, and all the other functions normally associated with a religion.

We might even think of philosophies as secular religions. That may seem like an oxymoron, but it makes sense once we know the generic meaning of the term *religion*. What is the one feature shared by all religions? It's not what you might expect.

Does a religion have to affirm the existence of a personal god or creator? Most Westerners would say yes. An atheist friend once argued on my Facebook page, "Religion is belief in a deity. No deity, no religion." Yet many beliefs that we classify as religions do not identify the divine with a being at all. In pantheist religions, such as Hinduism, the concept of the divine is not a personal Being but a non-personal, non-cognitive spiritual substance or essence—akin to energy, electricity, or the force in the *Star Wars* movies.

In its popular forms, pantheism often does include the worship of local gods and goddesses. But what Westerners often fail to understand is that these local gods are not identified with ultimate reality. They are merely beings in which the divine essence shared by all humans is more highly intensified or concentrated.

Buddhism goes even further, referring to the divine with terms such as *the Void* or *Nothingness*. That's why, odd as it may sound, Buddhism is sometimes called an atheistic religion. So are Taoism and Confucianism. As one philosopher explains, the founders of these religions are "not gods themselves; they identify with no deity, no revelation, no personal or transcendent Creator of any sort."[11]

Religion without Morality

If a personal deity is not required to qualify as a religion, what about morality? No, again. Many Eastern religions are *a*moral. They teach that everything must be accepted as parts of the One, the Whole—both yin and yang, both good and evil. The goal is the balance or union of opposites. The rituals associated with these religions do not aim at achieving holiness but enlightenment: the recognition that everything is equally part of the Whole.

When I was a college student during the countercultural 1970s, I was deeply impressed by Hermann Hesse's novel *Siddhartha*, about a Brahmin's son who undergoes a search for spiritual wisdom. In the end, he learns that "everything that exists is good—death as well as life, sin as well as holiness, wisdom as well as folly."[12] Pantheism teaches that it is a mistake to draw any moral distinctions. Everything merges into the One. The end result, however, is that you cannot distinguish good from evil—which means you have no basis for fighting against evil.[13]

The same pantheism is promoted today in movies like *Avatar*. On the mythical planet Pandora, all the flora and fauna are connected by a vast neural network that functions as a kind of collective unconscious, personified by a Gaia-like goddess called Eywa. Significantly, Eywa is portrayed as beyond good and evil. One of the natives says, "Our great mother does not take sides. She protects only the balance of life."

What about pagan or polytheistic religions? They, too, are typically amoral. Polytheistic religions may demand rituals to appease the gods and guarantee good health and good harvests, but often they say nothing about morality. Anthropologist Mary Douglas discovered in her research that there is no "inherent relation between religion and morality: There are primitives who can be religious without being moral and moral without being religious."[14]

Indeed, pagan gods are often outright *im*moral. The Greek and Roman gods were prone to greed, adultery, quarreling, jealousy, and deception. The philosopher Xenophanes complained that "Homer and Hesiod ascribed to the gods all [acts] that are to people disgraceful and shameful: stealing, committing adultery, and deceiving one another." Augustine echoed the same criticism of the pagan gods: "Their habit is to be instigators and instructors in vice, not its avengers."[15]

Some religions even require worshippers to engage in rituals that are immoral, such as temple prostitution or child sacrifice. In ancient Carthage, parents sacrificed their children as burnt offerings to the gods. Archaeologists have uncovered graves containing the tiny charred bones of infants buried under tombstones with inscriptions thanking the gods that they "heard my voice and blessed me."[16]

Do all theologies at least involve some kind of worship ritual then? No again. In ancient Greece, the Epicureans taught that the gods exist but take no interest in human affairs. They do not care if they are feared or worshipped. Aristotle conceived of the Prime Mover as a perfect and unchangeable mind, which therefore thinks only about what is perfect and unchangeable—namely, itself. It neither knows nor cares what humans do. Other religions that practice no worship include Brahmin Hinduism and Theravada Buddhism.

Search for the Divine

Are there *any* features shared by all religions, then? Surprisingly, only one. Based on empirical research, Clouser says, the only feature shared by all religions is that they acknowledge something as divine—using that word to mean the self-existent, eternal reality that is the origin of everything else. Obviously, they do not agree on *what* qualifies as divine; they agree only that *something* is divine. No other factor is genuinely universal among religions.[17]

As a result, religions are a lot more like philosophies than most people think. And philosophies are a lot like religions. Structurally, both start with a set of postulates about what is ultimately real or divine.

Think of the divine as whatever is furthest back, beyond or behind everything else. For example, in polytheism, the personal gods and goddesses are not the ultimate reality because they derive from some pre-existing primordial substance—and *that* is what actually functions as the divine (even if the term is not used).

For example, in ancient Greek mythology where did the gods come from? The essential story line is that the universe began as a divine primeval substance called chaos—an undefined, unbounded nothingness. Out of this initial state arose the first gods. The earth goddess (Gaia) mated with the sky god (Uranus) to produce the Titans, and from the mating of two Titans came the gods of Mount Olympus—Zeus, Apollo, Athena, Poseidon, and all the rest.[18]

Today it is crucial for Christians to understand paganism, and not just for historical reasons. In Western nations, paganism is growing in popularity again: Wicca, Druidism, Shamanism, and Native American religions. In Iceland, which converted to Christianity in the eleventh century, "Heathenry" has once again become a nationally recognized religion. In Britain, some public schools now teach paganism in their religious education courses, including "witchcraft, druidism and the worship of ancient gods such as Thor."[19] Only weeks ago, as I write, a mother contacted me, desperate to learn how to talk with her son who had joined a Wiccan group.

Most revived versions of paganism involve some form of pantheism combined with polytheism, in which the gods are regarded as aspects or emanations of a universal earth spirit. Consult a typical Wiccan website, for example, and you will read texts like this: "Divinity manifests itself through all living beings. Nature itself is divine."[20] The idol in paganism is Nature itself, or a spiritual substance interconnecting all of nature.

Philosophers and Their Gods

Identifying the idol gets to the core of any religion, whether ancient or modern. It also cuts to the heart of any philosophy. The earliest philosophers in the West, the pre-Socratics, ignored the Olympian gods and went back to the original primordial substance—which they called the *arché*, the source or first cause. At the time, four elements were recognized (water, fire, air, earth), and many of the early philosophers selected one of them as the most basic, then reduced everything else to that single element to arrive at a fundamental unity.

Thales observed that all living things need water, and he proposed that the fundamental starting principle, the *arché*, was water. Heraclitus noted that all living things generate heat and proposed that the *arché* was fire. For Anaximenes, the divine substance was air: "Air is God." Others went beyond the four elements. Pythagoras discovered that the order in nature can be represented by geometry and mathematics, and he concluded that the *arché* was number: "God is number; number is God."[21]

Does the Greek concept of the *arché* fit the biblical definition of an idol? Clearly. Whereas Scripture asserts that "all things hold together" in Christ (Col. 1:17), the early philosophers sought to identify some principle immanent within the cosmos that provided an underlying unity—that functioned as their ultimate explainer. Though they rejected the Olympian gods, the pre-Socratics still held a concept of the divine.

The most familiar names among the Greek philosophers are Plato and Aristotle. They taught that the ultimate formative principle within the universe was what they called rational forms. You can think of forms as abstract concepts that make it possible to categorize the world. Though there is vast variety among domestic dogs, from the Great Dane to the tiny Chihuahua, we recognize that they belong to the same category because they fit the abstract concept of "Dog."

Plato taught that the forms exist in an ideal realm separate from matter, whereas Aristotle argued that they inhere in matter. Yet both conceived the forms as eternal, uncreated, unchangeable, universal, and self-existent. Is this a divinity claim? Certainly. The forms were invoked to explain the nature of things—why things are what they are. Human nature is the form shared by all human beings, and it is what makes them human. Justice is the form shared by all just actions, and it is what makes them just.[22] Forms are the ultimate explainer.

Both philosophers even used the language of divinity. Speaking of the realm of the forms, Aristotle says, "Here must surely be the divine, and this must be the first and most dominant principle [the *arché*]." For Plato, the pre-eminent form is the form of the good; to see the good, involves "a conversion, a turning of the soul" from darkness to light. The true philosopher is the person who contemplates this "divine order."[23]

In Romans 1 we learn that idols result from divinizing something immanent within the cosmic order. That description certainly applies to the forms. They are not personal. And though they transcend the *material* world, they do not transcend the cosmic order as a whole. As one theologian explains, "Plato's Form of the Good is not divine" in the Christian sense; it "is divine because it is the highest being *in* the cosmos." Aristotle even defined God as pure form, which means that he (or it) is one pole in the form/matter dialectic that constitutes the cosmos.[24]

The Church of Physics: Idol of Matter

What about modern philosophies? Do they qualify as idols, too? The prevailing view among the New Atheists, along with much of the academic world, is scientific materialism. What is ultimately real is matter—molecules in motion. Materialism is committed to the dogma that physics explains all of chemistry, chemistry explains all of biology, and biology explains the human mind, with nothing left over. Therefore, physics alone explains the human mind. Physics is the ultimate explainer.

Not surprisingly, this view is sometimes called physicalism. A prominent spokesperson is biologist E. O. Wilson of Harvard, who insists that all phenomena, "from the birth of stars to the workings of social institutions, are based on material processes that are ultimately reducible ... to the laws of physics." Biologist Jerry Coyne defines physicalism as "the view that all sciences are *in principle* reducible to the laws of physics." This view, he says, "must be true unless you're religious."[25]

But is this view itself religious? Is it a divinity claim? Without a doubt.

Some materialists admit as much. John Searle says, "There is a sense in which materialism is the religion of our time." A science journalist writing in *The Scientist* is equally candid. In an article about the origin of life, he says, "I believe a material explanation will be found, but that confidence comes from my faith that science is up to the task of explaining, in purely material or naturalistic terms, the whole history of life." He concludes: "My faith is well founded, but it is still faith."

The materialist creed was captured nicely by the late philosopher Dallas Willard: "There is one reality, the natural world, and physics is its prophet."[26]

The now-classic expression of that creed was the popular television series *Cosmos*. It opened with Carl Sagan intoning, in liturgical cadences, "The Cosmos is all there is, or ever was, or ever will be." When the series was reinitiated in 2014 with Dr. Neil deGrasse Tyson as the new host, fans created a Facebook page to promote what they call "Tysonism," defined as "a secular religion based on the philosophy of astrophysicist Dr. Neil deGrasse Tyson." The page is listed under the category of "Church/Religious Organization."[27]

As we saw earlier, materialism is really a cluster or family of related philosophies. It is a religion, we might say, with several denominations. For example, when applied to the economic realm, materialism gives rise to theories like Marxism. What are the logical steps that lead from materialism to Marxism, with its economic determinism? Bear in mind that human nature is always defined by its relationship to ultimate reality. If the ultimate is matter, then humans are defined by the way they relate to matter. And how *do* people relate to matter? They make things out of it. They mold and manipulate it to manufacture the items they need to survive—clothing, houses, tables, cars.

In Marxism, the tools we use to shape matter are called "the means of production." Thus the history of civilizations hinges on who owns the means of production. The ownership class maintains its control and protects its interests by shaping the rest of society in its favor—laws, politics, morality, religion, and so on. In this way, economic relations determine everything else in a society. In Marxism, economic conditions are the ultimate explainer.[28]

Hume Meets the Klingons: Idol of the Senses

Another widely held idol today is empiricism, the claim that the only valid form of knowledge consists of empirically verified facts. You may not meet many people who say, "Hi, I'm an empiricist." Yet among those who have gone through the public education system, many hold empiricism as a kind of unexamined background assumption. They assume that what we can really rely on are empirical facts—what we can see, feel, weigh, and measure. They relegate everything else to the realm of personal opinion or preference. After all, moral and theological concepts cannot be stuffed into a test tube or studied under a microscope. As a result, empiricism does not consider those concepts to be truths at all, but merely individual values and preferences.

The *enfant terrible* of empiricism was the eighteenth-century philosopher David Hume, who declared that if a book contains anything beyond empirical science, it ought to be burned. Scrutinize every book on the library shelf, he wrote. If it covers subjects like metaphysics or moral theory, then "commit it then to the flames! For it can contain nothing but sophistry and illusion."[29]

Is this another idol? Certainly. Empiricism makes an idol of the sensory realm. Whatever is not susceptible to empirical testing is not real. Hume is not a household name, but among the intellectual elites today, he is enormously influential. A few years ago, a survey of philosophers at leading universities asked which nonliving philosopher they most identified with. The clear winner was David Hume.[30]

Philosophies also spill out of the classroom and into popular culture. In one episode of *Star Trek: The Next Generation*, the plot centers on whether a character named Kahless is the Klingon messiah who has returned from death in fulfillment of prophecy. The *Enterprise*'s Klingon security officer, Lieutenant Worf, has to decide whether the resurrected messiah is real. The android Data asks for empirical evidence supporting the messiah's claims.

"It is not an empirical matter," Worf replies. "It is a matter of faith."

"Faith," Data responds. "Then you do believe Kahless may have supernatural attributes. As an android, I am unable to accept that which cannot be proven through rational means."

Which assumptions are laced through this dialogue? That claims about the supernatural "cannot be proven through rational means." That "a matter of faith" cannot be supported with empirical evidence.[31]

By contrast, if you asked Christians for empirical evidence that Jesus was the Messiah, they would probably list historical evidence for his resurrection, factual evidence for the claims of the New Testament, manuscript evidence for the reliability of the biblical text, archaeological evidence for the events in Scripture, and so on. The Christian message rests on events that could be "seen ... heard ... touched" (1 John 1:1).

Yet the *Star Trek* screenwriters have captured a widespread bias—that any statement about the supernatural is by definition "irrational." You will find the same bias on display in the comments section under virtually any article on the Internet about Christianity. No matter how strong the evidence, any claim that there exists something beyond what can be known by empirical science is attacked as "irrational."

Yet to define what is rational solely by whether it fits the tenets of your own worldview is an invalid move because it rules out all other truth claims by definition. You do not even have to investigate the evidence. A serious search for truth does not start by stacking the deck.

Inside the Matrix

So far, empiricism sounds like another path to materialism. And often it is just that. If what is real is defined in terms of what can be known by the five senses, then reality seems to include only the material world. But if you track empiricism to its logical conclusion, it takes a surprising turn inward to the mind. It signals an important trend in Western thought from materialism to mentalism—from matter as the primary reality to mind as primary.

Think of it this way: Empiricism says the only source of genuine knowledge is sense impressions—sights and sounds. But how do we know whether our sense impressions are true and accurate? After all, we know that our senses can deceive us. Everyone has been subject to optical illusions. Put a spoon into a glass of water and the handle certainly *looks* bent. How do we test our sense experiences?

The answer is that, for the strict empiricist, we *can't* test them. It is impossible to step outside my own head to compare my internal images with the external world to see if they match.[32] How, then, can I be sure that my senses are telling me the truth?

Empiricist philosophers themselves soon recognized the problem. In the nineteenth century, John Stuart Mill concluded that we actually know nothing about the external world. If we examine a table, we might see that it is brown, we feel that it is smooth, we knock on the surface and hear that it is solid, and so on. But those are all sensations—color patches and sound pitches in our heads. According to empiricism, our minds construct the concept of a table out of a cluster of sensations. But we cannot step outside our minds to discover what the external world is like in itself. Mill concluded that the material world is nothing but "the permanent possibilities of sensation."[33]

In that case, however, how do we know that an external world even exists? The most radical of the empiricists admit that, given their premises, we cannot know. There is no way to rule out the possibility that we are characters in *The Matrix*, plugged into a supercomputer that is creating the illusion of a physical world.[34] The bundles of sense perceptions that we interpret as physical objects could be nothing but ... bundles of sense perceptions.

Empiricism ends by claiming that the only thing humans are capable of knowing is a succession of sensations—like a filmstrip running through our heads.

As Morpheus says in *The Matrix*, "How do you define 'real'? If you're talking about what you can feel, what you can smell, what you can taste and see, then 'real' is simply electrical signals interpreted by your brain."

Hume seems to have accepted this bizarre conclusion. He wrote, "Let us chase our imagination to the heavens, or to the utmost limits of the universe; we never really advance a step beyond ourselves." We live in "the universe of the imagination."[35]

The same radical conclusion was shared by physicist Ernst Mach (from whom we get the term "Mach 1" for the speed of sound). "The world consists only of sensations," he wrote. Fundamental physical entities that cannot be observed, like atoms and electrons, he dismissed as nothing but "useful fictions."[36]

The upshot is that if we *begin* solely with sense impressions, then we will *end* with sense impressions. Using sensory experience alone, there is no way to build a bridge from internal mental images to the external world. We are trapped in the prison house of our minds. That is the logical outcome of treating sensation as divine—the sole starting point and standard of knowledge.

Sensational Bacon, Dubious Descartes

Historically, the main rival of empiricism was rationalism. But it, too, ends up trapped inside the mind. Rationalism claims that the sole source and standard of knowledge are ideas in the mind known by reason. But it is impossible to step outside our reason to test whether those ideas are accurate. Like empiricism, it lacks a way to bridge the gap from internal ideas to the external world.[37]

How did so much of Western thought end up trapped in the mind? We must go back imaginatively in history and re-create the intense intellectual chaos at the close of the Middle Ages. The breakup of the medieval church after the Reformation unleashed a century of religious warfare. Thousands of religious refugees fled their homes as Christians literally shed one another's blood in disagreements over interpretations of biblical doctrine. Taking place around the same time was the Renaissance, spurred by the rediscovery of classical texts—Plato, Aristotle, Democritus, Epicurus. And *they* all disagreed with one another as well.

This clash of ideas erupted in what historians call a "skeptical crisis."[38] The urgent question of day was, How can we be certain *which* of these competing truth claims is really true? Philosophers began to search for some deeper source of truth—*not* in any of the theological authorities denouncing one another, not in any of the sacred books or ancient traditions competing for acceptance, and certainly not in any of the civic institutions engaged in armed warfare with one another.

In fact, not in any external source at all. Their hope was to find a method located solely within the individual, rooted in the immediate data of consciousness. They wanted to start over from scratch and rebuild the entire edifice of knowledge on secure foundations within the individual mind.[39]

This hope was the motivation behind both empiricism and rationalism. The founder of empiricism was Francis Bacon. He outlined a program designed to purge our minds of all the popular notions picked up from our education and environment, and to "begin anew from the very foundations."[40] What were those foundations? In his view, the simplest, most direct form of knowledge were sense perceptions—sights and sounds. Bacon proposed to rebuild knowledge on the foundation of sensations.

The founder of rationalism was René Descartes. He proposed a system to purge our minds of every fuzzy or half-baked idea, everything that can possibly be doubted, until we reach a foundation that cannot be doubted. What was that foundation? The one thing Descartes could not doubt was, well, his own mental process of doubting. Even if all my ideas are delusions, he argued there is still a self who is experiencing those delusions. This is the meaning of his famous phrase "I think, therefore I am" (*Cogito, ergo sum*).

He hoped that clear and distinct ideas in the mind would be the foundation on which to rebuild knowledge.

Both Bacon and Descartes expressed some level of Christian conviction.[41] Nevertheless, the philosophies they proposed did not treat God as the final source of truth. Instead they replaced God with the individual consciousness. As one philosopher says, they turned "the first-person standpoint" into the only path to certainty; they set up the "self as the locus and arbiter of knowledge."[42]

This is the core of the modernist project: the idea that if we strip away enough cultural debris—received traditions, speculative philosophies, religious claims—in short, anything humans can be mistaken about, we will finally reach something we *cannot* be mistaken about. Why not? Because it is known not by inference or reasoning, but by introspection into the immediate data of consciousness. Thus it would be immune to any external criticism or challenge. Like the foundation of a house, it would provide a solid, infallible foundation to build the edifice of knowledge.

Signposts or Dead Ends?

Clearly, Enlightenment thinkers were seeking a God substitute. Just as Romans 1 says, they fastened on something within creation to serve in the place of God as their secure and certain source of truth, their ultimate explainer, the fixed foundation of knowledge.

That's why philosopher Karl Popper speaks of the "religious character" of Enlightenment epistemologies. The authority of divine revelation was merely replaced by another form of authority, he writes. Baconian empiricism appealed to "*the authority of the senses*," while Cartesian rationalism appealed to "*the authority of the intellect.*"[43] Yet both hoped to find a method that would yield a truth that was as certain and universal as divine revelation. Both hoped to find a method by which the individual could transcend his or her limited niche in space and time to arrive at absolute, godlike knowledge—what philosophers call a God's-eye view of reality. As philosopher John Herman Randall writes, "They were trying to arrive at that complete and perfect understanding and explanation of the universe that only a God could possess."[44]

In the end, ironically, that search for godlike knowledge was restricted to the tiny universe of the self.

Most philosophies are born when someone stumbles on one of the undeniable facts of human experience and then claims to have discovered the ultimate, infallible foundation of all knowledge. Bacon recognized that, in practice, no one can deny the testimony of the senses. We cannot function in the world unless we trust the basic reliability of what we see and hear. The entire scientific enterprise is based on the assumption that our sensations provide a reliable picture of reality. But empiricism takes this fact of experience and absolutizes it—tries to make it carry a philosophical weight it is not able to carry. Thus it reaches a dead end. If you begin with sense data alone, you end with sense data—nothing but a filmstrip running through your mind.

Descartes stumbled upon another undeniable experience— our sense of self or personal existence. Even if we can be induced to doubt everything we know, there is still a self that is doing the doubting. Rationalism takes this fact of experience and absolutizes it, seeking to build a full-blown philosophy on it. But if you begin with ideas in the mind, that is where you will end. You will be trapped in the prison house of your own mind.

Every nonbiblical philosophy fastens on something in creation—something known by general revelation—and tries to build a system of truth on that foundation. Inevitably, however, it proves too limited to support such an edifice. Our experiences of the created world are merely data that need to be explained. They are signposts pointing to a transcendent Creator. We misread the signs if we treat them as sources of ultimate truth in themselves. Invariably they turn into dead ends.

Kant's Mental Prison: Idol of the Mind

If both empiricism and rationalism leave us trapped inside the mind, the next step was to claim that there *is* no external world—instead the mind creates the world. That step was taken by Immanuel Kant. His innovation was to suggest that the mind does not merely *reflect* the structure of the world; instead it actively *imposes* structure and order onto the world. For Kant, reality as we know it is largely a construction of the human mind.

After all, where do we get our knowledge of the material world? According to Kant, the raw materials of knowledge are sense impressions, flooding into the mind through our eyes and ears in a jumbled chaos. And how do those perceptions get organized into a coherent, intelligible whole? By the creative action of the human mind. Kant proposed that the mind supplies the necessary ordering principles, such as before and after, cause and effect, space and time, and so on. The world appears to be lawful and ordered only because the human mind creates that order, like pressing clay into a mold. In Kant's words, "mind is the law-giver to nature."[45] The human mind took over God's role as law-giver to creation.

This concept was revolutionary, and Kant knew it. He called it his own Copernican revolution. At the birth of modern science, Copernicus had moved the sun to the center of the planetary system. Now Kant moved human consciousness to the center of reality. The primary reality is not matter but mind, he said; the world of objects is largely given its shape and character by human consciousness. As philosopher Alvin Plantinga explains, "The fundamental thrust of Kant's Copernican Revolution is that the things in the world owe their fundamental structure and perhaps their very existence to the noetic activity of our minds."[46]

And if the mind imposes even the categories of space and time, then it must itself be *outside* time. Kant called this timeless, changeless mind the transcendental ego. It was not the ordinary, experienced self—your sense of personal identity—but a kind of higher self, a universal mind.

The philosophical label for this view is idealism. The term is not used in the ordinary sense of having high ideals. Instead it means that ultimate reality is the realm of *ideas*—the mental realm. Instead of deifying matter, idealism deifies the mind. Instead of making matter the basis of consciousness, it claims that consciousness structures matter as we know it. It makes consciousness the ultimate explainer.

Kant claimed that his system "rests on a fully secured foundation, established forever."[47] When you hear phrases like *secured foundation* and *established forever*, your idol detector should start beeping. Anything in creation that is proposed as the eternal, unchanging foundation of reality is an idol. Like Bacon and Descartes, Kant was a theist. But what really played the role of the divine in his system was not God but the human mind. The mind itself was granted godlike creative power.

Textbooks often say that Kant's philosophy combined empiricism and rationalism, so not surprisingly it shares the same major weakness. On its own premises, there is no way to step outside the human mind and test whether our ideas match external reality. The logical consequence is solipsism, the doctrine that the only thing I can know for sure is the existence of my own mind. "Common to both empiricism and idealism is the doctrine that the mind has no direct knowledge of anything but its own contents," writes philosopher Anthony Kenny. "The history of both movements shows that they lead in the direction of solipsism."[48] They leave us trapped within the mind.

The Artist as God: Idol of the Imagination

Despite the flaws in idealism, it was enthusiastically embraced by the Romantic movement. Many Romantics were artists, and they were attracted to idealism because it deified the mind or creative imagination. If the mind is the power that imposes order on the world—creating order from chaos—then the artist is no longer just an artisan but a creator.

For the Romantics, then, the ultimate foundation for truth was neither the senses (empiricism) nor reason (rationalism) but the creative imagination. They conceived of the imagination as an autonomous power "immune to any outside force," explains Alan Jacobs of Baylor University; it "generates its own distinctive kind of truth unchallengeable by other kinds of truth." Words like *autonomous*, *immune*, and *unchallengeable* should set your idol detector beeping. The Romantics were claiming that the imagination generates ultimate truth. It "performs a number of functions formerly reserved for God himself," Jacobs says.[49] It is a God substitute.

Poets began to say that art re-enacts the very work of God in creating a new world from nothing. Samuel Coleridge described artistic creation as "a repetition in the finite mind of the eternal act of creation in the infinite I AM." Johann Gottfried Herder wrote, "The artist is become a creator God."

Thus was born the now-familiar notion of the artist as a prophet or visionary. William Wordsworth felt that his spirit had been "clothed in priestly robe" and singled out "for holy services." William Butler Yeats said that art became for him "a new religion, almost an infallible Church of poetic tradition." A book on Romanticism is titled *The Imagination as a Means of Grace*, reflecting the religious status assigned to the creative imagination.[50]

It is often said that the two movements that kicked off the modern age were the Enlightenment and Romanticism—and both were built on idols.

Cure for Blind Philosophers

The cosmic drama unfolded in Romans 1 gives us powerful principles that apply to religions as well as philosophies, ancient as well as modern. Principle #1 tells us that the way to cut to the heart of any alternative to Christianity is to identify its idol. Each one carves out some aspect of creation and elevates it to a false absolute—a single, all-defining principle. This tendency to absolutize some part of creation is "the source of all isms," writes Christian philosopher Herman Dooyeweerd.[51] One part of the created order is treated as the whole. One piece of a puzzle is claimed to be the complete picture. One color in the spectrum is declared to be the entire rainbow.

Worldviews are a lot like the characters in the famous poem "The Blind Men and the Elephant." The blind man who caught hold of the waving trunk insisted that the entire elephant was like a snake. The blind man who grasped the tusk argued that the whole animal was like a spear. The man who found the tail insisted that the beast was like a rope. And so on. Idol-based worldviews work in much the same way. Each grabs on to a part of reality and declares it to be the whole show. That one part is treated as the set of conceptual categories that explains all of human experience, the key that unlocks the universe.

Anything it does *not* explain is either denied, redefined, or dismissed as unreal.

By contrast, Christianity does not start with anything in creation. It begins with the transcendent Creator. Therefore, it is not limited in scope. It does not have to reduce all of reality to a single set of categories. It does not see just the trunk or the tusk or the tail. It is a transcendent point of view that sees the whole elephant—the God's-eye view that philosophers and mystics have always sought. Though you and I are limited in our individual perspectives, we have access to the perspective of eternity.

The Joy of Critical Thinking

The philosophies you are learning in this book form the backbone of all of Western thought—the ideas that inform every subject area, every academic discipline, every profession. When our son took a college course on the history of psychology, I opened the textbook and could have sworn it was for a philosophy course. It started with the pre-Socratics, went on to Plato and Aristotle, covered empiricism and rationalism and Kant, then continued all the way to the most recent philosophical movements. The textbook was making the point that every *psychological* theory stems from the application of a *philosophy*.[52]

Other subject areas draw from the same well. Once you master the five principles from Romans 1, you will be equipped to think critically and creatively about any theory in any field of study or work. As one of my students said, using this method "is like the difference between driving around Los Angeles with just a set of directions (turn left, turn right) compared to having a map of the whole city. The map gives you the overall perspective." The five principles provide a map to navigate any system of ideas.

Students have sometimes told me that the main message they get from reading books on apologetics is "Everyone else is wrong." A Romans 1 approach offers a refreshing alternative. Because a counterfeit god is something within creation, it leads people to focus on that aspect of creation—which means they are likely to uncover some genuine truths. Consider the idols we have identified:

> **Materialism** is partly right because God did create a material universe. He even pronounced it "very good" (Gen. 1:31). So we should not be surprised that scientists who embrace materialism can tell us a great deal about the physical universe.
>
> **Rationalism** gets something right because God did create the world with a rationally knowable structure. He also created the human mind with a corresponding structure. Good reasoning leads to God. In C. S. Lewis's *The Screwtape Letters*, the experienced devil warns the younger devil to avoid arguments: "By the very act of arguing, you awake the patient's reason: and once it is awake, who can foresee the result?"[53]
>
> **Empiricism** gets some things right because God did create a world with a sensory dimension, and he equipped humans

with their five senses to function in that world. Jesus himself validated the need for empirical evidence. If you don't believe my words, he told his disciples, then believe "on the evidence of the miracles" (John 14:11 NIV[54]). When the Pharisees questioned his authority to forgive the sins of a paralyzed man, Jesus responded, "But that you may *know* that the Son of Man has authority on earth to forgive sins...." He left the sentence hanging, turned, and healed the paralytic (Mark 2:9–11). Jesus confirmed his identity by giving empirical evidence that was available to any seeking person.

When the apostles proclaimed the gospel, they treated their message as public truth, based on eyewitness testimony, open to cross-examination and testing—that "which we have heard, which we have seen with our eyes, which we have looked upon and have touched with our hands" (1 John 1:1). They did not preach "cleverly devised myths" but were "eyewitnesses" of events taking place in time and space (2 Pet. 1:16). What they witnessed were "many convincing proofs" of Christ's resurrection from the dead (Acts 1:3 NIV). What's more, as Paul reminded the Roman rulers, those events were not "done in a corner" (Acts 26:26). They were public events witnessed by many people who were still alive at the time— and who could therefore potentially refute the apostles' claim, if they had any contrary evidence to present.[55]

Romanticism was right to oppose Enlightenment worldviews that reduce humans to complex mechanisms. It was right to assert human freedom and creativity. Because we are made in the image of a Creator, Christians should be more committed than anyone else to supporting the creative arts. The imagination should soar.

A biblical worldview enables Christians to approach every viewpoint with a free and respectful attitude, knowing that virtually every perspective offers something of value. We can glean what is good wherever we find it. We can enjoy the best works of any culture. We can delight in the artistry and beauty found in classic works of art and literature. We can learn from the insights found in science and philosophy. We should refuse to allow good words like *empirical* and *rational* to be taken over by secular worldviews. Instead we should work to fill these terms with balanced biblical content.

All the while, we should be making the case that whatever is genuinely good and true finds its true home within Christianity. Every ism isolates one strand from the rich fabric of truth. Christianity alone provides what the greatest philosophers and sages have sought all along: a coherent and transcendent framework that encompasses all of human knowledge.

The Good, the True, and the Pagan

In every age, Christians have faced the task of identifying what is good and true in the surrounding culture. The Christian church was born into an intellectual climate shaped by Greek philosophy.

The challenge for the church fathers was to design a strategy for addressing that highly literate but pagan culture. Sifting through the prevailing ideas, they found much they had to reject as contrary to the Bible. But they also uncovered much that was good and right, which they could assimilate into a biblical worldview. They coined a phrase that is still in common currency today: "All truth is God's truth, wherever it is found."

The church fathers also passed on a phrase they borrowed from the Old Testament. In the exodus of the Israelites from Egypt, God urged them to "plunder the Egyptians" (Exod. 12:36). Metaphorically, the phrase came to mean appropriating the best of pagan society, including its art and scholarship.[56]

Paul himself provides a stunning example when he quotes the literature of his day while speaking to the Greek cultural leaders on Mars Hill in Acts 17. When the text says Paul "reasoned" with the philosophers of Athens, the word in Greek is *dialegomai*, the root of the English word *dialogue*. In other words, Paul's address was not a one-way street. He starts by acknowledging that his pagan listeners had some insight into truth, even if their groping toward the divine was hazy: "I found also an altar with this inscription, 'To the unknown god.' What therefore you worship as unknown, this I proclaim to you" (Acts 17:23).

Paul then quotes pagan poetry: "'In him we live and move and have our being'; as even some of your own poets have said, 'For we are indeed his offspring.'" (Acts 17:28). Close parallels to these lines are found in several ancient literary sources, which means Paul was tapping into assumptions that were widespread at the time. He was willing to appeal to the valid intuitions and insights of his Greek audience, even as he corrected and transformed those insights by incorporating them into the biblical universe of meaning. Paul was making the astounding claim that Christianity provides the context of meaning for the Greeks to understand *their own* culture.

The biblical worldview is so rich and multi-dimensional that Christians can learn and benefit from what is true in all philosophies of life, while at the same time critiquing their flaws and transcending their limitations.

First, however, we need to help people recognize those limitations. In Principle #2, we will learn how to show how cramped and dehumanizing idol-based worldviews are.

PRINCIPLE #2

・・・・・

HOW NIETZSCHE WINS

"Why does God let people go through the 'stupid years'?"

John Erickson was telling me, in self-deprecating tones, the story of what he calls his "stupid years"—the time spent turning his back on the church and looking for a more sophisticated creed to live by. It is a familiar trajectory, traveled by many young adults.[1]

"I grew up in a devout, church-going, King James Bible Southern Baptist home in West Texas," John told me. "But during my senior year in high school, I began reading Darwin and Freud. I immersed myself in the French poets, like Rimbaud and the other Decadents.

"When I asked questions about these secular ideas, the answer seemed to be that good Baptists didn't ask those questions. That did not satisfy me."

Coming of age in the 1960s counterculture, John was attracted by its heady idealism. He was morally outraged by the more than fifty thousand dead Americans in Vietnam while, as he saw it, the church wrapped itself in the flag. As a Southerner, John was also repulsed by the church's historical role in slavery and racial oppression. He veered left in his politics and his theology, grew his hair long, and joined protest marches against racism and the Vietnam War.

After college, John was awarded a Rockefeller Fellowship to attend Harvard Divinity School. There he studied under the leading liberal luminaries of the day, such as H. Richard Niebuhr and Harvey Cox. Also teaching at Harvard at the time was Joseph Fletcher, author of *Situation Ethics*, a book that alienated students from the idea that there are unyielding principles of right and wrong. For students like John, it seemed that Fletcher had achieved an intellectual tour de force: He had "put a scholarly gloss on what, for centuries, had been regarded as mere adolescent fantasy—that we are free to make up the rules as we go along and then call it Christian."

It was not until John was about to graduate that he finally encountered a challenge to his theological liberalism—not by reading the Bible but by reading Nietzsche.

"Vociferous Atheist"

The turnaround began when John wrote a paper on Nietzsche for one of his courses. "I knew that Nietzsche was a vociferous atheist and an enemy of the Christian faith, but I rather enjoyed watching him throw jabs in the face of flabby bourgeois Christianity. I figured it might be fun to spar a few rounds with him in my term paper."

But the sparring match turned into a rout. To John's surprise, he found himself agreeing with much of Nietzsche's scathing critique of the white-bread cultural Christianity so common in the West. Nietzsche denounced religion that had degenerated into sheep-like bourgeois respectability.

"I submitted my essay and made an appointment with the professor to discuss it," John told me. "I couldn't even look him in the eye. Looking down, I said, 'Nietzsche won. I could not answer his arguments.'"

You might expect a professor at a prominent divinity school to offer a robust counter-challenge to one of history's most notorious atheists. But to John's astonishment, the professor had nothing to offer. Except an A- on the paper.

Years later, John came to regret the years that he had spent captivated by Nietzsche's atheism and nihilism. As a rebellious college student, he had found it all too easy to flog the organized church for its failings, while ignoring Christianity's positive contributions. John eventually discovered that many of the freedoms and human rights enjoyed in the West are fruits of its Christian heritage. That modern science is largely a product of the biblically inspired concept of laws in nature. That just-war doctrine, developed by medieval theologians, did much to bring an end to unlimited slaughter, rape, looting, and enslavement. That a host of moral ideals, from anti-slavery to women's rights, have their roots in Christianity.

"As students, we took all of this for granted, like oxygen in a lecture hall, and we heaped harsh judgment on the Christian West," John recalled. "But we rarely asked, 'Compared to what?' The 'what' was always some form of utopian ideal. But utopian ideals have not fared so well. In the twentieth century, secular utopian idealists presided over the extermination of a hundred million people, killed for 'a higher good' by the apostles of Darwin, Marx, and Nietzsche. History has never produced a more efficient set of butchers."

John came to wish his Harvard professors had been a lot tougher on their students' faddish nihilism. "My professor should not have let me off so easy. He should not have allowed me to walk out of his office thinking that Nietzsche had obliterated nineteen hundred years of Christian intellectual and moral accomplishment. He should have said something like this: 'Nietzsche was a brilliant, tormented genius who gave us the blueprint for spiritual disintegration and Hell on earth. He beat you up because you're weak, rebellious, and ignorant. Worse, you're proud of it. Take your paper and write it again.'"

In the end, John grew disillusioned enough to pack his bags and leave Harvard, moving back to West Texas where he reconnected with his family and his roots. Over the years, he rethought his theology and became a committed Christian. Today he is a highly successful children's writer, author of the much-loved Hank the Cowdog series.

Have It Your Way

Why does God allow people to go through what John Erickson calls the "stupid years"? To answer that, we must listen again to the message of Romans 1. The text repeats a poignant phrase that speaks volumes: "God gave them up ... gave them up ... gave them up" (Rom. 1:24, 26, 28). The phrase does not mean God gives up on people. Just the opposite. It means he tries to get through to them by allowing them to play out the negative consequences of their idolatrous choices.

This divine strategy is apparent throughout Scripture. When the ancient Israelites turned to idols, God said, "So I let them follow their own stubborn desires, living according to their own ideas" (Ps. 81:12 NLT). Similarly, in the Song of Moses, God said, "I will hide my face from them; I will see what their end will be" (Deut. 32:20). In the Septuagint (the Greek translation of the Old Testament), the word for *see* means to show, point out, exhibit, teach, demonstrate, make known. Clearly, God's purpose is to reach out and communicate. In essence God is saying, Okay, have it your way, and see for yourself how destructive it is.

This strategy has obvious parallels in everyday life. Parents sometimes have to allow children to make bad choices and suffer the consequences. Teachers may have to let students fail due to bad study habits. Counselors know that addicts have to hit bottom before they are willing to change. In the same way, God gives people up so they will perceive the harmful consequences of their idols. From verse 26 to the end of the chapter, Romans 1 illustrates those consequences with a long list of destructive and self-destructive behavior. God uses these negative experiences to press people to the point of decision: Will they continue worshipping a counterfeit god that is destroying them, or will they repent and turn to the true God?

Principle #2
Identify the Idol's Reductionism

Why do idols invariably lead to destructive behavior? What is the connection? The link is that idols always lead to a lower view of human life. In Romans 1, the connection is captured in the word *exchanged*: They "exchanged the glory of the immortal God for images resembling mortal man and birds and animals and creeping things" (Rom. 1:23). When a worldview exchanges the Creator for something in creation, it will also exchange a high view of humans made in God's image for a lower view of humans made in the image of something in creation.

Humans are not self-existent, self-sufficient, or self-defining. They did not create themselves. They are finite, dependent, contingent beings. As a result, they will always look outside themselves for their ultimate identity and meaning. They will define human nature by its relationship to the divine—however they define divinity. Those who do not get their identity from a transcendent Creator will get it from something in creation.

We could say that every concept of humanity is created in the image of *some* god. And because that divinity will always be lower than the biblical God, its view of humanity will also be lower. Those who dishonor God will dishonor those made in God's image. Those who create idols eventually "become like them" (Ps. 115:8).

In philosophical terms, this is called reductionism—the process of reducing a something from a higher, more complex level of reality to a lower, simpler, less complex level. When an idol absolutizes some part of creation, everything else must be explained in terms of that one limited part—pulled down to that level, measured against that one yardstick, reduced to that lowest common denominator.

Principle #1 gave us the first step in engaging any nonbiblical worldview: Identify its idol. Now we move to Principle #2: Identify its reductionism. When God gives people up to their idols, the result is always a reductionistic view of humanity—which ultimately unleashes harmful and destructive behavior. When we reduce people to anything less than fully human, we will *treat* them as less than fully human.

When we define God as a *something* instead of a *Someone*, we will tend to treat humans as *somethings* too.

Dehumanize Thy Neighbor

It may be easier to recognize reductionism by starting on a personal level. Consider the idols that many of us live for. Do you live for financial success? Is that the most important goal in your life? If so, you will evaluate every activity by its economic payoff. You will size up other people by asking whether they are useful for advancing your economic interests. Your outlook on life will be one-dimensional and utilitarian.

Or is the most important thing in your life your relationships? Your physical appearance? Your professional accomplishments? No matter what your idol is, you will feel pressure to measure every part of life by that yardstick. An idol always leads to a reductionistic attitude that dehumanizes others and justifies using them for your own agenda.

Reductionism is often signaled by the phrase "nothing but." Think of some examples from everyday conversation. Haven't we all heard people say that religion is nothing but an expression of psychological need? A projection of a father figure in the sky? A myth invented by primitive people to assuage their fear of natural forces? In the typical college course or television science program, a reductionist theory of religion is simply assumed without argument.

Or haven't we all heard that love is really nothing but a product of chemical reactions? Current theories in neuroscience convey the impression that love can be reduced to neurotransmitters and circuits in the brain. A *Wall Street Journal* article suggests that Valentine's Day cards should not feature hearts but images of a squishy gray blob—the brain. "And instead of saying 'I love you,' the knowledgeable lover would say, 'Darling, dopamine floods my caudate nucleus' every time I look at you."[2]

Haven't we all met cynics who insist that morality is nothing but self-interest in disguise? In ancient Greece, the sophists argued that people do what serves their own advantage, and afterward invent a moral code to justify their behavior. Today an updated version of sophism is taking the college classroom by storm, a theory called evolutionary psychology. It claims that altruistic behavior has been programmed into our genes by natural selection because of its survival value. We are kind to others only so that they will be kind to us in turn (reciprocal altruism). Or we are kind to those who share our gene pool because we have a vested biological interest in passing our own genes on to the next generation (kin altruism). Evolutionary psychology reduces all human behavior to masked self-interest.

In practice, people often find ways to avoid the reductionistic implications of their worldviews. Because humans are made in God's image, they often do treat others with dignity and respect; they engage in humanitarian projects and advocate for human rights. The problem is that nonbiblical worldviews provide no logical basis for such altruistic behavior. For example, the late Richard Rorty was revered as a philosopher of democracy, yet he wrote, "I do not know how to 'justify' or 'defend' social democracy … in a large philosophical way."[3] He was acknowledging that he had no basis for his own highest ideals.

In evangelism, it can often be effective to walk people through the implications of their worldview to show that it provides no basis for *their own* highest moral and humanitarian ideals.

The Science of Cheating

Reductionism is the key to explaining why idols lead to immoral behavior—why Romans 1 ends with a list of destructive and self-destructive behavior. When we dehumanize people in our thinking, we will eventually mistreat, oppress, abuse, and exploit them in our actions.

The connection between thinking and behavior has even been investigated scientifically. An article in *Scientific American* describes an ingenious series of studies designed to test the practical consequences of holding the philosophy of materialism, with its corollary that humans have no free will. A group of enterprising researchers decided to test whether such a reductionistic view of humanity has any impact on moral behavior.

The results showed a clear yes. One experiment involved a quiz designed to make it easy to cheat. Some participants were randomly assigned to what was called a *determinism* condition. They were asked to read statements such as "A belief in free will contradicts the known fact that the universe is governed by lawful principles of science." Other participants were randomly assigned to what was called a *free-will* condition. They read statements such as "Avoiding temptation requires that I exert my free will."[4]

Which group of participants cheated more on the quiz? The *determinism* group, whose members were encouraged to think they had no capacity for moral choice—and thus no moral responsibility. By contrast, the *free-will* group, whose members were primed to exert their moral will, was less likely to cheat.

Another experiment involved managing money. Once again, the *determinism* group was more likely to steal money. *Scientific American* summarizes: "One of the most striking findings to emerge recently in the science of free will is that when people believe—or are led to believe—that free will is just an illusion, they tend to become more antisocial."[5]

When a person accepts materialism as a life philosophy, its effects do not stay neatly contained within the mental realm. It leads to destructive personal behavior and harmful public consequences.

In these experiments, science is catching up with what Paul said two millennia ago: Your worldview affects how you treat others. A reductionistic worldview leads to destructive behavior. Those who dishonor God will end up dishonoring themselves and others.

The Psychology of Suppression

Given the negative consequences of a reductionist worldview, you might wonder why anyone would adopt one. What's the appeal? Paul gives a clue: Recall that human nature is part of general revelation, giving evidence for God. The existence of beings with the capacity to reason, love, plan, and choose is evidence that the first cause that created them must have at least the same capacities.

The cause must be sufficient to produce the effect. The origin of personal beings is best explained by a personal Being.

How do sinful, fallen humans seek to avoid that conclusion? Paul says they "suppress the truth" (Rom. 1:18). That's what reductionism accomplishes. It denies one or more dimensions of human nature—so that the evidence from human nature no longer points as clearly to the biblical God.

If reductionism is like trying to stuff all of reality into a box, we could say the problem is that the box is always too small. Idols deify some part of the created order. But no matter which part they choose, a *part* is always too limited to explain the *whole*. The universe is too complex and multi-dimensional to fit into a box composed of just one part. Invariably something will stick out. Something will not fit into its restricted conceptual categories.

What then? Whatever does not fit into the box will be dismissed, devalued, or outright denied. Reductionist thinking can be summarized as saying, if my worldview does not account for X, so much the worse for X. Idols are popular precisely because they cut reality down to a size that can be stuffed into a box and controlled. They eliminate those dimensions of reality that would falsify the worldview. You can make any worldview appear successful simply by denying anything that does not fit into its box.

To use the Bible's term, people suppress anything that threatens their favored worldview. If general revelation is evidence for God, then every substitute religion will have to deny that evidence.

Yet suppression creates a deep chasm—a dualism or dichotomy—sometimes in theory but always in practice.[6] On one side of the chasm are the things that fit inside the box, which are accepted as real and objective. On the other side are the things that stick out of the box, which are reduced to the status of subjective illusions or mental constructs.

To switch metaphors, philosophers sometimes picture the dichotomy using the image of two stories in a building. Reductionists try to live in only one story. For example, materialists try to live strictly in the lower story, the material universe. They treat matter and energy as the only things that are real, knowable, and objectively true. The upper story becomes a sort of attic where they toss everything that does not fit into the materialist box—soul, spirit, mind, morality, freedom, love, God.

You might say these things are stashed away in the attic in dusty old trunks labeled "Superstition" and "Wishful Thinking" and "Educated People Know Better." We can picture the two-story divide with a simple diagram. If you have read the works of Francis Schaeffer, or my own earlier books, you will recognize this diagram:

Materialists try to live in the lower story

NON-MATERIAL WORLD
Subjective, Superstitious, Mental Constructs

MATERIAL WORLD
Objective, Scientific, Knowable Facts

Because people are made in God's image, however, in practice they cannot live strictly in one story. They cannot completely get rid of those troublesome old trunks in the attic. But that's jumping ahead to Principle #3, which argues that no one can live inside the limited box of an idol-based worldview.

Before we make that argument, we need to see how widespread reductionism is. As there are many different idols, so there are many forms of reductionism, and it is vital to hone our idol detectors to recognize them. Because it is easier to identify the dehumanizing impact when worldviews are developed to their most logical conclusions, we will consider two of them in their most recent versions—materialism and postmodernism. Then we will identify the reductionism inherent in two religions—pantheism and Islam. Finally, because negative consequences are especially visible when worldviews are expressed in public policy, we will end with two political theories.

Crick: "Nothing but a Pack of Neurons"

In recent years a radically reductionistic version of materialism has been advanced called *eliminative* materialism. It goes beyond the traditional materialist claim that material conditions determine the mental world to the more surprising claim that the mental world does not exist—that all of our thoughts, convictions, desires, intentions, perceptions, and decisions are fictions. They are illusions produced by the underlying brain chemistry, with no causal impact of their own, like foam whipped up by the sea or sparks created by a machine.

"Our starting assumption as scientists ought to be that on some level consciousness has to be an illusion," says Cambridge psychologist Nicholas Humphrey. "The reason is obvious: If nothing in the physical world can have the features that consciousness seems to have, then consciousness cannot exist as a thing in the physical world."[7] In his view, apparently, if something is not "a thing in the physical world," then it cannot exist.

But if consciousness is an illusion, then how is Humphrey conscious of that fact? And why should we trust the thinking of scientists who tell us there is no such thing as thinking? As one philosopher notes, eliminative materialism "refutes itself since even an illusion is the presence of an experience" within someone's consciousness.[8]

Despite these logical contradictions (which we will discuss in Principle #4), the same radical reductionism is held by several leading thinkers. Francis Crick, best known for cracking the DNA code, later undertook to disprove the existence of the soul or self. He writes: "'You,' your joys and your sorrows, your memories and your ambitions, your sense of identity and free will, are in fact no more than the behavior of a vast assembly of nerve cells and their associated molecules." Playing off a line in *Alice in Wonderland*, he concludes, "You're nothing but a pack of neurons."

In a similar vein, psychologist Daniel Wegner of Harvard argues that free will is an illusion and that all our actions are really the effects of unconscious physical causes. His book is aptly titled *The Illusion of Conscious Will*. In an interview he admits that free will is "a very persistent illusion; it keeps coming back." Yet he treats it as nothing more than a magician's trick: "Even though you know it's a trick, you get fooled every time. The feelings just don't go away."[9] (You might think that when a theory is contradicted by persistent experiences that "just don't go away," that persistence should count as evidence against the theory. We will develop this argument in Principle #3.)

It strikes most people as extreme to claim humans have no free will or consciousness or personal identity. Why would anyone come up with a theory so contrary to normal experience? The reasoning rests on a metaphor popular among cognitive scientists: that the brain is a computer. For example, Harvard neuroscientist Steven Pinker calls the human brain a complex machine for "information processing or computation." Now, we know that computers work perfectly well without being conscious. So why are *we* conscious? The reductionist answer is: We're not. The idea that there is an inner self that unifies our thoughts and experiences is an illusion. In Pinker's words, "There's considerable evidence that the unified self is a fiction."[10]

Where would such a fiction come from? The theory claims that natural selection has programmed it into our genes because it enables us to predict and control our environment more easily. For example, we can more easily predict that Sally will go to the refrigerator if we know she *wants* a drink and *thinks* a carton of milk is in the fridge. In reality, however, the theory says, internal states such as *wanting* and *thinking* do not exist. Ordinary language is just a convenient shorthand that we use because an accurate account, invoking the laws of physics that govern the neurons firing in Sally's brain, would be impossibly complex.[11]

"Deepest Irrationality"

We have to give eliminative materialism credit for being utterly logical: Having made an idol of matter, it rejects anything beyond the material realm. Yet not all materialists are happy with that outcome. They point to the obvious fact that we are conscious beings. Somehow, they say, consciousness must emerge from matter. This view is called emergentism.[12]

Yet the claim that mental properties emerge from brain states is highly implausible. After all, mental states are not at all like physical states. A physical object like a rose may be red and prickly, but your thought about the rose is neither red nor prickly. Physical objects are public: They can be observed by other people. But mental states (such as feelings of pain or joy) are private: They cannot be directly observed by anyone else. We explain physical states by invoking a general causal law (as in science). But we explain mental states by invoking personal intentions, desires, and choices. Finally, mental states are always *about* something, directed toward an object (you think about a person, you worry about a problem). But physical objects are not *about* anything. They just "are."[13]

It appears that consciousness and matter differ in kind (qualitatively), not merely in degree (quantitatively). Therefore, to claim that consciousness somehow emerges from matter seems like trying to get something from nothing—like pulling a rabbit from a hat. Philosopher Evan Fales calls it a mystery: "Darwinian evolution implies that humans emerged through the blind operation of natural forces. It is mysterious how such forces could generate something nonphysical."[14]

Philosopher Colin McGinn treats it as akin to a miracle. "We do not know how consciousness might have arisen by natural processes from antecedently existing material things," he writes. "One is tempted, however reluctantly, to turn to divine assistance: … It would take a supernatural magician to extract consciousness from matter." Resorting to a biblical analogy, McGinn asks, "How did evolution convert the water of biological tissue into the wine of consciousness?"[15]

Philosopher Mark Bedau says the idea of emergence "is uncomfortably like magic." Thus it "will discomfort reasonable forms of materialism."[16] More "reasonable" forms of materialism hold that if humans *came* from matter, then they *consist* solely of matter—and mind is an illusion.

Why do most people find it difficult to accept that "reasonable" conclusion? Because it runs counter to our most pressing everyday experience. In the words of philosopher Galen Strawson, the denial of consciousness "is surely *the strangest thing that has ever happened in the whole history of human thought.*" It shows "that the power of human credulity is unlimited, that the capacity of human minds to be gripped by theory, by faith, is truly unbounded." It reveals "the deepest irrationality of the human mind."[17]

This is a striking critique. Strawson is saying that eliminative materialism is a "faith"—one that is deeply "irrational" when measured against what we know by common-sense experience.

The eighteenth-century philosopher Thomas Reid argued that such extreme logical consistency in the face of contrary facts is a form of insanity. When you allow yourself to be reasoned out of what you know by common sense, just because some philosophical system requires it, he wrote, "we may call this metaphysical lunacy."[18]

After all, the goal of philosophy is to *explain* the facts of experience, not to deny them. Anything less is ducking the issue. The problem with reductionism is that instead of explaining things, it tries to explain them away.

Outside the ivory tower, ordinary people are not interested in a worldview that spins out a logically coherent system, and yet contradicts human experience. They are looking for a worldview that makes sense of the world we actually inhabit. They want one that explains the undeniable facts of human experience, not one that suppresses those facts for the sake of its own internal logical consistency.

Besides, the facts suppressed by materialism are exactly the things people care most about—the whole realm of conscious experience. Most of what makes life worth living consists of experiences: love, happiness, fulfillment, moral ideals, a sense of purpose, and so on.[19]

Finally, ordinary people are sensitive to the practical and moral consequences of worldviews. Radically reductionist views of the human person are not just harmless speculations—idle amusements for philosophers. What the dominant classes hold as true tends to shape social and political practice. If the elites hold a materialism that reduces humans to computers, then they will treat people like computers. Thinking will be reduced to computing: the neuroelectrophysiology of the brain. People will be judged solely by how well they perform their assigned functions. And when they stop functioning, they will be tossed in the garbage heap with the other electronic trash.

Revenge of the Romantics

In a typical university, this radical form of reductionism is likely to be held in the science department, where the expectation is that most professors embrace materialism. If you walk across campus to the arts and humanities buildings, however, there you will find that most professors embrace postmodernism. In many ways, the two worldviews are diametrically opposed. Yet both lead to a dehumanizing reductionism.

For many people, the term *postmodern* seems somewhat arcane, but it is easier to understand if we trace how it developed. Its roots reach back to the Romantic movement, touched on briefly in Principle #1. One of the heroes of Romanticism was Schopenhauer, who said, "Materialism is the philosophy of the subject who forgets to take account of himself."[20] That is, a materialist looks outward at the physical world, as though that were the sole reality, and "forgets" to look inward at the self. Yet the inner world of consciousness is equally part of the reality that worldviews are required to explain.

The Romantics were not interested in recovering only the individual mind, however. They were enamored of Kant's idea of a transcendental ego or universal mind, with its godlike powers to create the world of experience. For many, it was a springboard to pantheism. Theologian Ian Barbour says that, for the Romantics, "God is not the external creator of an impersonal machine, but a spirit pervading nature."[21]

The Romantics wanted to overthrow the Enlightenment image of the universe as a vast machine and replace it with an organic image—the universe as organism. In their vision, explains Randall, "the world was no machine, it was alive, and God was not its creator so much as its soul, its life."[22]

As we saw earlier, the philosophical label for this is idealism, the claim that the real causal power in the universe is the mental realm of ideas. The Romantics wanted to knock down the idol of materialism (ultimate reality is material), so they proposed the idol of idealism (ultimate reality is mental). They wanted to counter worldviews that absolutize matter, so they absolutized mind. Novelist Walker Percy says materialism stuffs everything into the "box of things," while idealism stuffs everything into "the mind box."[23] Or to return to the metaphor of two stories in a building, each movement tries to live in one story.

Western philosophy divides into two philosophical "families"

ROMANTICISM
The Box of Mind

ENLIGHTENMENT
The Box of Things

Each of these two streams grew into a richly interconnected network of philosophies, which today are called the analytic and the continental traditions. The analytic tradition traces its roots to the Enlightenment and tends to highlight science, reason, and facts. The continental tradition traces its roots to the Romantic movement and seeks to defend mind, meaning, and morality.[24]

Worldviews are not a scattershot of disconnected ideas; they tend to cluster in groups connected by family resemblances. When we learn each family's connecting themes, it will be easier to identify its form of reductionism.

Emerson's Over-Soul

When the Romantics reached out for conceptual tools to defend their spiritualized conception of the world, they revived neo-Platonism, a version of idealism with roots in the third century. University courses in philosophy often skip neo-Platonism. (I did not have a course on it until graduate school.) Yet it had a significant influence on Western history.[25]

As the name suggests, neo-Platonism started out with Plato's thought, which was patched together with bits and pieces from other Greek schools of thought and then spiced with Eastern pantheism. From these diverse sources, neo-Platonism crafted a "big tent" worldview. You might think of it as the New Age movement of the ancient world, combining elements from both East and West.

The central tenet of neo-Platonism was that the world is an emanation of a spiritual substance called the One or the Absolute. Like a fountain cascading down through multiple levels, the One emanated a descending series that flowed down through several levels: from spiritual entities to human beings, then to sentient creatures (animals), living things (plants), and finally material things (rocks). This was called the ladder of life or the great chain of being. The goal of the spiritual life was to re-ascend the ladder, escape from matter, and reunite with the One.[26]

What attracted the Romantics to neo-Platonism was the idea that nature is permeated by soul or spirit. For the idealists, says Eagleton, the Absolute served "as a form of secularized divinity." This was not a personal God who thinks, feels, wills, and acts. It was a non-personal spiritual essence or substance. Ralph Waldo Emerson called it the Over-soul: "the soul of the whole ... the eternal ONE."[27]

Hegel's Evolutionary Deity

Neo-Platonism was given a novel twist by the philosopher Hegel, who added the concept of historical development or evolution. Until then, the ladder of life had been static. It was a fixed list or inventory of the things that exist in the universe. But with Hegel, the ladder became dynamic. To picture the change, you might think of the ladder tilting over to become an escalator, with the entire universe progressing upward through a series of stages. Hegel called his pantheistic deity the Absolute Spirit or Universal Mind. And because it was the soul of the world, it was said to evolve along with the world.[28]

What Hegel was offering was a spiritualized version of evolution. (Nietzsche even said that "without Hegel, there would have been no Darwin.") The difference is that Hegel applied the concept of evolution not to biology but to the world of ideas. His claim was that all our ideas—law, morality, religion, art, political ideals—result from the gradual "actualization of the Universal Mind" over the course of history. Everything is caught up in a vast historical process advancing toward a final perfect state.[29]

For many people, the law of historical progress functioned as a substitute for divine Providence. "When science seemed to take

God out of the universe, men had to deify some natural force, like 'evolution,'" explains Randall.[30] A goal-oriented version of evolution comforted people with the hope that every event has a reason, a purpose, within the upward progress of the universe as a whole.

Hegel's philosophy is a form of historicism, the doctrine that all ideas are products of historical forces—that what is "true" at one stage of history will give way to a higher truth at the next stage.[31] In essence, Hegel surveyed all the conflicting philosophies and worldviews, all the competing religious claims, all the warring camps and cultures, and proposed to overcome the strife by treating each one as a partial and relative truth in the upward progression of Mind, the evolution of consciousness.

What is the logical flaw in historicism? It is self-refuting. The claim that every idea is a partial and relative truth must include its *own* claim. Like every other evolving idea, it is relative to its own moment in history, and therefore not true in any transhistorical sense. As philosopher John Passmore says, you cannot "maintain, as a timeless philosophical truth, that there are no timeless philosophical truths."[32]

Hegel avoided this devastating conclusion only by tacitly making an exception for himself. He wrote as though he alone was mysteriously able to rise above the evolutionary process—as though he alone was capable of an objective, timeless, complete view of the entire historical process.

But of course, by making an exception for himself, Hegel implied that there was one thing that his system did not cover—namely, his own thinking. In this way, he introduced a logical inconsistency into his system. And of course, any inconsistency within a system of thought discredits it. (Many worldviews are subject to this same logical flaw. We will probe it more deeply in Principle #4.)

Triumvirate of Race, Class, Gender

In our own day, we have progressed far beyond the Romantic era, yet the continental tradition continues to exert enormous influence. It moved from idealism through a series of successors (such as existentialism), which we will not take time to discuss. In recent decades, it has given birth to postmodernism. The tragic irony is that although Romanticism was embraced to counter Enlightenment reductionism, postmodernism has become equally reductionistic and inhumane.

In everyday life, we encounter postmodernism most often in the form of political correctness. Multiculturalism. Identity politics. Speech codes. Rules for politically correct speech have become de rigueur in most social institutions: schools, newspapers, law, politics. A Harvard professor complains that on many university campuses, students are "muzzled by speech codes that would not pass the giggle test if challenged on First Amendment grounds."[33] These rules define the accepted ways to speak about race, class, gender, ethnicity, sexual identity, and so on. Postmodernism virtually defines a person's identity in terms of the groups to which he or she belongs.

How did we get from Hegel to postmodernism? For Hegel, the real actor in history is not the individual but the Absolute

Mind or Spirit, which expresses itself through a community's laws, morality, language, social relationships, and so on. Hegel accepted Kant's idealism in which the world is constituted by consciousness, but for him it was a collective consciousness. As one philosopher explains, the Absolute Mind creates the world "through the shared aspects of a culture, a society, and above all through a shared language."

Indeed for Hegel, individuals do not even *have* original ideas of their own. Their thoughts are merely expressions of the Absolute Mind. In his words, individuals "are all the time the unconscious tools of the World Mind at work within them."[34]

Over time, Hegel's pantheism was secularized and his Absolute Spirit was reduced to a metaphor—the spirit of the age, the Zeitgeist.[35] (In German, *Zeit* means time or age; *geist* means spirit.) What remained, however, was the idea that individuals are "unconscious tools" of the Zeitgeist. They are not *producers* of culture so much as *products* of a particular culture.[36] Individuals are shaped by the communities they belong to, each with its own shared perspective, values, habits, language, and forms of life.

In our own day, this has led to the extreme conclusion that everyone's ideas are merely social constructions stitched together by cultural forces. Individuals are little more than mouthpieces for communities based on race, class, gender, ethnicity, and sexual identity.

What is the idol here? Postmodernism absolutizes the forces of culture or community. Dooyeweerd calls it the "ideology of community."[37] Truth has been redefined as a social construction, so that every community has its own view of truth, based on its experience and perspective, which cannot be judged by anyone outside the community. One postmodern theologian makes the claim in these words: "There is no absolute truth: rather truth is relative to the community in which we participate." Rorty says truth is merely "intersubjective agreement" among people within a particular community.[38]

Postmodernism is thus a form of anti-realism, the doctrine that reality depends for its character and possibly even its existence on our minds. The term *anti-realism* was coined by Nietzsche to describe his own view, which he summed up in the slogan "There are no facts, only interpretations." Or as one postmodern writer puts it, "Reality has now become a mere bunch of disparate and changing interpretations, a shifting loosely-held coalition of points of view in continual debate with each other."[39]

If reality has shattered into clashing interpretations, so has the concept of personal identity. Postmodernism says there is no unified self. Instead the self is simply the locus of the shifting points of view absorbed from various interpretive communities, each defining its own "truth." Recall that the Enlightenment treated the individual as a disembodied mind, capable of transcending time and space to achieve a God's-eye view (see Principle #1). In reaction, postmodernism tethers individual consciousness tightly to communities whose perspective is conditioned by history and geography.

Even science, the golden calf of modernism, is not considered true in any universal sense. Like all other forms of knowledge, science is a social construction. Postmodernists agree with Nietzsche, who wrote, "All that conformity to law, which impresses us so much in the stars and in chemical processes, coincides at bottom with those properties which *we* bring to things."[40] If science is just another creation of the human mind, why should it be granted any special status over other ways of thinking?

And if there is no objective or universal truth, then any *claim* to have objective truth will be treated as nothing but an attempt by one interpretive community to impose its own limited, subjective perspective on everyone else. An act of oppression. A power grab.

Roots of Political Correctness

Like other idols, postmodernism gets some things right. It has done good service in countering the lonely individualism of the Enlightenment's autonomous self. It rejects the modernist project of thinkers like Bacon and Descartes to start history over from scratch within the isolated individual consciousness. It denies that we can reach an infallible foundation for knowledge by direct intuition into the contents of the individual mind.[41]

In the process, postmodernists have debunked Enlightenment claims to neutral, timeless, value-free knowledge. They insist that real, living individuals always bring to the table a complex panoply of prior commitments, interests, goals, and ambitions—even in fields like science, where objectivity is the expected norm.

The same insight, however, was offered long ago by Christian thinkers. Scripture itself is replete with warnings that idolatry leads to a kind of spiritual and intellectual blindness. Romans 1 tells us that when we refuse to acknowledge God, our minds become "futile" and our hearts are "darkened" (Rom. 1:21) Theologians call this the *noetic* effects of sin, from the Greek word *nous*, which as we saw earlier means not just the mind but the core of our being. The Protestant Reformers taught that when we turn away from God at the core, then everything we do is affected, including our thinking. We come to our desks or laboratories with a complex set of motivations and predispositions already in place, which predetermine to some degree what we accept as plausible or true. Far from being neutral blank slates, our minds are predisposed to interpret new data in light of the convictions we already hold—what we *want* to be true.

Yet postmodernism typically goes further than this commonsense biblical insight to the much more radical claim that there *is* no extra-mental truth. It reduces truth claims to social constructions. And it reduces individuals to puppets of social forces. The implication is that people hold certain ideas not because they have good reasons but because they are black or white, a man or a woman, Asian or Hispanic, or whatever.

This is radically dehumanizing. It implies that individuals are powerless to rise above the communities to which they belong. It is a form of reductionism that dissolves individual identity into group identity. And the list of group identities keeps growing. Harvard's Kennedy School of Politics recently announced that all incoming students will be required to take "a mandatory power and privilege training that examines components of race, gender, socioeconomic class, sexual orientation, ability, religion, international status, and power differentials."[42]

At many universities, liberal arts departments no longer teach the classics but immerse students in contemporary works on racial and sexual politics. And if classic books of literature and philosophy *are* taught, they are likely to include "trigger warnings." An omnibus edition of Kant's three *Critiques* includes a warning label on the title page: "This book is a product of its time and does not reflect the same values as it would if it were written today. Parents might wish to discuss with their children how views on race, gender, sexuality, ethnicity, and interpersonal relations have changed since this book was written before allowing them to read this classic work." The irony is that Kant had enormous influence on the development of the anti-realist concept of truth. But that's not what educators are concerned about. They're worried about Kant's violations of political correctness.[43]

Postmodernism is leagues away from the materialism rampant in the science department, but it is equally dehumanizing. Materialism reduces humans to products of *physical* forces. Postmodernism reduces them to products of *social* forces. Whenever a philosophy absolutizes something less than God—no matter what it is—the result is reductionism, a lower view of the human person. Postmodernists themselves label their view "anti-humanism," by which they mean the human subject has no power to transcend social and historical conditions—the Zeitgeist.

In that case, however, the individual can have no independent stance from which to *critique* the Zeitgeist. As Dallas Willard points out, "postmodernism hardly leaves you a logical leg to stand on to oppose ... the spirit of the age."[44]

By contrast, Christianity offers a transcendent truth—a perspective not bound by the spirit of the age. It liberates individuals to think critically about the prevailing ethos.

The Fall of Postmodernism

I was speaking at an evangelical college when a student asked, "We live in a postmodern age when no one cares anymore about truth. How do we talk to people who are not persuaded by facts and reasons?" It's true that postmoderns may not be impressed by fact-based apologetics. But they *can* be reached by arguments using their own conceptual language.

Start with their view of truth. Postmodernists reject any claim to a truth that is universal, objective, or eternal. They insist that everyone's perspective is "situated" within a context that is particular, local, and historically contingent. But of course, the same critique applies to postmodernists' own claims—they, too, are "situated" within a particular, historical context. After all, where did postmodernism come from? As we have seen, it is an offshoot of modern European culture. It stems from post-Hegelian continental philosophy with its notion that individuals are socially constituted by their communities and forms of life.

Postmoderns often accuse Christians of being narrow and closed-minded. But postmodernism is itself confined within a particular strand of Western intellectual history. Thus postmodernists are just as restricted by their own historical horizons as the more traditional people whom they tend to look down on. And they are just as exclusive as anyone else in insisting that *their* view captures the way things really are.

In short, the same reasoning that postmodernists use to debunk traditional concepts of truth applies to their own views.

Some postmodernists have updated Hegel's historicism by linking it to science-based theories of evolution. An example is Rorty, who argues on the basis of Darwinian evolution that there are no eternal truths—that all our ideas are "a product of time and chance."[45] But his conclusion rests on the assumption that Darwinian evolution is true—in precisely the sense he denies that anything can be true.

I was once invited on a radio program to debate a seminary professor who described himself as postmodern. My question was, why would a Christian *want* to embrace postmodernism? Granted, it deflates modernist claims to universal truth by showing that modernism is a limited, historically conditioned point of view. But then, so is postmodernism. As a Christian, why would I want to commit myself to any idea that is merely a social construction?

The Bible describes idols as human inventions, "the work of human hands" (Ps. 115:4; 135:15). Their "craftsmen are only human" (Isa. 44:11). Those who worship idols "bow down to the work of their hands, to what their own fingers have made" (Isa. 2:8). Why would Christians want to build their lives on *any* idea that is a product of human thinking—"the wisdom of the world" (1 Cor. 1:20)? The human heart hungers for a truth that is transcendent and eternal. God has "set eternity in the human heart" (Eccles. 3:11 NIV).

The finite cannot reach to the infinite, so the only way it is possible to know eternal truth is if God has communicated to the human race—giving his own transcendent perspective. And that's exactly the earth-shaking claim that Christianity makes: that Scripture is communication from God, giving us information about himself, the cosmos, and history. Even Christians typically take this concept far too much for granted. For it amounts to the astonishing claim that we do have access to a God's-eye view of the world, a perspective beyond merely human knowledge, a timeless and transcendent truth.

Of course, our comprehension of that truth is never complete or exhaustive. Our understanding is filtered through our fallible, fallen human minds, influenced by our culture and circumstances. Yet there are windows to transcendence. God's word in Scripture gives us access to truths that are "not of human origin" (Gal. 1:11 NIV). Over against postmodern historicism and relativism, Christianity makes the liberating claim that humans have access to *trans*historical truths because God himself has spoken.

In a striking passage, Rorty admits that the very concept of objective truth is grounded in the Christian conviction that the universe was "created by a person." The idea of a truth beyond human subjectivity, he writes, "is a remnant of the idea that the world is a divine creation, the work of someone who ... Himself spoke some language in which He described His own project."[46] In other words, objective truth is possible only if the Creator has spoken to the human race, giving us his eternal, transcendent perspective—not about matters of salvation only but also about history and the cosmos. To adapt the titles of Schaeffer's books, it is not enough that *God Is There*; it is also crucial that *He Is Not Silent*.

Only if God has communicated, the infinite reaching down to the finite, is it possible to break free—no longer trapped in our individual minds, as modernist thinkers are, or trapped in a communal mind, as postmodern thinkers are. A biblical apologetics strategy will equip you to help liberate those who have been taken captive "through hollow and deceptive philosophy, which depends on human tradition" (Col. 2:8 NIV). It will teach you how to "unmask the temporal idols"[47] and turn people toward eternal truth.

Pantheism versus You

So far we have traced two very different forms of reductionism, resulting from two widespread philosophies: materialism and postmodernism. A Romans 1 apologetics strategy also gives us tools to diagnose reductionism resulting from religion. Let's practice applying those tools to Eastern pantheism and Islam.

Earlier we learned that Romantic thinkers embraced a Western version of pantheism. So it is not surprising that they were also open to Eastern versions. In the late nineteenth century, Schopenhauer became the first philosopher to import full-blown Buddhism into the West. In our own day, the New Age movement has elevated Eastern religions to the status of Hollywood chic.

Pantheism is typically summarized as the doctrine that god is the universe and the universe is god (*pan* means all; *theism* means god). God is called the One or the All. The world is seen as a manifestation or emanation of the divine essence.

Is this an idol? Obviously.

Pantheists typically argue that the biblical teaching of a transcendent God has alienated us from nature—that it has caused Western culture to rape and plunder the earth. If we cultivate a sense of spiritual oneness with nature, they claim, we will have a greater reverence for all life.

Is that claim true? Not at all. The reason is that, like all idols, pantheism is reductionistic. It leads to a lower view of life.

Whatever a worldview identifies as the divine becomes the lens through which it sees everything, the sieve it uses to sift out what is real. In pantheism, the divine is an underlying spiritual unity, the One. What slips through the sieve, then, is diversity, difference, individuality. In Hinduism, your individual identity is actually called *maya*, which means illusion. It is regarded as the cause of evil, selfishness, greed, and war. The goal of meditation is to dissolve your sense of being a separate self by merging with the cosmic One, the undifferentiated All, like a drop of water dissipating into the ocean. In Buddhism, the word *nirvana* means literally "to become extinguished."[48]

The loss of the self is expressed in a poem by the Chinese poet Li Po. The poem is about the coming of evening, and it ends with these words:

> We sit together, the mountain and I
> until only the mountain remains.

This poem is often quoted in books on meditation as a moving expression of our oneness with nature. But notice that in this oneness, the "I" is lost—dissolved into the rock of the mountainside. As a contemporary poet explains, the mountain represents the eternal One: "Watching this 'mountain' of eternal presence long enough, in deep stillness you find that you are nowhere to be seen. You are surprised to discover that everything you reflexively called 'me' was never really there in the first place."[49]

The implicit message is that the individual self has so little value that it ought to dissolve into the One. For it "was never really there in the first place." It was an illusion.

Another reason pantheism leads to a low view of human life is that the divine is non-personal. In classic pantheism, the concept of the divine is not a personal deity who thinks, wills, feels, and acts. Instead it is a non-personal, non-thinking, non-acting spiritual substratum underlying all things. A former Zen Buddhist (who converted to Christianity) explains that, in pantheism, the divine is "an unconscious and impersonal essence, which may be called God, Nature, the Absolute, Oneness."[50]

As a result, surprisingly, pantheism is not all that different from materialism. It is the flip side of the same coin. Materialism claims that everything consists of *material* stuff. Pantheism claims that everything consists of *spiritual* stuff. Both are non-personal. Thus both fail to account for the personal dimensions of human nature. And what they cannot account for, they will suppress and ultimately deny.

This is the reductionist pattern. Every idol-based worldview seeks to stuff all of reality into a box. Inevitably, however, something will stick out of the box. Something will fail to fit within its conceptual categories. Both materialism and pantheism define ultimate reality in non-personal terms—and therefore both fail to account for human personhood. Thus they end up denying, denigrating, and devaluing the unique features of human persons. Humans are reduced to products of non-personal forces. The individual dissolves into the rock of the mountainside.[51]

Any system that begins with non-personal forces will, in the end, suppress human personhood. It will reduce persons to components of a blind, unconscious matrix of being. Water cannot rise above its source.

The puzzling question is why these worldviews are at all popular. After all, what we long for most of all is to be known and loved for who we are as unique persons—a longing that can be met only if the divine is a Person. The God of Christianity does not erase our individual identity but actually affirms it. He calls us to become ever more fully the unique individuals we were created to be. Contrary to Eastern mysticism, the goal is not to *suppress* our desires but to *direct* them to what truly satisfies—to a passionate love relationship with the ultimate transcendent Person.

Islam versus Human Dignity

All the religions we have considered—whether Eastern or pagan—fit the diagnosis of Romans 1. They worship the creature instead of the Creator. They absolutize something immanent within the cosmos. Because their god is something lower than the biblical God, they lead to a lower view of the human person. As Principle #2 says, they lead to reductionism.

The exceptions to this rule are the other monotheistic religions, Judaism and Islam, which share with Christianity a concept of a transcendent Creator. They also accept at least some of the same scriptures. I am going to leave Judaism aside because of its complex relationship to Christianity. Christians hold that doctrines such as the Trinity are found in the Old Testament, even if taught more explicitly in the New Testament. That's why the gospel went "to the Jew first" (Rom. 1:16). The term "Judeo-Christian" emphasizes the many continuities and similarities.

What about Islam? Today Islam has become a powerful geopolitical force, and Christians are searching for better ways to understand it. Islam accepts segments of the Christian Scripture as divinely revealed (the Hebrew Torah, the psalms of David, and the Gospels).[52] Nevertheless, its concept of God is unitarian—it rejects the classic Christian concept of the Trinity.

The Koran teaches that Jesus is not divine but is "only a messenger of Allah."[53] Islamic scholar Seyyed Hossein Nasr writes, "The Quran continuously emphasizes the Unity and the Oneness of God, and it can be said that the very raison d'être of Islam is to assert in a final and categorical manner the Oneness of God and the nothingness of all before the Majesty of that One." Due to Islam's emphasis on the oneness of God, some scholars even maintain that it is closer to the pantheism of neo-Platonism and Hinduism than to Christianity.[54]

And a pantheist or unitarian concept of divinity lacks key elements of personhood—in particular, the qualities associated with relationship. Only within a relationship can God express interpersonal attributes such as love, sympathy, intimacy, self-giving, and communication. Only between distinct persons can there be giving and taking, initiating and responding, sharing and self-revelation, union and communion.

For God to be fully personal, then, capable of love and community, there must be genuine plurality within the divine being itself. Historic Christian theology teaches that these interpersonal attributes were expressed from all eternity among the three Persons of the Trinity. In this way, Christianity is able to maintain within the Godhead the highest conception of what it means to be a personal being.

"All sorts of people are fond of repeating the Christian statement that 'God is love,'" writes C. S. Lewis, "But they seem not to notice that the words 'God is love' have no real meaning unless God contains at least two persons. Love is something that one person has for another person. If God was a single person, then before the world was made, He was not love."[55] (Or if he did have the capacity for love, he had no way to exercise it. To fulfill his nature, he would *need* to create a world—in which case, he would be dependent on creation, which is not the kind of deity taught by either Islam or Christianity.)

Only a God of love is fully personal. Thus the Trinity is crucial for maintaining a fully personal concept of God. As theologian Robert Letham writes, "Only a God who is triune can be personal.... A solitary monad cannot love and, since it cannot love, neither can it be a person." Therefore it "has no way to explain or even to maintain human personhood."[56]

Astonishingly, *The Stanford Encyclopedia of Philosophy* reports that Islam does not even have a concept of the person: "There is no conceptual equivalent of the Western philosophical concept of 'person' in Arabic and in classic Islamic philosophy." This fact seems "to confirm the importance of the specifically Christian ... origins of the term."[57]

If it's true that Islam lacks even a clear concept of the person, this would explain why it tends to be fatalistic, emphasizing sheer submission to the will of Allah (*islam* means submission). As Udo Middelmann explains, "Islam is a religion of resignation.... Allah made the world, and you must accept the way it interacts with you, even should it kill you. You are allowed no questions, no doubt, no individual responsibility. Negation of self is your salvation."

This also explains why a great deal of Muslim worship consists of near-mechanical rituals: Worshippers recite the Koran, in unison, word for word, by memory, in the original Arabic. (The word *Koran* means "that which is recited.") To quote Middelmann again, "Its spirituality is repetitious and impersonal, not a chosen and deliberate love of God with all your heart, mind and soul."[58]

Muslims are not even required to understand what they recite. Many are not Arabic and do not speak the language. A book by two Muslim authors says, "It is not uncommon to meet people who know a great deal of the text by heart but have not the slightest understanding of the world view that permeates it." But this is acceptable, the authors say, because in Islam "understanding is secondary" to recitation and ritual.[59]

Thus Islam proves the reductionist principle once again—that a lower view of God leads to a lower view of the value, status, and dignity of the human person.

From Secular Idols to Death Camps

One of most powerful ways to engage with seekers and skeptics is to help them identify their own idols. And idols are easier to recognize when lived out in practice—especially when they are incarnated in politics and public policy. We have applied Principle #2 to philosophies and religions; now let's show the impact of reductionism when fleshed out by two political theories—Nazism and Communism. Both illustrate the dark and destructive power of idols.

Western history is often retold in the form of a religious epic, says anthropologist Richard Schweder. "The Enlightenment story has its own version of Genesis, and the themes are well known: The world woke up from the slumber of the 'dark ages,' finally got in touch with the truth and became good about 300 years ago in Northern and Western Europe." This secular faith offers its own version of salvation: "As people opened their eyes, religion (equated with ignorance and superstition) gave way to science (equated with fact and reason)."

For centuries, this Enlightenment myth was held up as the blueprint for progress and liberty. Yet "as a theory of history,"

Schweder comments dryly, the "story has had a predictive utility of approximately zero."[60] For the rise of secularism did *not* lead to ever-increasing liberty. On the contrary, it turned the twentieth century into a bloodbath of death and destruction. Most of the atrocities were perpetrated by regimes devoted to political ideologies such as National Socialism (Nazism) and Marxism (Communism).

Historians have often wondered how such mind-staggering barbarism could emerge in modern civilized Europe. The answer lies in the power of idols. Nazi doctrine was organized around the idol of race. An individual's race (Aryan or Jewish or Slavic) was said to determine that person's views, character, and even worth. Communist ideology was organized around the idol of economic class. A person's economic class (capitalist or proletarian) was held to be the all-determining factor.

As we have seen, in every idol-based worldview, some parts of creation will not fit in its box. Some facts of general revelation will be suppressed. But when idol-centered worldviews are applied in the political realm, there will be some *people* who do not fit in the state's prescribed box—and who will literally be suppressed and even killed. Under Nazism, those who did not fit in the prescribed box of race included Jews, Gypsies, Slavs, Serbs, Poles, Ukrainians, and others. They were transported to concentration camps where about twenty-five million died or were shot to death. Under Communism, those who did not fit the prescribed box of economic class included capitalists, kulaks, and others. They were subject to forced famines or to hard labor camps where an estimated eighty-five to a hundred million died or were shot to death. (Both regimes rounded up dissenting Christians.)[61]

In World War II, these same false absolutes led to global conflict. As Gilson observed at the time, "Millions of men are starving and bleeding to death because two or three ... deified abstractions are now at war. For when gods fight among themselves, men have to die."[62]

The lesson is that idol-based ideologies are invariably dehumanizing, and if unchecked they lead to repression, coercion, oppression, war, and violence. In the twentieth century alone, they have taken far more lives and created more havoc than all the religiously motivated witch hunts, inquisitions, and wars of the previous centuries.

"Materialists are ready to worship their own jerry-built creations as though they were the Absolute," writes Aldous Huxley. This "makes it possible for them to indulge their ugliest passions with a clear conscience and in the certainty that they are working for the Highest Good."[63] The bloodshed and death camps produced by idolatrous ideologies were not a violation of their principles (as religious wars were violations of Christian principles); they were logically consistent outworkings of the worldview.

Philosopher John Gray, though himself an atheist, writes that "when atheism becomes a political project, the invariable result is an ersatz religion that can only be maintained by tyrannical means"[64]—by secret police and death camps.

From Liberators to Despots

The study of worldviews is not merely a theoretical subject to be discussed hypothetically in the classroom. Idols have life-and-death consequences. When Romans 1 says God gives people up to the destructive impact of their idols, that does not mean only personal behavior. Worldviews are also incarnated in the classroom, the boardroom, the courtroom, the legislative chamber, and the theater of war.

Modern totalitarianism illustrates Paul's teaching that those who do not know God will fall under the yoke of idols. They will be "enslaved to those that by nature are not gods" (Gal. 4:8).[65] When a group of famous ex-Communists wrote a book about their disillusionment, they titled it *The God That Failed*.

Historian Isaiah Berlin once observed that every philosophy offers a model of reality that promises to liberate people from error: "But they almost invariably end by enslaving those very same people, *by failing to explain the whole of experience*. They begin as liberators and end in some sort of despotism."[66]

To create a humane society, we must identify the idols that "fail to explain the whole of experience"—that lock people into partial, one-dimensional models of reality. The only basis for genuine human rights and dignity is a fully biblical worldview. Instead of absolutizing one piece of the puzzle, Christianity offers the entire puzzle with all the pieces in harmony, creating an image of enchanting beauty. It gives a far richer, fuller, more complex vision of reality than any other worldview. Christianity includes the valid insights of all other worldviews, while avoiding their weaknesses.

More Than Is Dreamed of in Your Philosophy

What is the common thread running through all the examples in this chapter? Religions and worldviews that deny the biblical God must treat something else as the ultimate reality (Principle #1). With the exception of the other monotheistic religions, they deify something immanent within the cosmos. They absolutize some aspect of creation as the ultimate explainer. Then they reduce everything else to that single category (Principle #2). Reductionism is like trying to see the world through a single lens. G. K. Chesterton called reductionism a mental prison, "the prison of one thought."[67] Whatever does not fit in that prison is denied and suppressed.

The result is always a vision of the world that is narrower, poorer, darker, and less humane than the biblical picture. A worldview's concept of humanity cannot be higher than its concept of the divine.

Romans 1 starts its teaching on idols by saying that the "wrath of God" is revealed from heaven. There is probably nothing that modern people hate more about religion than talk of the wrath of God. It suggests a picture of an angry, vengeful deity. But the biblical concept of wrath often refers simply to God's implacable opposition to evil and injustice. It does not necessarily mean a catastrophic event, like a lightning bolt from heaven. In fact, it does not necessarily mean divine intervention in human affairs at all. As we have seen in Principle #2, God's judgment often consists in giving people what they want and letting them experience the self-inflicted consequences of their choices. He allows them to choose ways of thinking and living that are self-destructive, tearing down the honor and dignity of others and themselves.

I cannot think of a better description of reductionistic worldviews.

When Romans 1 warns that idols lead to behavior that is dishonoring, we often overlook the implication—namely, that people are meant to *honor* others and themselves. As Thomas Johnson writes, the text implies "that there are proper ways for people to honor themselves," namely, by accepting God's view of them. "When people accept their status as image-bearers of the Creator, placed in this world to fulfill his mandates, there is honor for all." But when they create God substitutes and recast their self-understanding in the image of an idol, then there is dishonor and destruction for all.[68]

Our hearts should break for people whose worldviews are dark, dehumanizing, demeaning, and dishonoring to the human person. An opportunity is wide open to present Christianity as radically positive and humane. A biblical worldview does not divinize any aspect of creation or set up a false absolute. As a consequence, it does not lead to a reductionism that devalues or denies the other dimensions of creation. It does not have to shove the universe into a box and slice off whatever doesn't fit. It is not exclusive but inclusive, affirming the goodness and reality of all God's diverse and multi-faceted creation.

Christianity agrees with Hamlet when he said to Horatio, "There are more things in heaven and earth than are dreamed of in your philosophy." Reductionistic worldviews insist that there are *fewer* things in heaven and earth. Living according to these worldviews is like living in a concrete bunker with no windows. Communicating a Christian worldview should be like inviting people to open the door and come out. Our message ought to express the joy of leading captives out of a small, cramped world into one that is expansive and liberating.

We understand better now why Paul could stand before the Roman Empire and proclaim that he was "not ashamed of the gospel." He was confident that Christianity is not only more convincing than any competing religion or worldview but also more appealing. In Scripture, the phrase "put to shame" does not usually mean to be psychologically embarrassed. It means to trust in something that lets you down, that fails to come through. "Let me not be put to shame; let not my enemies exult over me" (Ps. 25:2). Because "the Lord GOD helps me ... I know that I shall not be put to shame" (Isa. 50:7). So when Paul says he is "not ashamed of the gospel," he is saying that a Christian worldview will not let you down. It will not disappoint.[69] Christianity fulfills the human hunger for a unified, integrated worldview to live by. It has the intellectual resources to provide a holistic, internally consistent guide to life.

Of course, being attractive does not mean a worldview is true. To test whether it is true or false, we need to move to Principle #3. When we ask whether an idea is true, typically what we mean is, Does it fit the world as we know it? Does it match up with the facts? In Principle #3, we'll see how Romans 1 outfits us with a powerful set of tools to test worldviews and uncover truth.

PRINCIPLE #3

·····

SECULAR LEAPS OF FAITH

A few years ago, CNN published an article titled "Why I Raise My Children without God." Instantly it went viral. The author, a young mother named Deborah Mitchell, listed several reasons why she shielded her children from learning about God—most of them variations on the problem of evil. Mitchell argued that a loving God would not allow "murders, child abuse, wars, brutal beatings, torture and millions of heinous acts to be committed throughout the history of mankind."[1]

The classic Christian answer to the problem of evil is that God created humans with free will—and they have made a horrific mess of things. This is called the free-will defense, and it acknowledges the tragic reality of sin and suffering, while at the same time affirming human dignity. It portrays humans as genuine moral agents whose choices are so significant that they alter the direction of history, and even eternity.

Having rejected the Christian answer, what did Mitchell offer as an alternative? She proposed a materialistic worldview in which humans are completely determined, without free will. "We are just a very, very small part of a big, big machine," she intoned, "and the influence we have is minuscule." We must accept "the realization of our insignificance."

Is *that* meant to be an appealing alternative to Christianity? That humans are little machines trapped in a big machine? That their actions are insignificant? Mitchell claimed that her materialist view leads to "humbleness." But it is not humbling; it is dehumanizing. It essentially reduces humans to robots.

More importantly, it is not true. Its view of humanity runs counter to the data of human experience. All civilizations throughout history have recognized that humans are moral agents capable of making responsible choices. There is no society without some moral code. The testimony of universal human experience is that humans are not merely little robots.[2]

After all, what is a worldview intended to explain? A worldview is meant to give a systematic explanation of those inescapable, unavoidable facts of experience accessible to all people, in all cultures, across all periods of history. In biblical terms, those facts constitute general revelation. Philosophers sometimes refer to them collectively as the life-world, or lived experience, or pre-theoretical experience.[3] The whole point of building *theoretical* systems is to explain what humans know by *pre-theoretical* experience. That is the starting point for any philosophy. That is the data it seeks to explain. If it fails to explain the data of experience, then it has failed the test. It has been falsified.

The Gravity of Fact

You might think of this as the practical test of a worldview. Just as scientists test a theory by taking it into the lab and mixing chemicals in a test tube to see if the results confirm the theory, so we test a worldview by taking it into the laboratory of ordinary life. Can it be lived out consistently in the real world, without doing violence to human nature? Does it fit reality? Does it match what we know about the world? Does life function the way the worldview says it should?

We could say that the purpose of a *worldview* is to explain what we know about the *world*. If a worldview contradicts our fundamental experience of the world—what we know by general revelation—that is a good sign that it should be scrapped. As Dooyeweerd put it, every philosophy "ought to be confronted with the datum of naive experience in order to test its ability to account for this datum in a satisfying manner." Any philosophy that "cannot account for this datum in a satisfactory way must be erroneous."[4]

Philosopher J. P. Moreland says we test worldviews by how well they explain "recalcitrant facts," those stubborn facts that every theory must explain—or else be considered falsified.[5]

And we can be confident that all idol-centered worldviews *will* be falsified. All will fail to account for at least some of those stubborn facts. Why? Because, as we learned in Principle #2, they are reductionistic. They try to define the whole in terms of a part. Inevitably their conceptual categories will be too narrow and limited. Some parts of reality will stick out of the box.

Consider the CNN article that went viral. It proposed a materialist philosophy that reduces humans to machines, determined by material forces. What sticks out of that box? Human freedom. The undeniable fact is that humans do make choices. This fact serves as evidence that a person is *not* "a very, very small part of a big, big machine." Instead humans are personal beings capable of willing and choosing—which means their origin must be a personal Being, not the blind forces of nature.

Recall that in philosophy, *personal* does not mean warm and friendly; it means a being with the capacity to think, feel, choose, and act, in contrast to a non-thinking substance whose action is automatic. Consider what happens when you combine sodium with chlorine: the atoms react with one another to produce sodium chloride (table salt). The atoms do not make a conscious decision to interact. They do not choose to transfer electrons to form an ionic bond. The process takes place by purely automatic physical forces. Materialism claims that human behavior can likewise be explained solely by physical forces at work in our brain chemistry. The existence of free will counters that theory. It constitutes evidence that humans were not created by automatic physical forces but by a personal Agent.

It is ironic that people who reject Christianity—who think that without God they can finally be free—end up with philosophies that deny human freedom.

To become familiar with the practical test, we will walk through several examples. The benefit of working with examples is that you will learn to analyze the actual wording and reasoning used by secular thinkers in real-world situations. The most surprising thing we will discover is that many of them, when pressed, actually acknowledge that their worldview does not fit the facts. The examples in this chapter will help you make the case using their own words.

I, Robot—We, Machines

Do not be tempted to think that worldview questions like these are esoteric—irrelevant to ordinary people. When I was a teenager, I was already wrestling with the same questions raised by the young mother writing for CNN. After rejecting my Lutheran upbringing, I embraced physical and social determinism. I saw it as one more nail in the coffin of Christianity, for the Bible clearly teaches that humans exercise moral responsibility: "See, I have set before you today life and good, death and evil.... Therefore choose life, that you and your offspring may live" (Deut. 30:15, 19).

Of course, theologians debate the exact nature of human freedom. The Reformers, Luther and Calvin, emphasized that humans can do nothing to contribute to salvation. The liberating message of the gospel is that we do not have to earn or work for salvation; that both justification and sanctification are by "hearing with faith" (Gal. 3:2, 5). But the Reformers did not mean that we cannot choose whether to have ham or turkey on our sandwich for lunch. By contrast, materialism holds that humans only *think* they are choosing ham or turkey. In reality their behavior is driven by natural forces such as neurons firing in the brain—just like sodium reacting with chlorine. All Christians agree in rejecting this materialist conception of humans as mere robots or meat machines.[6]

The Bible teaches that humans are fallen sinners, but the fall did not make us less than human. It did not make us machines.

Obviously, humans are not free to do anything we might dream up, because we are creatures and not the Creator. We are also embedded within a physical universe and a social world; we each have a personal history that affects our choices. Yet within those parameters, we have some range of genuine choice and accountability. Our actions are not simply links in a closed chain of causally connected physical events. We have the capacity to be first causes, starting a new chain of cause and effect.

It was not until I went to L'Abri, however, that I heard cogent arguments in favor of free will. The arguments centered on the universality of human experience. The testimony of all known cultures through all of recorded history is that humans do exercise moral freedom and responsibility. From time to time, quirky individuals have raised objections, but civilizations as a whole cannot survive without the conviction that people can be held responsible for their actions.

Even materialists often admit that, in practice, it is impossible for humans to live any other way. One philosopher jokes that if people deny free will, then when ordering at a restaurant they should say, "Just bring me whatever the laws of nature have determined I will get."[7] It seems that we are forced to accept the reality of free will. Humans are so constituted that they cannot function without it. It is one of those stubborn facts that must be accounted for by any worldview.[8]

These were some of the arguments I encountered while studying at L'Abri. As a result, I began to seriously consider whether my deterministic worldview might be mistaken. It began to look as though humans do have moral freedom after all. And if my worldview did not account for it, well, I needed to look for one that did. It was the beginning of an intellectual turnaround. Christianity began to look considerably more plausible.

How can we make Christianity more plausible for our own friends and family members who are seekers, agnostics, or skeptics?

Principle #3
Test the Idol: Does It Contradict What We Know about the World?

We have worked through two principles in worldview analysis. First we identify its idol. Second we identify its reductionism. Now we will ask whether idol-centered worldviews fit the real world.

Let's stay with the questions of free will because it is so central to human dignity. The ability to choose from among alternatives makes a host of other distinctively human capacities possible—creativity and problem solving, love and relationships (robots do not love), even rationality itself (if our minds are preprogrammed to hold an idea, then it is not a rational decision). "Unless human beings are morally responsible," says law professor Jerome Hall, "justice is only a mirage." Unless humans have free will, we will not develop a sense of identity or self-worth (because everything *I* do is really the work of unconscious, automatic forces).[9]

What is at stake is nothing less than our *"respect for persons,"* says one philosopher. For if determinism is true, then "we are, in the final reckoning, merely playthings of fortune."[10]

Free will has thus become a stand-in for the whole range of human qualities that depend on it. If you take a course in Philosophy 101, your textbook is almost certain to include a section on free will versus determinism. In recent years, the topic has moved to center stage in philosophy.[11] Therefore it is one of the most salient facts of general revelation that can be used in testing worldviews.

Why Secularists Can't Live with Secularism

Let's practice applying Principle #3 to several examples, using secularists' own words and writings. An especially clear example is Galen Strawson, a philosopher who states with great bravado, "The impossibility of free will ... can be proved with complete certainty."

Yet in an interview, Strawson admits that, in practice, no one accepts his deterministic view. "To be honest, I can't really accept it myself," he says. "I can't really live with this fact from day to day. Can you, really?"

But if humans "can't really live with" the implications of a worldview, is it a reliable map to reality? Watch for phrases like this as you read through other examples. Often they are clues that someone is trying to live out a worldview that does not fit the real world—that he or she has bumped up against one of the intractable facts that point to the biblical God.

Moreover, Strawson insists that he is not alone, that even cognitive scientists who publish books and journal articles favoring determinism do not accept it as a workable theory to live by. They "may accept it in their white coats, but I'm sure they're just like the rest of us when they're out in the world—convinced of the reality of radical free will."[12]

In short, their *practice* contradicts what they *profess*. They are trapped in cognitive dissonance.

Strawson states the conflict in striking terms: "Powerful logical or metaphysical reasons for supposing we can't have strong free will keep coming up against equally powerful psychological reasons why we *can't help believing* that we do have it.... It seems that we *cannot live* or experience our choices as determined, even if determinism is true."[13]

What are the telltale phrases here? That there are ideas "we can't help believing." That "we cannot live" on the basis of contrary ideas, even if we think they are true. When a concept (like free will) keeps bubbling up inescapably and irresistibly even in the mind of someone who disavows it—*whose worldview directly denies it*—that's a good clue that it is a truth of general revelation that is being suppressed. The created order refuses to fit inside the box of any idol-based worldview.

No matter how hard people work to suppress their knowledge of God, creation itself keeps challenging them. "Human life is a continual wrestling match with God and his created order," writes Thomas Johnson.[14] When talking with skeptics and agnostics, we can show that their worldview fails to account for reality as *they themselves* experience it. The truths of general revelation cannot be ultimately suppressed.

A worldview is like an internal map that guides us in navigating reality. Because idols deify a *part* of creation, they produce maps that cover only *part* of reality. As a result, in the course of ordinary life, humans keep walking off the map. It happens whenever they are "compelled to believe" in free will or moral responsibility or anything else not covered by their cognitive map—whenever they "cannot live" within the map's cramped borders. Life itself keeps pushing them off their own map. No one can live consistently on the basis of such a limited worldview map.

Double-Minded Secularists

Consider a few more real-life examples. In *What Science Offers the Humanities*, Edward Slingerland, identifies himself as an unabashed materialist and reductionist. A reviewer for the journal *Science* expressed hope that the book will "initiate conversion experiences" to a materialist worldview. (Conversion experiences? And you wondered whether materialism could really be labeled a religion?)

Slingerland argues that Darwinian materialism leads logically to the conclusion that humans are robots—that our sense of having a will or self or consciousness is an illusion. Yet, he admits, it is an illusion we find impossible to shake. No one "can help *acting* like and at some level *really feeling* that he or she is free." We are "constitutionally incapable of *experiencing* ourselves and other conspecifics [humans] as robots."

One section in his book is even titled "We Are Robots Designed Not to Believe That We Are Robots."

Do you recognize the language of general revelation? It consists in those fundamental truths that humans "can't help" experiencing and feeling, even when those truths contradict their own worldview. In one passage Slingerland writes, "We are constituted in such a way" that we "unavoidably" and "inescapably" experience the "lived reality" of being moral agents.

How does Slingerland propose to resolve the contradiction between his "lived reality" and his deterministic philosophy? He does not even try. Instead he says "we need to pull off the trick of ... living with a dual consciousness, cultivating the ability to view human beings simultaneously under two descriptions: as physical systems and as persons."[15] In other words, he explicitly recommends constructing a mental dichotomy, a two-story division:

Cultivating a "dual consciousness"

PERSONS
Free Agents

PHYSICAL SYSTEMS
Robots

Such compartmentalized thinking is what George Orwell famously called "doublethink," and it functions here as a philosophical coping mechanism. When a worldview fails to account for all of reality, what do adherents do? Do they say, "I guess my theory has been falsified; I'd better toss it out"? Most people do not give up that easily. Instead they suppress the things that their worldview cannot explain, walling them off into a conceptual area separate from reality—an upper story of useful fictions. Wish fulfillment. Illusions.

A dual consciousness is a signal that contrary evidence from general revelation is being suppressed. As we saw in Principle #2, *every* nonbiblical worldview ends up with some form of "dual consciousness" or dualism. There will always be a contradiction between the realities it acknowledges (what fits in the box) and the realities it denies (what sticks out of the box). A conflict between what it professes and what it suppresses.

Losing Total Truth

The price of accepting such a sharp dichotomy, however, is the loss of a unified truth. Slingerland's two views of the human person are logically contradictory. For if we really are robots operating by purely material causes, then freedom is impossible. There is no logically coherent, unified worldview that can encompass both these contradictory views of the human person.[16]

From time immemorial, people have held to the ideal of the unity of truth. The universe itself is an integrated, coordinated whole and therefore the truth *about* the universe must be an integrated, coherent whole. We may not be able to see yet how it all fits together. But we know that two contradictory statements cannot both be true.

Until roughly the 1930s, American higher education was based on what was explicitly called "the unity of Truth"—"the conviction that all truths agreed and ultimately could be related to one another in a single system," writes Harvard historian Julie Reuben.[17] Yet today even well-educated people have come to accept a contradictory, fragmented two-story view of truth. On one hand, they embrace a worldview that is radically reductionistic. On the other hand, they cannot deny the truths pressed on them by everyday experience—the truths of general revelation. So they have done what earlier generations would have found unthinkable: They have given up the ideal of the unity of truth.

A Leap of Doubt

The thinkers we have covered so far are surprisingly frank. They recognize the sharp contradiction between what they practice and what they profess. It is unusual, however, for people to be so clear-sighted. Many stop short of working out the full implications of their worldview. They simply live with a patchwork of conflicting ideas. An effective strategy in apologetics is to help people see more clearly where their worldview really leads. When they realize that idol-centered worldviews fail the practical test, that insight may open them to the case for a biblical worldview.

Consider Marvin Minsky of MIT. He is best known for his pithy phrase that the human brain is nothing but "a three-pound computer made of meat." Obviously, computers do not have the power of choice; the implication is that neither do humans. Surprisingly, however, Minsky then asks, "Does that mean we must embrace the modern scientific view and put aside the ancient myth of voluntary choice? No. We *can't* do that."

Why not? Minsky goes on: "No matter that the physical world provides no room for freedom of will; that concept is essential to our models of the mental realm." We cannot "ever give it up. We're virtually forced to maintain that belief, *even though we know it's false*."[18] False, that is, according to Minsky's materialist worldview.

This is an amazing case of Orwellian doublethink. Minsky says people are "forced to maintain" the conviction of free will, even when their own worldview tells them that "it's false." Clearly, he is not referring to merely cultural customs or traditions that can differ from society to society. These are truths that humans can't *not* know.

The inescapable fact that we are personal beings constitutes evidence that our origin is a personal Being. How does Minsky escape the force of that evidence? He reduces it to the status of a necessary falsehood. He moves it to the upper story:

"Ancient myths" that we are "forced to maintain"

NECESSARY FALSEHOODS
Freedom of Will

SCIENTIFIC VIEW
Computer Made of Meat

This is nothing less than a secular leap of faith. Materialists start by affirming the lower story as an account of what is real and true. But when the facts of experience fail to fit their worldview, they take a leap of faith to the upper story and embrace those facts in an ambiguous manner as false—yet necessary—beliefs.[19]

We must emphasize that this is a far cry from the biblical concept of faith. The Bible does *not* define faith as a leap to something that has no logical ground within its own worldview—a useful falsehood. When Paul writes, "We walk by faith, not by sight" (2 Cor. 5:7), some Christians seem to think he is speaking metaphorically and means "by faith, not *reason*." But Paul is speaking literally and he means sight. Non-material realities are invisible. They cannot be seen. Faith is "the evidence of things not seen" (Heb. 11:1 KJV). It can take tremendous faith to act on the basis of realities we cannot see, but it is not a logical contradiction. Given the evidence, such actions can even be eminently reasonable, just as it is reasonable for physicists to count on the reality of forces and fields that they cannot see.

The secular project leads to the suicide of the intellect and the disintegration of the person. By contrast, the Christian worldview is amazingly positive, affirming both the unity of truth and the holistic commitment of the thinking person.

Atheism versus Civilization

In Romans 1, Paul warns that idols lead to destructive behavior, to moral and social breakdown. Amazingly, some secular thinkers recognize the truth of Paul's warning.

Philosopher Saul Smilansky is a determinist who regards free agency as an illusion. Yet he considers it a "fortunate" illusion because it makes civilized life possible. He urges society's elites to persuade people that they are responsible agents (though in reality they are not) in order to maintain a healthy sense of moral duty and responsibility. Otherwise they could excuse hostile behavior by saying they had no choice in the matter. Free will is a necessary fiction—"morally necessary"—to undergird the social order.

Smilansky summarizes by saying, "We *cannot live* adequately with ... a complete awareness of the absence of free will." Thus "we ought to hold on to those central but incoherent or contradictory beliefs in the free will case."[20]

What are the telltale phrases that he is being challenged by general revelation? His admission that "we cannot live" on the basis of what his worldview teaches. That "we ought to hold on to" a contradictory belief in free will.

Of course, Smilansky's materialistic worldview gives no basis for any moral "ought" because that word implies that humans are capable of making moral choices. A review of his book points out that he is advocating "a two-tiered" system: "There are those in the know (mostly philosophers and scientists) who realize the naturalistic truth about ourselves, and then there's the rest of us—the vast majority who must be misled as to our real nature, lest we become demoralized."[21]

When we hear people talk about ideas that are false, yet necessary for a humane social order, that is a signal that they have bumped up against the hard edge of a reality that does not fit their worldview. They have stumbled upon the truths of general revelation. And they are seeking to suppress those truths by demoting them to useful fictions. It's remarkable how Paul's description in Romans 1 of the dynamics of suppression makes sense of the latest modern worldviews.

Dawkins's "Intolerable" Worldview

The best known of the New Atheists is Richard Dawkins. In his books, he argues that humans are merely "survival machines—robot vehicles blindly programmed" by their genes. Therefore it makes no sense to hold anyone responsible for what they do. After all, he says, "When a computer malfunctions, we do not punish it. We track down the problem and fix it." He urges an overhaul of the entire criminal justice system: "Isn't the murderer or the rapist just a machine with a defective component?"

Dawkins likes to illustrate with an episode from the British comedy show *Fawlty Towers*. When Basil Fawlty's little red car won't start, first he scolds the car, like a parent with a disobedient child. Then he counts to three. Finally he picks up a tree branch and gives the car a good thrashing. "Of course we laugh," Dawkins writes. But, "Why don't we laugh at a judge who punishes a criminal? ... Doesn't a truly scientific, mechanistic view of the nervous system make nonsense of the very idea of responsibility?"[22]

In Dawkins's mind, a person has no more freedom than a little red car.

When a young man pressed him on the issue after a public lecture, however, Dawkins admitted that he does not practice what he preaches. He does not treat the very idea of responsibility as nonsense. He does hold people responsible for their actions: "I blame people, I give people credit."

"But don't you see that as an inconsistency in your views?" the young man asked. Dawkins replied, "I sort of do, yes. But it is an inconsistency that we sort of have to live with, *otherwise life would be intolerable*."[23]

It was an astonishing admission that in practice no one can live by the naturalistic worldview that he himself promotes—that its consequences would be "intolerable."

Einstein's Dilemma

What we learn from these examples is that many prominent thinkers live a two-story or bipolar existence. In their professional work, they adopt a reductionistic philosophy that regards people as essentially little red cars. But when they leave their laboratories and go home for the day, they have to switch to a contrary paradigm in order to treat people justly and humanely—to avoid a life that is "intolerable."

Even the great Albert Einstein was caught in the same dilemma. On one hand, he writes, "human beings in their thinking, feeling, and acting, are not free but are as causally bound as the stars in their motions." Yet on the other hand, he said, "I am compelled to act *as if* free will existed because if I want to live in a civilized society I must act responsibly."[24]

Einstein's phrase "as if" is a giveaway that he is talking about an irrational leap of faith. The source of the phrase is the writings of Immanuel Kant. On one hand, Kant thought science led to the conclusion that humans are elements in a vast machine operating by the laws of physics. On the other hand, he said, to salvage morality, we must act *as if* we were free. And to ratify our moral standards, we must act *as if* God existed. And because morality makes no sense unless justice prevails in the end, we must act *as if* there were an afterlife. Otherwise, "all moral laws are to be considered as idle dreams."

In Kant's view, it is impossible to *know* whether these theological teachings are true. But to encourage moral behavior, he said we must live *as if* they were true. The phrase *as if* signals a concept that has been moved to the upper story.[25]

Living "as if" Christianity were true

WHAT WE ACCEPT "AS IF"
Freedom, God, Morality, Afterlife

WHAT WE KNOW
Materialism, Determinism

Ever since Kant, the phrase *as if* has come to signal truths that people are compelled to hold, even though they cannot account for those truths within their own worldview. They live *as if* Christianity were true, even though their worldview denies it.

Instead of giving up their worldview in the face of contrary facts, they endure a severe mental schizophrenia.

Secular Mysticism

We still live in the shadow of Kant. In *What Is Thought?*, computer scientist Eric Baum argues that the mind is essentially a computer program produced by evolutionary processes; thus free will is an illusion. The logical argument is "airtight," Baum insists. Astonishingly, he then adds, "But who really cares, for all practical purposes? It's much more reasonable and practical for my genes to build me believing in free will, and for me to act and think *as if* I have free will." It is a useful fiction.

But a useful fiction is still a fiction. And to hold it, when your own worldview denies it, is irrational. We might even call it a form of secular mysticism. Baum admits as much. "Free will is a very useful theory" for describing human behavior, he writes. Yet it is still "wrong." To be precise, it is "not even wrong"—because it "cannot be given any logical interpretation" (at least, not within his worldview). Thus Baum concludes, "The belief is simply mystical."[26]

One group of thinkers has even been labeled "mysterians." They argue that human intelligence is simply not equipped to solve the mystery of consciousness—that it evolved to solve purely practical problems like obtaining food and making tools. A representative of this group, Colin McGinn, writes, "Consciousness *must* have evolved from matter somehow but nothing we could contrive or imagine seem[s] to offer the faintest hope for explanation.... We just don't have the faculties of comprehension that would enable us to remove the sense of mystery."[27]

Francis Schaeffer in *The God Who Is There* observes that every worldview containing a two-story dualism leads ultimately to "mysticism" in the sense that adherents must affirm truths that their own worldview cannot rationally explain.[28] It is ironic that many thinkers who pride themselves on being champions of rationality have accepted a form of mysticism—driven to that extreme position by the impulse to suppress the facts that contradict their preferred worldview.

Darwinian Psychopaths

Romans 1 says God "gives people up" to pursue their idols ever further, increasing the gap between what they profess and what they practice. We can picture worldviews falling along a continuum: The more consistently people work out the logic of their worldview, the more reductionistic the result will be, the wider the gap, and the further its leap into irrational mysticism. The choice facing them becomes ever clearer: Will they follow the evidence of general revelation? Or will they cling to their theories in the face of the evidence?

Let's follow a series of examples to watch for ourselves how the gap grows ever wider—and more disturbing.

We began with Slingerland; now let's see where he ends. As a Darwinist and materialist, he acknowledges that his reductionist view of humans as essentially robots is contrary to ordinary experience. It is "alien and often repugnant, from any sort of normal human perspective." Gesturing toward his own daughter, Slingerland writes, "At an important and ineradicable level, the idea of my daughter as merely a complex robot carrying my genes into the next generation is both bizarre and repugnant to me." Such a reductionistic view "inspires in us a kind of emotional resistance and even revulsion."

Indeed, he writes, if you do *not* feel that revulsion, something is wrong with you: "There may well be individuals who lack this sense, and who can quite easily and thoroughly conceive of themselves and other people in purely instrumental, mechanistic terms, but we label such people 'psychopaths,' and quite rightly try to identify them and put them away somewhere to protect the rest of us."[29]

What can we say when someone urges us to adopt a view of humanity that he himself admits is bizarre and repugnant? A view that ought to inspire revulsion? A view so dangerous that, when acted on, it would justify us in labeling people "psychopaths" and locking them up?

There is a severe clash between what his Darwinian materialism tells him (in the downstairs) and what his lived experience tells him (in the upstairs). Which one will he accept as true?

To describe this clash, we've been using the term *cognitive dissonance*, but that word may be too tame. This is a searing contradiction. Paul writes that those who build their lives on idols become "futile in their thinking, and their foolish hearts

[are] darkened" (Rom. 1:21). The Greek word for *futile* means unproductive, ineffectual, failing to achieve its purpose. As this example clearly shows, idol-based worldviews do not produce what a philosophy of life is meant to give us—a coherent, logically satisfying worldview that makes sense of all of life.

The Greek word for *foolish* reinforces the theme. Its root (*syniēmi*) means to synthesize, to put things together in the mind, and therefore to understand, to be wise. Thus to be foolish is to fail to connect ideas or link them into a meaningful structure, a coherent whole. Scripture is giving a spot-on description of the fragmented, fractured, internally contradictory two-story worldviews that result from embracing idols.

No wonder Paul writes that those who reject the Creator "are without excuse" (Rom. 1:20). The phrase means "without a defense," and it originally referred to a legal defense in a courtroom. In the Greek, the word is *anapológetos*, which has the same root as the word *apologetics*. The passage implies that those who adopt Creator substitutes end up with two-story worldviews that are not defensible as logically consistent, coherent, or realistic. Their worldviews do not fit reality as they themselves experience it.

The strength of this approach is that it shows why worldviews fail on their own terms. It is rarely persuasive to criticize other views from within your own perspective. All that really shows is that those other views disagree with *you*. Instead you must step imaginatively inside other perspectives to show from within why they lack explanatory power.

MIT Prof: My Children Are Machines

When God gives people up to their idols, they experience a growing conflict between their worldview and their lived reality. When I teach these concepts in the classroom, an example my students find especially poignant is *Flesh and Machines* by Rodney Brooks, professor emeritus at MIT. Brooks writes that a human being is nothing but a machine—a "big bag of skin full of biomolecules" interacting by the laws of physics and chemistry.

In ordinary life, of course, it is difficult to actually see people that way. But, he says, "when I look at my children, I can, when I force myself, ... see that they are machines."

Is that how he treats them, though? Of course not: "That is not how I treat them.... I interact with them on an entirely different level. They have my unconditional love, the furthest one might be able to get from rational analysis." Certainly if what counts as "rational" is a materialist worldview in which humans are machines, then loving your children *is* irrational. It has no basis within Brooks's worldview. It sticks out of his box.

How does he reconcile such a heart-wrenching cognitive dissonance? He doesn't. Brooks ends by saying, "I maintain two sets of inconsistent beliefs."[30] He has given up on any attempt to reconcile his theory with his experience. He has abandoned all hope for a unified, logically consistent worldview. He has no defense.

This is the tragedy of the postmodern age. The things that matter most in life, that are necessary for a humane society—ideals like moral freedom, human dignity, even loving our own children—have been reduced to nothing but useful fictions. They are tossed into the attic, which becomes a convenient dumping ground for anything that a materialist paradigm cannot explain.

The Bible teaches that, without God, people are morally lost. But they are also intellectually lost because they are trying to live within the limits of a worldview that is too cramped and narrow to account for *their own humanity*. They are forced to place their entire hope for dignity and meaning in an upper-story realm that they themselves regard as irrational and unknowable—nothing but necessary falsehoods.

Tragically, over time those humane ideals will inevitably lose their hold. After all, we are made in God's image as logical beings; thus we tend to follow the logical consequences of our premises. It is psychologically impossible to accept concepts that we regard as fictions, no matter how useful. If someone like Brooks genuinely thinks his children are just mechanisms operating by whirring gears, that conviction will eventually erode the "unconditional love" he feels for them. If the leadership classes in a society genuinely think people are machines, that conviction will eventually erode political liberty. Idols have practical consequences.[31]

Chesterton: Christianity "Too Good to Be True"

Today Christians have an unprecedented opportunity to present the biblical worldview as positive and life affirming. If you begin with matter operating by blind, mechanical forces, then logically humans cannot ultimately be anything *but* complex mechanisms. Your starting assumptions limit the categories available to you.

But if you begin with a transcendent personal Agent, then you have a perfectly logical explanation for why humans are likewise personal agents. The cause is adequate to the effect. The very phenomena that are so problematic for scientific materialism—like free will, consciousness, love—can be logically accounted for within a Christian worldview. No part of human experience falls outside its categories. Nothing sticks out of the box. The human person is no longer a misfit in a deterministic world. There is no division into an upper and lower story because you don't need a mystical attic to stash things that don't fit in your worldview. Christianity continues to affirm the unity of truth as a coherent, logically consistent whole. In Christ, all things still "hold together" (Col. 1:17).

G. K. Chesterton wagers that secularists reject Christianity not because it is a bad theory but because it seems "too good to be true." For the materialist, "the universe is a universal prison." It shackles humans in an interlocking chain of cause and effect. Thus when a secularist encounters the biblical view, "it is like believing in fairyland to believe in such freedom."

If secularists find Christianity "incredible," Chesterton concludes, that is because it is so incredibly positive in affirming a high view of human freedom and dignity.[32]

Secular thinkers often criticize Christianity for being irrational. Yet ironically, today it is a biblical worldview that coheres in a logically consistent system. It liberates us from cognitive dissonance, imparting a profound inner unity and peace. It accords with the natural human longing for a life of integrity and wholeness. (The word *integrity* comes from the Latin word for wholeness.) When talking with secular people, we can show them how Christianity fulfills *their own* highest hopes and ideals.

Of course, not everyone who accepts materialism or naturalism goes on to accept determinism. But I suggest that's only because they are not as careful to work out the logical outcome of their premises. Often people accept ideas that sound attractive or sophisticated but do not follow those ideas all the way to their final implications. By giving examples of scientists and philosophers like those we have met in Principle #3, we can provide a reality check. People are more likely to be persuaded when they learn the negative consequences of materialism and atheism from the writings of materialists and atheists themselves.

Walking Off the Postmodern Map

So far we have applied the practical test to Enlightenment worldviews. What happens when we apply Principle #3 to the other side of the coin—the continental tradition that stems from the Romantic movement? As we saw earlier, instead of absolutizing the lower story (matter), philosophical idealism absolutizes the upper story (mind). It claims that ultimate reality is the mental realm of ideas. Schopenhauer describes idealism by saying it takes the "eternal truths" that were the foundation of all previous philosophy, "investigates their origin, and then finds this to be in man's head."[33]

But if the eternal truths really are "in man's head," then the logical conclusion is that they are *not* eternal after all. They are merely human constructs, relative and changing. In our day, postmodernism has drawn that conclusion. It holds that humans have no access to an objective or extra-mental world. In Rorty's succinct phrase, truth is "made rather than found."[34]

If materialism keeps its old trunks in the attic, we might say postmodernism keeps its old trunks in the basement, labeled with postmodern jargon like "Logocentric," "Post-Colonialist," "Metanarrative," and "False Consciousness."

Let's ask the same question we posed to Enlightenment worldviews: Does postmodernism account for the facts of universal human experience? Can it be lived without contradiction in the real world? Or does it lead to an untenable dualism?

The answer is that in practice postmodernists do not live consistently on the basis of their own philosophy. They do not treat all ideas as human constructs. Instead, like every other normal person, they test their mental concepts against extra-mental states of affairs in dozens of ways. They *thought* the bread was in the refrigerator but found it was on the counter. They *thought* their keys were on the table but found they were in a pocket. How? By comparing their internal thoughts with a state of affairs in the external world.

In everyday life, postmodernists are just as concerned about objective truth as anyone else. Dallas Willard comments, "I have noticed that the most emphatic of Postmodernists turn coldly modern when discussing their fringe benefits or other matters that make a great difference to their practical life."[35] If we use the metaphor that a worldview is a mental map, postmodernists keep walking off their map. It is too small to account for the full geography of who they are.

As we saw in Principle #2, postmodernism is a form of anti-realism, the view that reality is a social construction. Yet humans cannot help functioning as though the external world is real and our knowledge of it is basically reliable. Those who deny that we have access to an external reality still look both ways before crossing the street. They avoid jumping off balconies. They hold their breath under water. In other words, they know that there is an extra-mental reality to which they must adapt their behavior; otherwise the consequences will be disastrous.

We all learned this basic truth from the time we were tiny. As toddlers, when we bumped into the wall or tipped over our chair and crashed to the floor, we discovered in a painful way that the universe has an objective structure. When the toy box did not contain the toy we wanted, we discovered that reality does not bend to our subjective desires. Anything that we are compelled to affirm, simply in order to function in the world, is part of general revelation.

Christianity explains *why* truth is not merely a human construction. The world is not a creation of my own mind. It is the handiwork of God. The human mind cannot usurp the Creator's role and function. The biblical concept of creation gives logical grounds to support what humans inescapably conclude by experience from the time we are toddlers.

Remarkably, Rorty concedes that the very idea of objective truth—a truth that is "out there"—makes sense only on the basis of a Christian worldview. "The suggestion that truth is out there ... is a legacy of an age in which the world was seen as the creation of a being who had a language of his own," a "non-human language" written into the cosmos.[36] Rorty is harkening back to an image that Christians have embraced since the church fathers—the idea that there are two books: the book of God's word (the Bible) and the book of God's world (nature). And because the world itself is a kind of book, there is a message and meaning written in the cosmos itself. Humans should be able to "read" certain fundamental truths in creation. We should be able to discern evidence for God in general revelation, just as Romans teaches.

Don't Impose Your Facts

Earlier we learned that all idols lead to a mental dichotomy or dualism—and postmodernism is no exception. Philosopher William Lane Craig points out that virtually no one applies postmodernism consistently across the board: "People are not relativistic when it comes to matters of science, engineering, and technology; rather, they are relativistic and pluralistic in matters of *religion* and *ethics*."[37]

In short, they apply their postmodern skepticism selectively.

Think of it this way: We often hear people say, "Don't impose your religion on me." But we never hear people say, "Don't impose your facts on me." Why not? Because facts are assumed to be objective and universal, binding on everyone.

The upshot is that most people function as modernists *and* postmodernists—depending on the situation. When dealing with religion and morality, most people no longer think in terms of true and false. They no longer look to religion for an explanatory system to answer the cosmic questions of life. Instead they choose a religion the way they choose a wallpaper pattern or an item on the menu, says philosopher Ernest Gellner. It has become an area of life where it is considered acceptable to act on the basis purely of personal taste or feelings. By contrast, Gellner says, when "serious issues are at stake" like making money or meeting medical needs, then people want solutions based on "real knowledge." They want to know the tested outcomes of objective science and research.[38]

What this means is that most people live fragmented lives. In the private world of home, church, and relationships, they operate on a postmodern view of truth as subjective and relative. But in the public world of work, business, and finance, they operate on a modernist view of truth as objective and verifiable. In short, they no longer live as whole persons with a consistent, coherent philosophy of life.

No wonder philosopher Louis Dupré says that the central challenge of our age is the lack of any integrating truth: "We experience our culture as fragmented; we live on bits of meaning and lack the overall vision that holds them together in a whole." As a result, people feel an intense need for self-integration. Christianity has the power to integrate our lives and create a coherent personality structure, but only if we embrace it as the ultimate, capital-T truth that pulls together all lesser truths. Our commitment to Christian truth "cannot simply remain one discrete part of life," Dupré says; it must "integrate all other aspects of existence."[39] Anything less is neither beautiful nor compelling enough to ignite our passion and transform our character.

A Harvard Professor's Admission

I once delivered a presentation that included several of the examples in this chapter. Afterward a Harvard professor came up to me from the audience, visibly upset. After all, I had criticized the work of university professors at places like Harvard—his own colleagues. "*They know* their theories don't explain ordinary life outside the lab," he said emphatically. "But why throw it in their faces?"

The first thing that struck me was that he had let slip an amazing admission. These scientists and philosophers *know* that their theories do not fit the real world? In Romans 1, Paul says the testimony of general revelation is knowable by everyone. Was this professor unwittingly confirming what Paul says?

When we read in Romans 1 that those who worship idols are "without excuse," those words may seem harsh. In this chapter, however, we have met several scholars who openly acknowledge that their reductionist theories clash with the facts of experience. They are aware, at some level, that they harbor a severe contradiction. Derek Parfit says this type of inner conflict is actually quite common. Addressing his fellow philosophers, he writes, "At a reflective or intellectual level, we may be convinced that some view is true; but at another level, one that engages more directly with our emotions, we may continue to think and feel *as if* some other view were true." He concludes, "Many of us, I suspect, have such inconsistent beliefs about the metaphysical questions that concern us most," such as free will, consciousness, and the self.[40]

How do philosophers justify living with "inconsistent beliefs"? Yale philosopher Karsten Harries ventures to say many hold a "double truth" theory. They are "hard-wired" to hold certain ideas as true in terms of first-person experiences—but they hold the same ideas to be false according to science. Here's how Harries puts it: "As intelligent agents we are *compelled to believe* certain things, most importantly that our will is free, that we are selves that persist through time, that there are moral truths that can be universalized, beliefs which as individuals committed to science we yet *know to be false*." That is, "false" according to a materialist conception of science.[41]

You would think that when people realize they hold inconsistent beliefs, they would look for better ones. As we have seen, however, many scholars entrench themselves even more deeply in their reductionism. To acknowledge the evidence from general revelation would point them toward the biblical God—and so they suppress the evidence.

Fascinatingly, there are even a few who admit that getting rid of God is precisely the goal of their reductionist theories. Take Francis Crick, who became a household name after he and James

Watson discovered the double-helix structure in DNA. Crick freely admits that he sought out reductionist theories because he wanted to discredit religion. "I went into science because of these religious reasons, there's no doubt about that," he said in an interview. "I asked myself what were the two things that appear inexplicable and are used to support religious beliefs." The two things, he decided, were the origin of life (physical nature) and of consciousness (human nature). His goal was to explain away both of them by reducing them to physical-chemical causes.

In the same interview, Watson also expressed his religious motivation. The discovery of the double helix, he said, gives "grounds for thinking that the powers held traditionally to be the exclusive property of the gods might one day be ours."[42]

At least for some people, the purpose of proposing reductionist theories is to deny the Creator and to expropriate his divine power.

Secularism Is Too Small for Secularists

The second thing that struck me about the Harvard professor's comment was that he characterized an analysis of someone's worldview as "throwing it in their faces." The goal of testing worldviews should never to be attack those who hold them but to open their minds to a better alternative. People often hold half-baked ideas that they would reject if they understood more clearly where those ideas lead. So they erect a kind of buffer zone to protect themselves from recognizing the illogical and inhumane consequences of their worldviews. An effective method of apologetics can be to gently press people to think more critically by peeling away the protective layers so they can see the implications of their views more clearly. Only then will they be truly free to make tough choices about their fundamental convictions.

When pressing people to the logic of their conclusions, however, we must act with love and empathy, for when people feel the full force of their views, it can be deeply unsettling.[43]

Scripture says that when Paul noticed the many idols dotting the landscape in Athens, he was "provoked," a word that is also translated stirred, distressed, troubled, or grieved (Acts 17:16). A Christian's motive in apologetics should be a God-inspired grief for the lost. We should be brokenhearted over the dehumanizing reductionisms that dishonor and destroy our fellow human beings. We should weep for people whose dark worldviews deny that their life choices have meaning or moral significance. We should be moved by sorrow for people whose education has taught them that their loves, dreams, and highest ideals are ultimately nothing but electrical impulses jumping across the synapses in their brains. We should mourn for postmoderns who think that (as Schopenhauer said) the "eternal truths" are only in one's head.

When talking to people trapped in a secular worldview, we can help them to see that it gives no basis for the realities of life that they themselves care most about. The very fact that they cannot live within its cramped confines is a sign that they were made to live in a larger, richer conceptual universe. Secularism is too small for secularists. We should begin by expressing solidarity with their deepest longings for meaning and significance—and then show that in a biblical worldview, those longings are not merely illusions or useful fictions but living realities.

We often hear stereotypes that Christianity is negative and repressive; that it regards human nature as corrupt and worthless; that it places little value on life in this world. But in reality the Christian worldview has a much higher view of human life than any competing system. It gives a logical basis for the facts of experience that are denied by the dominant secular worldviews of our day: freedom, creativity, love, personal significance, genuine truth. How can we be anything but loving and joyful in communicating such a life-giving message?

Another common negative stereotype is that Christianity is irrational and obscurantist. In the next chapter, you will learn how to turn the tables on that charge—to show that in reality it is idols that lead to irrational and self-contradictory worldviews. You will learn a simple yet devastating strategy to demonstrate how idolatrous worldviews shoot themselves in the foot.

PRINCIPLE #4

·····

WHY WORLDVIEWS COMMIT SUICIDE

Do Christians have to check their science at the church door? Michael Egnor, a leading brain surgeon, used to think so. After years of rigorous scientific training, he was sure a scientific worldview was incompatible with any form of religion.

Ironically, it was science itself that showed him how mistaken he was.

"I was raised as an agnostic and grew up pretty much as a scientific materialist," Egnor told me.[1] He came to regard Christianity as an inspiring set of moral tales—lessons that were spiritually uplifting but not true.

Why was he so certain? Because, in his view, science had decisively disproved all theistic claims. "As a science major in college," Egnor said, "I was steeped in Darwinian evolution, which seemed to demonstrate that life could be explained perfectly well by material mechanisms alone. There was no reason to invoke God."

Darwin's theory seemed to have discredited the classic argument from design.

Egnor's studies also covered Freud, whose theories persuaded him that "religion is wish fulfillment—a product of the search for a father figure, a way of working out our internal fears and desires." As a result of his university studies, he told me, "Every time I even considered Christianity, I was stopped cold by the thought that it would mean abandoning scientific integrity."

Over the years, Egnor rose to the top of his field. He was appointed professor and vice president of neurosurgery at State University of New York, Stony Brook, and became an award-winning brain surgeon, named one of New York's best doctors by *New York Magazine*. One of his specialties is the treatment of hydrocephalus ("water on the brain"), and while developing a theory of blood flow to the brain, his research took a surprising turn. He realized the cranial system he was studying was like an ingeniously designed gadget. The filter that protects the delicate capillaries from the pulsating force of the heartbeat "is a finely tuned mechanism analogous to vibration dampers widely used in engineering. In fact, most of what I needed to know was not in biology textbooks but in *engineering* textbooks."

And what engineers do, of course, is design things.

Eventually Egnor realized that virtually all biological research operates on the presumption of design. For example, a standard procedure in biology is called "reverse engineering," which is modeled on the kind of thinking you would do if you came across a widget and did not know how it functioned. You would take it apart piece by piece, working backward to reproduce the engineer's thought process when he originally designed it. That's exactly the kind of analysis that biologists do in the laboratory. They tease apart molecules like proteins or genes, asking what each part does and how they interact to achieve their function.

In essence, biologists operate on the basis of design all the time—in practice at least—regardless of which theory they hold.

Philosopher Michael Ruse, though himself an outspoken Darwinist, says biology unavoidably relies on "design-type thinking." Living things are best explained by discovering what purpose their parts serve. The purpose of the heart is to pump blood. The purpose of the eye is to see. Fins are designed for swimming, and wings for flying. All the components work together in a coherent, coordinated fashion to achieve a goal.

"We treat organisms—the parts at least—*as if* they were manufactured, *as if* they were designed, and then we try to work out their functions," Ruse writes. "End-directed thinking—teleological thinking—is appropriate in biology because, and only because, organisms seem *as if* they were manufactured, *as if* they had been created by an intelligence and put to work."[2]

Surprisingly, even Darwin did not deny that the world looks as if it were designed. He merely argued that the appearance of design is misleading—that the same teleological order can be created by material forces instead.[3]

As we saw in Principle #3, the phrase *as if* signals cognitive dissonance. It indicates that certain ideas are inescapable in practice, no matter what a person's worldview says. When a concept (such as design) has to be assumed in order to understand living systems, that is a clue that it is a part of general revelation.

It's Not Brain Surgery ... Oh Wait, Yes It Is

In Egnor's work in the lab as a medical researcher, he ran into the same cognitive dissonance again and again. "I was surprised at how little the Darwinian paradigm contributed to my work," he told me. "By contrast, the design paradigm aligned nicely with the most important aspects of my research." Eventually he had to make a decision. When theory and facts contradict one another, which would he follow?

Egnor's guiding principle was to follow the evidence wherever it leads. He decided the best explanation for why living things function as if they were designed is that they *were* designed. "I came to see that Darwinism is a philosophical bias more than coherent science. Darwinian processes may explain some patterns and changes in gene frequency in populations, but the evidence does not even remotely support the claim that chance and necessity fully account for the appearance of complex design in living things."

What about Freud? "Freud's notion that religion is wish fulfillment can be turned against his own theory," Egnor said. "In fact, it is much more plausible that atheism, rather than Christianity, is a form of wish fulfillment. For if there is no God, then no one is watching, there is no moral accountability, and you can do what you want (as long as you can get away with it)." As Polish poet Czesław Miłosz observes, there is great relief in "a belief in nothingness after death—the huge solace of thinking that for our betrayals, greed, cowardice, murders *we are not going to be judged*."[4]

Egnor finally realized that if he were to follow the facts wherever they lead, he would have to accept Christianity. And having a scientist's respect for facts, that's what he did. Immediately he discovered a new sense of unity and wholeness. The biblical God proved to be a sufficient integration point to unify all areas of his life, both professional and personal. Christianity is a worldview conceptually rich enough to account for all of human experience.

"Now I see science as another way to appreciate the beauty of God's creation," he told me. "I bring science into church with me. Truth is unitary."

Tests for Truth

Egnor's story illustrates the two major ways to test a philosophy or worldview: Does it fit the facts? And is it logically consistent? These are the same questions we raise in testing any idea—whether in a science lab, a court of law, or when asking a friend why she showed up late. First, does the explanation match what we know about the world? That's the question we asked in Principle #3. Second, does the explanation hold together logically? That is the question we will consider now in Principle #4.

Internal contradictions are fatal to any worldview because contradictory statements are necessarily false. "This circle is square" is contradictory, so it has to be false. Scripture assumes that logical contradictories cannot both be true: "No lie is of the truth" (1 John 2:21); God "never lies" (Titus 1:2); God "cannot deny himself" (2 Tim. 2:13).

An especially damaging form of contradiction is self-referential absurdity—which means a theory sets up a definition of truth that it *itself* fails to meet. Therefore it refutes itself.

You've probably heard the argument from self-referential absurdity in ordinary conversation, even if you didn't call it that. To the relativist who says there are no absolutes—are there *absolutely* no absolutes? To the skeptic who says we can't know anything for sure—do you know *that* for sure? In each case, the critic is turning the claim back on itself to show that it undercuts itself. It is self-defeating.

Apologist Greg Koukl likes to say this is how a philosophy commits suicide. When its own criteria are applied to itself, it kills itself. It slits its own throat.[5]

People sometimes dismiss this kind of argument as nothing but a snappy put-down, a parlor game. A university student who had recently abandoned his Christian upbringing told his parents he now realized there are no absolute truths. When they asked whether that statement itself was absolutely true, he dismissed their response as a rhetorical trick and refused to engage any longer. In Principle #4 we will discover why it is not a trick but a valid and powerful form of argument.

In fact, we will discover that virtually *all* idol-based worldviews are self-refuting. Why? Because they are reductionistic. When reductionism is applied to the human mind, it reduces reason to something *less* than reason. It says the ideas in our minds are products of natural selection (Darwinism) or economic conditions (Marxism) or electrochemical responses in the brain (contemporary neuroscience). Yet the only way a worldview can build its *own* case is by using reason. Thus when it discredits reason, it undercuts its own case. It is self-defeating.

Of course, most worldviews are plagued by a variety of logical difficulties and contradictions. To track each one individually would seem an endless task. But because idol-centered worldviews are all reductionistic, this one fundamental flaw is predictable.[6] Learning to identify it will empower you with a laser-focused strategy that you can apply to any and every worldview you encounter.

As soon as Christians raise the problem of contradictions, we are likely to get pushback from people claiming that Christianity itself contains contradictions. They point to the doctrine of the Trinity or to Jesus's paradoxical statements such as "You must lose your life in order to save it." But these are not genuine logical contradictions. In logic, the law of non-contradiction states that two antithetical propositions cannot both be true at the same time and in the same sense. Biblical theology does not say that God is One *in the same sense* that God is Three. And Jesus was using paradoxical language to make a point (a paradox is an *apparent* contradiction). His statements were plays on words to catch people's attention, but they were not logical contradictories.

More to the point, Christianity is not self-referentially absurd. Because it is not reductionistic regarding human reason, it is not self-refuting. It does not commit suicide.

Principle #4
Test the Idol: Does It Contradict Itself?

To see why the argument from self-referential absurdity is not just a rhetorical trick, let's start with a historical example. Throughout much of the twentieth century, American academia was dominated by an extreme form of empiricism called logical positivism. As we saw earlier, classic empiricism puts everything into the box of the senses. Any statement that cannot be traced back to sense impressions is rejected as false. Logical positivism took this claim a step further: it insisted that any statement not reducible to sense impressions is not just false, but cognitively meaningless—that is, not even subject to standards of true and false.

Take, for example, a moral statement such as "Slavery is unjust." Justice is not something you can stuff into a test tube or study under a microscope. The logical positivists argued that therefore the sentence "Slavery is unjust" has no cognitive content. It is merely an expression of personal feelings or preference. It really means "I don't like slavery." This view of morality is sometimes called emotivism because it reduces moral statements to expressions of emotion, like saying "Boo!" or "Hooray!" And "Hooray!" is not something that can be true or false. A moral statement may be important to the person saying it, but according to logical positivism, it is cognitively meaningless. It is literally nonsense.

The emotivist view of morality has percolated through all levels of society. After all, it is much easier to dismiss someone's views by saying "That's just a value judgment" and treating it as a subjective preference instead of examining it seriously as a valid candidate for truth.

What happened, though, when the test of logical positivism was applied to itself? Its central claim was that statements are meaningful only if they are empirically testable. But is *that* statement empirically testable? Of course not. It is not an empirical observation. It is a metaphysical rule—an arbitrary definition of what qualifies as knowledge. Thus when the criterion of logical positivism was applied to itself, it was discredited. It stood self-condemned.

Logical positivism had been so influential for such a long time that its collapse sent shock waves all through the intellectual world. Its fall "was the most important philosophical event of the 20th century," says William Lane Craig.[7]

The strategy of applying a philosophy's own standard of truth to itself proved to be no mere rhetorical trick. It is a powerful tool for testing truth claims. And it can be applied to many other philosophies to show that they self-destruct in the same way.

Hitting the Marx

The key to identifying where a worldview commits suicide is to uncover its particular form of reductionism. Any theory that says, "Truth claims are nothing but X" is susceptible to self-refutation. For example, Karl Marx said that truth claims are nothing but rationalizations of economic interests: Laws are created by the rich to protect their property. Religion is the "opiate of the people," placating the poor with false promises of a happy afterlife.[8] But what happens if we apply Marx's rule to his own theory? Did he create it merely to rationalize his own economic interests? If so, we can dismiss it as a serious truth claim. The theory commits suicide.

Or take Friedrich Nietzsche. He held that all human action is driven by the will to power: Morality is invented by the weak to give them leverage over the strong. Religion is a "holy lie" used to control people.[9] But what about Nietzsche's own theory? Was it driven by his own will to power? Then why should the rest of us pay any attention to it? The theory undercuts itself.

Sigmund Freud insisted that our thoughts are shaped by unconscious emotional needs: Personality is shaped by things like early toilet training. Much of human behavior is a result of sexual repression. But what does that imply about the origin of Freud's own theory? Onto the couch yourself, Dr. Freud.

The behaviorist B. F. Skinner held that humans are nothing but stimulus-response mechanisms, responding to rewards and punishments: Their behavior is explainable in terms of operant conditioning, like the pigeons in his experiments, pecking at levers to get a pellet of food.[10] But is Skinner's theory a product of his own conditioning? The theory refutes itself.

What these philosophies all share is a refusal to take truth claims at face value. Instead they interpret them as cover-ups for hidden motives and disguised self-interest. This penchant for debunking has been labeled the "hermeneutics of suspicion" (hermeneutics is the science of interpretation). Those who practice it have been dubbed the "masters of suspicion."[11] To be logically consistent, however, the masters should practice equal suspicion toward their own views—which they rarely, if ever, do.

As a tool of critical thinking, a hermeneutics of suspicion can be useful to highlight common human failings—to diagnose the ways our thinking may be distorted by things like economic interests or psychological impulses. Scripture teaches that we deceive ourselves all the time about our true motives: "The heart is deceitful above all things, ... who can understand it?" (Jer. 17:9). Taken on its own terms, however, a hermeneutics of suspicion is radically reductionistic. It simply abandons the question of truth, reducing it to questions of power and desire.

Debunking the Debunkers

The principle of self-referential absurdity should be in everyone's toolbox. It is used regularly by apologists and philosophers, but with no underlying rationale or method. What is unique about the Romans 1 approach is that it explains *why* the argument works and how to apply it to any worldview. Find the reductionism: That's the point where it will commit suicide. A lower view of humanity will include a lower view of the mind—logic, reason, rationality. It will reduce human rationality to some *non*-rational force or process. Yet if ideas are products of non-rational forces, that must apply to *all* ideas—including the theory itself. The debunkers end up debunking their own theories.

Or they would, if they were consistent. To avoid discrediting their own views, the debunkers tacitly exempt themselves from the critique they use to discredit everyone else. They act as if *they* are not blinded by the same irrational forces that distort and bias everyone else's views—*they* are mysteriously able to rise above the forces that enslave everyone else—*they* alone are capable of achieving an untainted insight into reality. Even though they have stuffed the entire universe into a box, strangely they themselves are not trapped in that box. They somehow have the power to float above the box, rendering their own theories objectively valid and true.

But of course, by carving out an exception for themselves, they have introduced a logical inconsistency into their system. They have stated that there is one thing (namely, their own thinking) that their system does not cover.

Either way, then, idol-based worldviews are logically contradictory—which means they fail.

By contrast, a Christian worldview is not reductionistic. It does not reduce reason to something less than reason, and therefore it does not self-destruct. A Christian epistemology (theory of knowledge) starts with the transcendent Creator, who spoke the entire universe into being with his Word: "And God said" (Gen. 1:3). "In the beginning was the Word" (John 1:1). John uses a Greek word, *Logos*, that means not only Word but also reason or rationality—the underlying principle that unifies the world into an orderly cosmos, as opposed to randomness and chaos. The Greeks who heard John's gospel understood that he was claiming that Christ is the source of the order and coherence of the universe.

This biblical view has two crucial implications. First, the intelligible order of the universe reflects the mind of the Creator. Second, because God created humans in his image, *our* minds correspond with that order as well. There is a congruence between the structure of the world and the structure of human cognition—a correlation between subject and object in the act of knowing. As Plantinga writes, "God created both us and our world in such a way that there is a certain fit or match between the world and our cognitive faculties."[12]

The medievals used the phrase *adaequatio intellectus ad rem*, which means the intellect is adequate to reality. Of course, humans are broken, fallen creatures, and as a result our thought processes are darkened and distorted. Nevertheless, even after the fall, we are still human. We still retain the image of God. Throughout history, the Bible has inspired confidence in the essential reliability of human cognitive faculties.

Biblical epistemology is backed up experientially by general revelation. To function from day to day, humans have to assume that we *do* know a great many things—that the material world is real (the chair I'm sitting on will hold me up), that the universe works by cause and effect (if I drop this computer, it will fall), that mathematical truths hold universally (5 plus 7 will always equal 12), that our memories are basically reliable (I did eat a sandwich for lunch today), that other people have minds (even though I cannot directly see them), and that the laws of logic are valid (to discredit logic, I have to argue using logic). In our daily actions, we have to assume the basic reliability of human cognition. If we were complete skeptics, we would be paralyzed, unable to act.

Anything we must assume in order to function in the world is part of general revelation. The undeniable facts of experience reflect the created structure of physical nature or human nature, or both. They are signposts pointing to the biblical God. Only a biblical worldview explains why it is possible for humans to have trustworthy knowledge.

The upshot is that all worldviews have to borrow a Christian epistemology—at least at the moment they are making their claims. They must tacitly assume the reliability of reason and rationality, which only a biblical worldview supports. They have to function *as if* Christianity is true, even as they reject it.

C. S. Lewis Unmasks Materialism

To practice the skill of detecting self-referential absurdity, let's dissect a few more examples. Because materialism or naturalism is the unquestioned assumption in much of academia, let's begin with it. Materialism claims that my thoughts are products of physical events. What does that mean? It means that when I calculate that 5 plus 7 equals 12, or when I perceive a rose as red, or when I judge that torturing people is evil, what is really happening is that my brain is doing physical things, like producing chemical reactions and causing neurons to fire.

As a case in point, a recent book expounding materialism claims that ideas are "physical states of matter within our brains." Thus a thought process is "a series of brain states—a series of physical configurations of matter—each causing the next in accordance with the deterministic laws that govern the interactions of physical objects."[13] In other words, the thought produced by your brain is akin to the sweat secreted by your glands or the digestive juice produced by your stomach.

The problem is that digestion is not something that can be true or false; it is just a biological fact. If our thoughts are also biological facts, determined by biological laws, then they are not the sort of thing that can be true or false either.

But that has to include our thoughts about materialism—which undercuts its claim to be true. When the implications of materialism are applied to itself, it commits suicide.

C. S. Lewis makes a similar argument in several of his writings. Here is an example: "If minds are wholly dependent on brains, and brains on biochemistry, and biochemistry (in the long run) on the meaningless flux of the atoms, I cannot understand how the thought of those minds should have any more significance than the sound of the wind in the trees." Lewis then shows how this view defeats itself: "But if I can't trust my own thinking, of course I can't trust the arguments leading to Atheism, and therefore have no reason to be an Atheist, or anything else."[14]

How do atheists or materialists avoid that self-refuting conclusion? They make what Lewis calls a "tacit exception" for their own theory—at least, at the moment they are stating their claims. In building their case, they must implicitly trust their own thinking. They must exempt themselves from their own reductive categories of analysis. As one philosopher says, the materialist functions as though he were an "angelic observer" somehow able to float above the determinist cage in which he locks everyone else.[15]

In essence, materialists must tacitly assume a Christian epistemology, at least when they are arguing for their claims.

Indeed, the sheer act of *asserting* materialism contradicts itself. If I say, "Everything that exists is material," is that statement itself material? Is it merely a series of sound waves? If I write out the statement, is it nothing but marks on a piece of paper? Of course not. The statement has a linguistic meaning. It has logical properties. It has a social function (communicating to others)—all of which transcend the material dimension. Ironically, materialism cannot even be stated without refuting itself.

Because humans are whole and integrated beings, we should expect our thoughts to be *accompanied* by physical events in the brain. But if we *reduce* thought processes to brain processes, the result is a logical contradiction.

Evolution Cannot Survive Itself

Another example of self-referential absurdity is a theory called evolutionary epistemology, a naturalistic approach that applies evolution to the process of knowing. The theory proposes that the human mind is a product of natural selection. The implication is that the ideas in our minds were selected for their survival value, not for their truth value.

But what if we apply that theory to itself? Then it, too, was selected for survival, not truth—which discredits its *own* claim to truth. Evolutionary epistemology commits suicide.

Astonishingly, many prominent thinkers have embraced the theory without detecting the logical contradiction. Philosopher

John Gray writes, "If Darwin's theory of natural selection is true, ... the human mind serves evolutionary success, not truth."[16] What is the contradiction in that statement?

Gray has essentially said, if Darwin's theory is true, then it "serves evolutionary success, not truth." In other words, if Darwin's theory is true, then it is not true.

Self-referential absurdity is akin to the well-known liar's paradox: "This statement is a lie." If the statement is true, then (as it says) it is not true, but a lie.

Another example is Francis Crick. In *The Astonishing Hypothesis*, he writes, "Our highly developed brains, after all, were not evolved under the pressure of discovering scientific truths but only to enable us to be clever enough to survive."[17] But that means Crick's own theory is not a "scientific truth." Applied to itself, the theory commits suicide.

Of course, the sheer pressure to survive is likely to produce *some* correct ideas. A zebra that thinks lions are friendly will not live long. But false ideas may be useful for survival. Evolutionists admit as much: Eric Baum says, "Sometimes you are more likely to survive and propagate if you believe a falsehood than if you believe the truth." Steven Pinker writes, "Our brains were shaped for fitness, not for truth. Sometimes the truth is adaptive, but sometimes it is not."[18] The upshot is that survival is no guarantee of truth. If survival is the only standard, we can never know *which* ideas are true and which are adaptive but false.

To make the dilemma even more puzzling, evolutionists tell us that natural selection *has* produced all sorts of false concepts in the human mind. In Principle #3 we read about evolutionary materialists who maintain that free will is an illusion, consciousness is an illusion, even our sense of self is an illusion—and that all these false ideas were selected for their survival value.

So how can we know whether the theory of evolution itself is one of those false ideas? The theory undercuts itself.

A few thinkers, to their credit, recognize the problem. Literary critic Leon Wieseltier writes, "If reason is a product of natural selection, then how much confidence can we have in a rational argument for natural selection? ... Evolutionary biology cannot invoke the power of reason even as it destroys it."[19]

On a similar note, philosopher Thomas Nagel asks, "Is the [evolutionary] hypothesis really compatible with the continued confidence in reason as a source of knowledge?" His answer is no: "I have to be able to believe ... that I follow the rules of logic because they are correct—not *merely* because I am biologically programmed to do so." Hence, "insofar as the evolutionary hypothesis itself depends on reason, it would be self-undermining."[20]

Darwin's Selective Skepticism

People are sometimes under the impression that Darwin himself recognized the problem. They typically cite Darwin's famous "horrid doubt" passage where he questions whether the human mind can be trustworthy if it is a product of evolution: "With me, the horrid doubt always arises whether the convictions of man's mind, which has been developed from the mind of the lower animals, are of any value or at all trustworthy."

But, of course, Darwin's theory itself was a "conviction of man's mind." So why should *it* be "at all trustworthy"?

Surprisingly, however, Darwin never confronted this internal contradiction in this theory. Why not? Because he expressed his "horrid doubt" selectively—only when considering the case for a Creator.

From time to time, Darwin admitted that he still found the idea of God persuasive. He once confessed his "inward conviction ... that the Universe is not the result of chance." It was in the next sentence that he expressed his "horrid doubt." So the "conviction" he mistrusted was his lingering conviction that the universe is not the result of chance.

In another passage Darwin admitted, "I feel compelled to look to a First Cause having an intelligent mind in some degree analogous to that of man." Again, however, he immediately veered off into skepticism: "But then arises the doubt—can the mind of man, which has, as I fully believe, been developed from a mind as low as that possessed by the lowest animal, be trusted when it draws such grand conclusions?"

That is, can it be trusted when it draws "grand conclusions" about a First Cause? Perhaps the concept of God is merely an instinct programmed into us by natural selection, Darwin added, like a monkey's "instinctive fear and hatred of a snake."

In short, it was on occasions when Darwin's mind led him to a theistic conclusion that he dismissed the mind as untrustworthy.[21] He failed to recognize that, to be logically consistent, he needed to apply the same skepticism to his own theory.

Modern followers of Darwin still apply the theory selectively. Harvard paleontologist Stephen Jay Gould wrote, "Darwin applied a consistent philosophy of materialism to his interpretation of nature," in which "mind, spirit, and God as well, are just words that express the wondrous results of neuronal complexity."[22] In other words, God is an idea that appears in the human mind when the electrical circuitry of the brain has evolved to a certain level of complexity.

To be logically consistent, however, Gould should turn the same skepticism back onto Darwin's ideas, which he never did. Gould applied his evolutionary skepticism selectively—to discredit the idea of God.

Applied consistently, Darwinism undercuts not only itself but also the entire scientific enterprise. Kenan Malik, a writer trained in neurobiology, writes, "If our cognitive capacities were simply evolved dispositions, there would be no way of knowing *which* of these capacities lead to true beliefs and which to false ones." Thus "to view humans as little more than sophisticated animals ... undermines confidence in the scientific method."[23]

Just so. Science itself is at stake. John Lennox, professor of mathematics at the University of Oxford, writes that according to atheism, "the mind that does science ... is the end product of a mindless unguided process. Now, if you knew your computer was the product of a mindless unguided process, you wouldn't trust it. So, to me atheism undermines the rationality I need to do science."[24]

Of course, the atheist pursuing his research has no choice but to rely on rationality, just as everyone else does. The point is that he has no philosophical basis for doing so. Only those who affirm a rational Creator have a basis for trusting human rationality.

The reason so few atheists and materialists seem to recognize the problem is that, like Darwin, they apply their skepticism selectively. They apply it to undercut only ideas they reject, especially ideas about God.[25] They make a tacit exception for their own worldview commitments.

Why Science Is a "Miracle"

It is clear now why Christianity played a significant role in launching the scientific revolution in the first place. Only a biblical worldview provides an adequate epistemology for science. First, a rational God created the world with an intelligible structure, and second, he created humans in his image. In the words of historian Richard Cohen, science required the concept of a "rational creator of all things," along with the corollary that "we lesser rational beings might, by virtue of that Godlike rationality, be able to decipher the laws of nature." Theologian Christopher Kaiser states the same idea succinctly: the early scientists assumed that "the same Logos that is responsible for its ordering is also reflected in human reason."[26]

For the early scientists, the image of God was not a dry doctrine to which they gave merely cognitive assent. Nor was it a purely private "faith." They treated it as a public truth, the epistemological foundation for the entire scientific enterprise. Their goal, they said, was to think God's thoughts after him.[27] At the time of the scientific revolution, biblical epistemology was the guarantee that the human mind is equipped to gain genuine knowledge of the world.

And it still is today. A widely quoted essay by Eugene Wigner is titled "The Unreasonable Effectiveness of Mathematics in the Natural Sciences." Wigner asks why the mathematical formulas we devise in our heads work so well in describing the external universe. The match between them "is something bordering on the mysterious." Indeed, "there is no rational explanation for it." No explanation, that is, within scientific materialism.

"It is difficult to avoid the impression that a miracle confronts us," Wigner muses. At the very least, "certainly it is hard to believe that our reasoning power was brought, by Darwin's process of natural selection, to the perfection which it seems to possess."[28]

By contrast, a biblical worldview offers a perfectly reasonable explanation for the effectiveness of mathematics—namely, that a rational God created humans in his image to think his thoughts after him.

In fact, looking at history, we find that a biblically inspired confidence in the mathematical structure of the universe came *first*, before any actual scientific discoveries. Mathematician Morris Kline writes, "The early mathematicians were sure of the existence of mathematical laws underlying natural phenomena and persisted in the search for them because they were convinced *a priori* that God had incorporated them in the construction of the universe."[29]

People must first be convinced there *is* a mathematical order in nature. Otherwise they will not go searching for it—and science will not get off the ground.

What this means is that even today, anyone who wants to pursue science has to adopt an epistemology derived from a biblical worldview—at least in practice. To do science, even the most hard-boiled atheist must function *as if* Christianity were true.

Postmodern Prison

What about postmodernism? What happens to it if we apply the test of self-referential absurdity?

As we saw earlier, postmodernism absolutizes the social group. It claims that individuals are largely constituted by their membership in a community. When we absorb the language of our community, in the process we absorb its worldview—the story line or narrative it invokes to explain the world. Thus when we speak, we are only externalizing a story line that we have first assimilated.

Postmodernists express this idea using paradoxical statements like, "Language speaks us, rather than we speak it."[30] Their point is that we cannot even think apart from the language we have assimilated from our community. Nietzsche, with his typical flair, wrote that we are trapped in the "prison house of language."

Because worldviews are transmitted through language, postmodernists use the metaphor of "language games." Just as baseball and football are games with virtually no rules in common, so worldviews are said to be language games, each with its unique set of rules. Each community has its own language game for making sense of the world—what Jean-François Lyotard calls little narratives. But there is no universal narrative—no "metanarrative"—that is valid for all human beings at all times. In Lyotard's words, "There is no possibility that language games can be unified or totalized in any metadiscourse."[31]

Yet what reasons can Lyotard give us for accepting his theory? Isn't his own view just one more language game like all the others? Isn't he trapped in the prison house of his own language, just like everyone else? Then why should we pay any attention to it?

Postmodernism is an example of what is called a "performative contradiction," which means that a position is contradicted in the very act of being asserted.[32] Everyday examples of a performative contradiction include saying (in English), "I cannot speak English." Or, "I do not exist" (to make the statement, I must exist). When a postmodernist asserts that there is no universally valid truth, he is implicitly claiming that his *own* assertion is universally valid and true. To make the statement, he has to occupy the transcendental position that postmodernism says is not there to be occupied. Thus every time a postmodernist states his position, he contradicts it. The position is self-refuting.

Barthes Busted

When postmodern thought was applied to literary theory, it gave rise to an offshoot called deconstructionism. Recall that for postmodernism, individuals are constituted by their membership within a community. The implication is that individuals do not really have original or creative ideas but merely reflect the ideas of their communities. For example, literary critic Roland Barthes says a piece of writing is merely a "tissue of quotations" absorbed from the surrounding culture.

Barthes is best known for his slogan "the death of the author"—by which he means the death of the very concept of individual creativity. In his view, writers are akin to the bards or shamans of old, who were not inventors of their own stories so much as transmitters of the stories of their clan, tribe, or community. Jacques Derrida means the same thing in his paradoxical statement "Texts have no author."[33]

Moreover, we all belong to a variety of communities based on attributes such as race, class, gender, ethnicity, and sexual identity—all with conflicting outlooks and interests. As a result, every author will unconsciously reflect conflicting social messages. For Barthes, a text is a mix "in which a variety of writings, none of them original, blend and clash."[34] The goal of the literary critic is to dig beneath the surface of the text to excavate and disentangle those clashing meanings.

This is called *deconstructing* the text—hence the term *deconstructionism*.

What reason does Barthes give for accepting such a theory? As Alan Jacobs writes, "As soon as deconstructionists get in the business of providing reasons, they are perforce in the business of making claims and thus are subject to their own critique."[35] What happens if we subject Barthes's views to his own critique? We have to conclude that he, too, is merely a mouthpiece for social forces such as race, class, and gender. His own writings do not offer original or creative insights but are merely collages of conflicting quotations absorbed unconsciously from the communities to which he belongs. The "death of the author" must include Barthes himself.

In practice, the only way deconstructionists can function is to tacitly exempt themselves from the critique they apply to everyone else. They presume to stand above the fray, with unique insight to deconstruct *everyone else's* statements as products of underlying interests and power struggles, while treating their *own* writings as immune to the process of deconstruction. They write as though they alone are able to transcend the social forces of race, class, and gender that render everyone else a victim of false consciousness.[36]

Thus ironically, postmodernists contradict their own views every time they write a book or article. Deconstructionists hope their own work will be treated as a serious contribution from a creative mind, not merely a replay of cultural messages. They continue to author books arguing that there is no author.

Theologian Mark C. Taylor, himself a postmodernist, explains that the death of the author was an inevitable result of the death of God: "The death of God was the disappearance of the Author who had inscribed absolute truth and univocal meaning in world history." And because humans are made in the image of God, Taylor concludes, "the death of God implies the disappearance of the author."[37] For if there is no Creator, then humans do not have the dignity of being sub-creators. They are merely products of social and historical forces.

Postmodernism and Terror

To understand the source of postmodernism, we must place its founders in their historical context. Why were they so opposed to grand metanarratives? The answer is that they viewed them as the source of brutal, oppressive political regimes. Most of the founders of postmodernism were Europeans who had witnessed firsthand history's bloodiest and most oppressive political systems—Nazism and Communism. As we saw in Principle #2 both of these systems centered on a single principle: race (Nazism) or economic class (Communism). Both embraced a grand vision of history moving inexorably toward some ideal society. And both became totalitarian, using their utopian visions to justify secret police and death camps.

After World War II, many European thinkers who had suffered under these oppressive regimes decided that the source of totalitarianism lay in "totalizing" metanarratives. By "totalizing" they meant a worldview that focuses on a single dimension of human experience, elevating it to a false absolute and subordinating everything else to its categories. When a one-dimensional, totalizing worldview gains political power, those who disagree will be marginalized, oppressed, left out, silenced, dominated, co-opted, controlled, and coerced. They will be stigmatized as different, perceived as "the other," locked up in concentration camps. All must bow to the state-enforced idol—or be burned in the fiery furnace of oppression.

Postmodernists' insight into the dynamics of false absolutes should sound familiar. We have been making a similar critique, showing how idols are created when some part of creation is absolutized. The mistake postmodernists made was to think the source of the problem was a commitment to any comprehensive truth. In *The Postmodern Condition*, Lyotard says the conviction that there is only one truth, the whole truth, leads inevitably to "terror": "The nineteenth and twentieth centuries have given us as much terror as we can take. We have paid a high price for the nostalgia of the whole and the one [truth]."

Postmodernists concluded that the way to challenge claims to absolute *power* was to challenge claims to absolute *truth*. As Eagleton puts it, postmodernism "makes the mistake of supposing that all passionate conviction is incipiently dogmatic" and will "end up with the Gulag."[38]

Why is that a mistake? Because it is self-refuting. By rejecting any universal truth, postmodernism undercuts its *own* claim to truth.

Moreover, without some universal standard of justice, there is no way to stand against injustice and oppression—the very things postmodernists were so concerned about. As one philosopher writes, "Without timeless and universal moral principles, it seems that we cannot criticize the values of different cultures or times, no matter how repugnant they may seem."[39]

Think of it this way: If all claims can be deconstructed, then what about the claim that the rich should not oppress the poor? Or that we should resist bigotry and racism? Those claims, too, can be deconstructed. Thus postmodernism may appear to be radical, but as Jacobs writes, "it is in fact unable to offer resistance to the political status quo."[40] Lived out consistently, postmodernism leads to complicity with evil and injustice.

The Tyranny of Diversity

Lived out consistently, the theory also leads to the coercive suppression of diversity. That may sound ironic at first, because it was postmodernism that made *diversity* such a potent buzzword in the first place. Postmodernists decided that if totalitarianism results from totalizing metanarratives, then the way to prevent concentrations of power is to maintain a variety of mini-narratives. By celebrating the diversity of communities and their language games, postmodernists hope to avoid the coercion of a society organized by a single absolutized category.

In practice, however, only select groups are singled out to represent "diversity"—certified victim groups based on things like race, class, gender, ethnic group, and sexual identity. Rarely is there a push for intellectual or political or theological diversity, when those views run counter to postmodernism. And the analysis of the problem is typically derived from Marxism: some group is said to be victimized and oppressed, and the path to liberation is to revolt against the oppressors, often through political activism.

This explains why the typical university campus has become thoroughly politicized. In many English departments, literary criticism no longer deals with issues of aesthetics such as style, structure, and composition. Instead the trend is to apply Marxist criticism or feminist criticism or whatever the critic's preferred theory is. Writing in the *Chronicle of Higher Education*, one English professor said the goal of literary study is to help students decide "which side of the world-historical class struggle they take: the side of the owners of the means of production, or the side of the workers. This and only this is the real question in textual literacy."[41]

Frank Lentricchia, a critic so radical he was once dubbed the "Dirty Harry of literary theory," was finally disillusioned when he observed his own students develop a suffocating sense of moral superiority. They would pass judgment on authors as racist or sexist or capitalist or imperialist or homophobic *before even reading their works*. In dismay, Lentricchia said, "Tell me your [literary] theory, and I'll tell you in advance what you'll say about any work of literature, especially those you haven't read."[42]

Politically correct university courses are not liberating students to think for themselves. They are turning students into cadres of self-absorbed reactionaries ready to take orders from the faddish theorist of the moment.

Bruno Latour, a sociologist of science, likewise grew concerned about the oppressive impact of the critical theory that he himself helped found. The attraction of postmodern criticism, he writes, is that it allows you to pose as the superior thinker who humiliates "naïve believers" by deconstructing their beliefs. "You are always right!" Latour says. "Their behavior is entirely determined by the action of powerful causalities coming from objective reality they don't see, but that you, yes you alone can see."[43]

Postmodernism began with the noble goal of unmasking the implicit imperialism of modernist worldviews. But, ironically, it has itself become imperialist, insisting that postmodernists alone have the ability to unmask everyone else's underlying interests and motives—to deconstruct and debunk them. It thereby essentially silences every other perspective.

Worse, if you do not share postmodernism's specific definition of diversity, it is likely to be imposed by force. An article in the *Atlantic* observes that "political correctness morphed into a tyranny of speech codes, sensitivity training, and book banning."⁴⁴ The drive for diversity, which was supposed to be the safeguard for liberty, has itself become coercive and homogenizing. Diversity has become a code word for a new form of tyranny.

Losing Your Self

I recently met friends who were grieving because their daughter had rejected her Christian upbringing—surprisingly, at a conservative Christian college. Her major was English, a subject most parents regard as relatively "safe," where students read Shakespeare and Dickens. Even at evangelical colleges, however, many faculty members have embraced elements of postmodernism and deconstructionism. Within a short time, my friends' daughter came to question whether there was any such thing as truth at all—including the biblical truth she had been taught in her home and church.

How can we prepare young people for the postmodern theories they will encounter in the classroom?

Like every worldview, postmodernism offers genuine insights—especially in its critique of modernism. The Enlightenment held an exalted view of the autonomous individual in possession of disembodied Reason (often capitalized), which supposedly lifted him above his tiny slot in time and space to deliver a timeless, objective truth. By contrast, postmodernism insists that knowledge is always contextual. Persons are not disembodied consciousnesses. They are physical beings situated within communities, and their worldviews are colored by cultural traditions, economic interests, and power relations.

Yet in reacting against the Enlightenment, postmodernism falls off the horse on the other side. It reduces the individual to a patchwork of historical and social forces, with no stable personal identity. The reason goes back to Hegel's historicism, the idea that humanity is caught up in the ceaseless flux of evolution. The implication is that there is no such thing as human nature—no stable, ideal blueprint for what it means to be human, no universal standard to tell us who we are and how to fulfill our true nature.

As the existentialist Jean-Paul Sartre put it, "There is no human nature because there is no God to have a conception of it."[45] Just as species are constantly changing and evolving, so individuals must leave behind all stable standards and immerse themselves in the ceaseless flux of life, constantly creating and re-creating themselves.

To use postmodern terms, the self is fluid and fragmented. Michel Foucault says his goal is "the dissociation of the self" by showing that our sense of being a coherent self is in reality an "empty synthesis" of past events. What exactly does that mean? One philosopher explains that for Foucault, "our identities are fictional anyway—each of us is plural, a congeries of forces pulling in many directions."[46]

But if our identities are "fictional," then who is Foucault? And who is really speaking in his writings? When a postmodernist states that it is impossible to attain objectivity, is *that* an objective statement? The theory undercuts its own claims.

Moreover, it runs contrary to human experience. Each of us experiences the inescapable, irresistible sense of being a coherent self—an active center of consciousness—not merely a passive locus of colliding social forces. Even as we undergo life changes, we are aware of an enduring core personal identity. The universality of this first-person awareness, even among those whose worldview denies it, is a clue that it is intrinsic to human experience. We are so constituted that we cannot live consistently on the basis of the postmodernists' radical reductionism. And neither can they. The truths of general revelation cannot ultimately be suppressed.

The Trinity for Postmoderns

The problem of how to balance our individual identity with our membership in communities is a perennial question known in philosophy as the one and the many, or unity and diversity. Christianity offers an answer that is surprising and unique. It teaches that the human race was created in the image of a God who is a tri-unity—three Persons so intimately related as to constitute one Godhead. God's own nature consists in reciprocal love and communication among the Persons of the Trinity (Father, Son, and Spirit). Both the one and the many, both individuality and relationship, exist within the divine nature.[47]

The perfect balance of unity and diversity within the Trinity offers a model for human social life—and a solution to the opposing poles of postmodernism and modernism. Against postmodernism's dissolution of the self, the Trinity implies the dignity of the individual self. Just as each Person within the Trinity is distinct and plays a unique role in the drama of salvation, so each human person has a unique identity and purpose.

Yet against modernism and its radical individualism, the Trinity implies that we are not disconnected and autonomous but were created for relationship. Sociality is built into the very essence of human nature. Aside from the effects of sin, there is an intrinsic harmony between what fulfills us as individuals and what fulfills us in our relationships—marriage, family, work, church, ethnic group. There is no inherent conflict between being true to oneself and participating in the God-ordained relationships that connect us to one another.

Christianity agrees with the postmodernist critique of the Enlightenment's notion of the disembodied consciousness. The Bible teaches that God created humans as embodied beings, biologically connected to families, living in particular nations at particular periods in history. We are rooted in the physical, material world— and that is not a negative limitation that must be transcended. On the contrary, Genesis states repeatedly that the material creation is intrinsically good: "And God saw that it was good."

In the book of Acts, Paul even teaches that our physical, social, and historical situatedness is intended by God as a means to draw us to him. Speaking about the nations (from the Greek *ethnos*, the root of *ethnic group*), Paul says God "determined the times set for them and the exact places where they should live, ... so that men would seek him and perhaps reach out for him and find him" (Acts 17:26–27 NIV[48]). Our biological and social identity is intended to be a blessing, to inspire us to search for God.

At the same time, Christianity refuses to reduce individuals to their communities, as postmodernism does. Christians are reborn into a redeemed community that transcends all natural communities. Even the family, the most basic biological community, does not determine our primary identity. All who become Christians are "children of God—children born not of natural descent, nor of human decision or a husband's will [to have a child], but born of God" (John 1:12–13 NIV). The Bible's liberating message is the promise that we can transcend the sin and brokenness of our natural communities because our primary identity is to be children of God.

This trinitarian view produces a wonderful balance in practice. Within the church, diversity based on physical origins—birth, family, gender, ethnicity, nationality—can be celebrated with gratitude as gifts from God. At the same time, these things do not ultimately define us: "Here there is not Greek and Jew, circumcised and uncircumcised, barbarian, Scythian, slave, free; but Christ is all, and in all" (Col. 3:11). Remarkably, an atheist Marxist philosopher has written movingly of the gospel's liberating legacy. Slavoj Zizek says Christianity teaches that we are not "bound by the chains of our past"—that we can "disengage ourselves from the inertia that constrains us to identify with the particular order we were born into."[49]

Christianity offers a unique balance of unity and diversity, of particularity and universality.

The church itself is intended to be a powerful apologetic—a visible, living expression of the Bible's balanced view.[50] Every local church is "a letter from Christ ... written not with ink but with the Spirit of the living God" (2 Cor. 3:3). When outsiders "read" that letter, they should see the trinitarian view of community lived out—not perfectly, but in a credible way. Jesus even said that people will judge whether Christianity is true by the trinitarian love they witness in the church. As the Father and the Son are one, so Jesus prayed that all Christians "may become perfectly one, *so that the world may know* that you sent me" (John 17:23).

Francis Schaeffer called the visible manifestation of love among Christians "the final apologetic," the single thing most likely to attract the attention of a jaded world.[51] The message of our words will bear fruit only when confirmed by the message of our lives.

Escape from Reductionism

Understanding reductionism equips us with a powerful means to "destroy arguments ... raised against the knowledge of God" (2 Cor. 10:5). In Principle #3, identifying reductionism was key to showing how idol-based worldviews contradict reality. In Principle #4, identifying reductionism is the clue to showing how worldviews self-destruct.

As we topple idols, it is imperative that we replace it with something better. If the core flaw is reductionism, then the way to build a positive case for Christianity is to show that it is *not* reductionistic. Because it does not deify any part of creation, it does not have to cram everything into a single set of categories. The result is that Christianity has a very rich ontology (theory of what exists). It offers a greater respect for creation than any of competing worldview. Consider how positive it is by comparison:

Materialism: To counter materialism, we can show that a biblical worldview teaches an even greater respect for the material world. The physical universe is not just a product of chance. The earth is not a rock spinning through empty space, with no higher purpose or meaning. Instead, the physical universe was brought into being by a God of love and beauty. It is a product of plan and design.

Fascinatingly, the early church also had to defend a high view of the material world, though for different reasons. Ancient Greek culture was permeated by philosophies such as Gnosticism and neo-Platonism that regarded the material realm as the realm of death, decay, and destruction. Gnosticism taught that the world was so evil that it could not be the creation of the highest, supreme deity but must be the handiwork of an evil sub-deity. The supreme God would not demean himself by mucking about with matter. Gnosticism denigrated the physical body as the "prison house of the soul." The goal of salvation was to *escape* from the physical realm and leave it behind.

In this context, Christianity was nothing short of revolutionary. It teaches that there is only one God, and that he created matter. It is therefore intrinsically good. Christianity's greatest scandal, however, was the incarnation—the claim that God himself took on a physical body. He was not an avatar who just *appeared* to be human (as the Gnostics taught). He actually *became* human. The incarnation grants an astonishingly high dignity to the material world.

Even more revolutionary, after Jesus had "escaped" the physical world—after he died—he *came back*. In a bodily resurrection. To the Greeks, this was not spiritual progress; it was *re*gress. Why would anyone want to come back to the material world, the realm of evil and corruption? The whole idea was utter foolishness to the Greeks (1 Cor. 1:23 KJV).

Finally, what will happen at the end of time, according to Scripture? God is not going to scrap the idea of a physical universe and replace it with a purely ethereal plane of being, as though he made a mistake the first time. Instead he is going to replace it with "a new earth" (Rev. 21:1). And you and I will live on that new earth in new physical bodies. In the Apostles' Creed, Christians affirm "the resurrection of the body." This is an astonishingly high view of the physical world. Christianity imparts greater value to the material realm than any version of materialism.[52]

Empiricism: To counter empiricism, Christians can show that a biblical worldview offers a better basis for trusting our senses. As we saw earlier, the flaw in empiricism is that it cannot give any guarantee that what we perceive through the senses is true. We cannot stand outside our heads to gain an independent vantage point from which to test sense data against the external world. The only adequate basis for confidence in sensory knowledge is the biblical teaching that a Creator designed our sensory apparatus to function reliably in the world he created.

The doctrine of creation is the epistemological guarantee that the constitution of our human faculties conforms to the structure of the external world. It is part of the "human design plan," writes Plantinga, to trust our sense perceptions. When our perceptual faculties are in good working order, and functioning in the environment for which they were designed, we naturally trust that the colors and shapes we perceive are real objects in a real world.[53]

The high value placed on empirical knowledge was one of the crucial preconditions for the rise of modern science. Christians had to stand against a long tradition going back to the ancient Greeks that had denigrated the empirical world as a shifting realm of shadows. For Plato, it was impossible to gain genuine knowledge of the sensory realm because it was the realm of "appearance," not reality. Many historians suggest that this low view of the empirical world is one reason the ancient Greeks did not develop modern science—and why Christianity was necessary to lay the groundwork for the empirical methodology of science.[54]

Rationalism: To counter rationalism, we can show that Christianity honors human rationality as part of the image of God. It is no historical accident that the Middle Ages, when Christianity flourished, was the age of great rational system builders like Anselm and Thomas Aquinas. Their confidence in reason was unsurpassed because they regarded it as a gift from God. They were certain that the world is the creation of a reasonable God, and therefore it has an intelligible structure knowable by reason. Even today, as we have seen, Christianity stands for a unified, logically coherent truth against the upper-lower story divide that fragments modern worldviews.

Christianity also stands against the "masters of suspicion" who claim that human rationality is swamped by non-rational forces. The biblical God invites us to "reason together" (Isa. 1:18). Sanctification comes through "the renewal of your mind" (Rom. 12:2), and the goal is to learn to love God "with all your mind" (Matt. 22:37). The word *logic* comes from *Logos*, the word used to describe Jesus in John 1:1. The implication is that logic reflects the nature of God's own mind and character.

Postmodernism: To counter postmodernism, Christianity offers an even more radical insight into the contingency of human knowledge. Postmodernism reduces knowledge claims to expressions of interest and power based on race, class, gender, ethnicity, and sexual identity. But the biblical teaching on idols cuts much deeper—to the ultimate spiritual commitments at the core of human motivation. The Bible teaches that the overriding factor in the choices we make is our commitment to a concept of the divine. Our lives are shaped by the god we worship—whether the God of the Bible or some substitute deity.

In every area, Christianity encompasses the valid insights of all other worldviews, while avoiding their weaknesses. It incorporates the best insights of idol-centered philosophies, without falling into any limited, life-denying reductionism. This is genuinely good news.

In fact, Christianity is so attractive that atheists keep reaching over and borrowing from it. In the next chapter, we will find out what makes Christian truth so appealing—and why even atheists keep trying to claim parts of it for themselves.

PRINCIPLE #5

FREE-LOADING ATHEISTS

A few years ago I visited a large urban church that attracted students from universities across the city. The leader of the college and career group told me that he was earning a doctoral degree in chemistry.

"Excellent!" I said. "Have you considered the ways chemistry relates to your understanding of Christianity? For example, have you studied theories of chemical evolution and the origin of life?"

"Oh no," he responded. "That's why I went into *synthetic* chemistry—so I would not have to deal with those issues."

Later that evening while mingling with other students, I met a young woman majoring in biology. "Great!" I said. "Have you read up on some of the controversial issues related to your field, like evolution and intelligent design?"

To my surprise, her response was almost identical to the young chemist's. "Oh no. That's why I went into pre-med—so I won't have to deal with those issues."

These were bright, well-educated young adults who could be using their gifts to educate the church on how to enter into public discourse with an informed voice. Yet they were refusing to step up to the plate.

Many Christians seem at a loss in constructing a biblical worldview suitable for the public arena. Typically they simply restate biblical *theology*. For example, George Barna conducts surveys to measure how many Christians hold a biblical worldview. His definition, however, consists of theological statements: that the Bible is "totally accurate," that Jesus "lived a sinless life," that Satan is "real," that "people cannot earn their way into Heaven by trying to be good," and so on.[1] But a worldview is not the same thing as a theology. A worldview *applies* theological truths to fields such as philosophy, science, education, entertainment, and politics.

Principle #5
Replace the Idol: Make the Case for Christianity

One of the best ways to craft biblical answers is to listen more closely to the questions. The Christian message will be most relevant when it is articulated at the specific points where people recognize the flaws and failures of their own worldviews. In Principle #3, for example, we met thinkers who recognize that their reductionistic worldviews have outcomes that they themselves regard as "alien" and "repugnant." Outcomes that they themselves "cannot live" with. In Principle #4 we met people who rely implicitly on a biblical view of human reason. We could say that reductionists cannot live within the confines of their own worldview box, so they smuggle in ladders from a Christian worldview to climb out of the box. They are hungry for a fuller, more humane worldview than their idols give them.

Surprising as it sounds, the Christian worldview is so appealing that even those who reject it often borrow from it, whether consciously or unconsciously.

To craft a case for Christianity in every field would take another book. But we can get started by identifying those elements that people smuggle in from a Christian worldview. They are showing us where their own worldviews break down and, at the same time, what they find most appealing about Christianity. These provide strategic starting points for framing a biblical worldview attuned to the questions of our day.

Can a Relativist Oppose Racism?

Let's start with a few widespread examples. Many people today claim to be moral relativists, arguing that there is no universal, timeless moral law. Yet they are likely to turn around and insist that acts of racism or abuse are wrong—not just unpleasant or personally offensive, but genuinely wrong. And they will protest vigorously if they themselves are cheated or violated in any way. Indeed, people cannot function for even a few hours without making moral evaluations: *He shouldn't say that. She is so mean.*

Ironically, moral relativists even pride themselves on being morally superior to others. After all, *they* are tolerant and nonjudgmental. *They* are not like other people who are insufferably bigoted and closed-minded, deserving the harshest condemnation.

Every person draws a line in the sand somewhere that allows him or her to feel morally superior, like the Pharisee in Jesus's parable who thanked God that he was not like other people (Luke 18:11).

Moral relativism may claim to be about tolerance and humility, but in reality it often fosters a highly judgmental, condemning attitude.

The upshot is that many people imbibe the *language* of moral relativism, but their words do not match who they really are as fully functional human beings. Instead it is the Christian worldview that fits who they are. Because humans are made in the image of God, they are hardwired with an intrinsic moral sense. Romans 2 says those who do not have God's law in written form have the moral law "written on their hearts" (Rom. 2:15). They cannot help making moral claims—claims that have no basis in their own relativistic worldview, claims that make sense only on the basis of the biblical worldview they reject.

You might say they function *as if* Christianity is true. The recognition of moral truths is an aspect of general revelation. No matter how vigorously people suppress that knowledge, it keeps rising to the surface.

Another example are people who claim to be skeptics with regard to knowledge. On one hand, they claim we cannot be sure of anything. On the other hand, they are likely to insist that science has proved their own favorite theories. In practical life, they probably check their bank statements to verify that the figures are correct. In short, they live and act as though they do have access to genuine knowledge.

No matter how skeptical someone is, some things are virtually impossible to doubt—at least in practice. No one really doubts that the material world is real. (We all look both ways before crossing the street.) No one doubts inner experiences like pleasure or pain. (If I say I have a headache, you don't ask, "How do you know?") We do not doubt the reality of cause and effect. (We trust that fire will heat and ice will cool.) No one doubts his or her personal existence (we use the word "I"). If anyone does deny these basic facts, we call him insane—or a philosopher.

And even philosophers deny such elemental facts only provisionally. As we saw earlier, David Hume is the poster boy for extreme empiricism, which led him to extreme skepticism. Yet Hume found it impossible to maintain his skepticism when he left his study (when he joined his friends for a game of backgammon, as he put it). In "the occupations of everyday life," Hume wrote, skeptical doubts "vanish like smoke, and leave the most determined skeptic in the same condition as other mortals."[2]

You might say there are no skeptics in the foxholes of real life. When they have to function in the ordinary world, their skepticism "vanishes like smoke." They are compelled to act *as if* they have access to genuine knowledge in a way that their own worldview denies is possible.

In short, they must act *as if* a Christian epistemology is true. Christianity teaches that humans are made in God's image. Our minds and senses are designed to function in God's world. Even those who hold to extreme skepticism are forced by the sheer circumstances of life to act *as if* the biblical view of human cognition is true.

Why do people hold ideas that are not supported by their own worldview? Scripture says all people are made in God's image, live in God's world, and experience God's common grace. As a result, in practice they experience the living truths of general revelation, even if they selectively suppress that knowledge. As psychologists tell us, suppressed knowledge eventually works its way to the surface. At those times, Thomas Johnson says, "people act and talk according to their repressed knowledge, which they receive from God's general revelation, instead of acting according to the beliefs they claim to accept."[3]

The fact that everyone has to function as though Christianity is true opens a creative opportunity for addressing the secular world. Christianity provides the basis for the way humans can't help behaving anyway. In making the case for a biblical worldview, a strategic place to start is by showing that it alone gives a basis for the ways we *all* have to function, no matter which worldview we hold.

The Confession of Richard Rorty

One challenge to building a case for Christianity is that its principles underlie so much of our shared culture that we no longer recognize them as distinctively biblical. For example, Westerners often pride themselves on holding noble ideals such as equality and universal human rights. Yet ironically, as we saw in earlier chapters, the dominant worldviews of our day deny the reality of human freedom and give no basis for moral ideals such as human rights.

So where did the idea of equal rights come from?

The nineteenth-century political thinker Alexis de Tocqueville said the idea came from Christianity. "The most profound geniuses of Rome and Greece" never came up with the idea of equal rights, he wrote. "Jesus Christ had to come to earth to make it understood that all members of the human species are naturally alike and equal."[4]

The nineteenth-century atheist Friedrich Nietzsche agreed: "Another Christian concept ... has passed even more deeply into the tissue of modernity: the concept of the 'equality of souls before God.' This concept furnishes the prototype of all theories of equal rights."[5]

The contemporary atheist Luc Ferry says the same thing. We tend to take the concept of equality for granted; yet it was Christianity that overthrew ancient social hierarchies between rich and poor, masters and slaves. "According to Christianity, we were all 'brothers,' on the same level as creatures of God," Ferry writes. "Christianity is the first *universalist* ethos."[6]

A few intrepid atheists admit outright that they have to borrow the ideal of human rights from Christianity. Richard Rorty was a committed Darwinist; and in the Darwinian struggle for existence, the strong prevail while the weak are left behind. So evolution cannot be the source of universal human rights. Instead, Rorty says, the concept came from "religious claims that human beings are made in the image of God."[7] He cheerfully admits that he reaches over and borrows the concept of universal rights from Christianity. He even calls himself a "free-loading" atheist: "This

Jewish and Christian element in our tradition is gratefully invoked by free-loading atheists like myself."[8]

At the birth of our nation, the American founders deemed it self-evident that human rights must be grounded in God. The Declaration of Independence leads off with those bright, blazing words: "We hold these truths to be self-evident—that all men are created equal, that they are endowed by their Creator with certain unalienable rights."

In the summer of 2013, a beer company sparked controversy when it released an advertisement for Independence Day that deleted the crucial words "by their Creator." The ad said, "They are endowed with certain unalienable rights." (Endowed by whom?) The advertisement is emblematic of what many secularists do: They borrow ideals like equality and rights from a biblical worldview but cut them off from their source in the Creator. They are free-loaders. Christians should reclaim those noble ideals, making the case that they are logically supported only by a biblical worldview.

Atheists often denounce Christianity as harsh and negative. But in reality it offers a much more positive view of the human person than any competing religion or worldview. It is so appealing that adherents of other worldviews keep free-loading the parts they like best.

What Makes Science Possible?

Another element of Western culture so widespread that we no longer recognize it as distinctively Christian is the scientific enterprise itself. The common stereotype is that religion and science are at war with one another. But historians have turned that stereotype on its head.

Consider, for example, the idea of "laws" in nature. Today that idea is so familiar that it strikes us as common sense. Yet historians tell us that no other culture—East or West, ancient or modern—came up with the concept of laws in nature. It appeared only in Europe during the Middle Ages, a period when Western culture was thoroughly permeated by Christian assumptions. As the respected historian A. R. Hall notes, the use of the word *law* in the context of natural events "would have been unintelligible in antiquity, whereas the Hebraic and Christian belief in a deity who was at once Creator and Lawgiver rendered it valid."[9]

Of course, all societies have recognized cause-and-effect patterns in nature, which enabled them to construct buildings and bridges. The difference is that they regarded those patterns as merely practical rules of thumb. The intrinsic order of nature itself was thought to be inscrutable to the human mind. And when people do not think there *are* rational laws behind natural phenomena, they will not go looking for them—and science will never get started.

Philosopher Mary Midgley even describes Christianity as science's "own worldview." She writes, "Science does have its own worldview that includes guiding presuppositions about the nature of the world. The founders of modern science expressed these very plainly for their time. Cosmic order (they said) flows wholly from God, so science redounds to his glory."[10]

Paul Davies makes the same point even more strongly. "All the early scientists, like Newton, were religious in one way or another," he writes. "They saw their science as a means of uncovering traces of God's handiwork in the universe." What we now call the laws of nature they regarded as thoughts in the mind of God. "So in doing science, they supposed, one might be able to glimpse the mind of God—an exhilarating and audacious claim."

Audacious perhaps, but a claim that remains a central underpinning for the scientific enterprise right to our own day. Science still has to assume that the world has an intelligible order. Yet the materialist or naturalist worldview cannot account for that order. If the universe is the product of *non*-rational processes, why does it have a rational order? If the universe is not the product of a mind, why it is comprehensible to the human mind? Among most scientists today, "the underlying order in nature—the laws of physics—are simply accepted as given, as brute facts," Davies writes. "Nobody asks where they come from; at least they do not do so in polite company. However, even the most atheistic scientist accepts as an act of faith that ... there is rational basis to physical existence manifested as law-like order in nature."

Science requires an "act of faith"? What is that "faith" based on? Davies draws this stunning conclusion: "So science can proceed only if the scientist adopts an essentially theological world view."[11]

In short, every atheist has to adopt a biblical worldview to pursue science at all.[12] Christians should confidently reclaim the biblical principles that made science possible in the first place—and that continue to provide its philosophical underpinnings today.

An Atheist Decries Humanism

To track down additional cases of free-loading, we can eavesdrop on atheists' in-house debates. For example, John Gray regularly castigates his fellow atheists and materialists for their habit of free-loading. Logically, he points out, materialism leads to reductionism—the conclusion that humans are nothing but animals. But most materialists do not want to accept that bleak conclusion. They want to grant humanity a higher status and dignity; they want to believe that humans have "consciousness, selfhood, and free will," Gray writes. That high view of humanity he labels *humanism*—and he denounces it as a prime example of free-loading.

"Humanists never tire of preaching" the gospel of human freedom, Gray complains. But "Darwin has shown us that we are animals," and therefore "the idea of free will does not come from science." Instead "its origins are in religion—not just any religion, but the Christian faith against which humanists rail so obsessively." Thus humanism "is only a secular version" of Christian principles.[13]

We could say that humanists do not want to live within the confines of their own materialist box. So they smuggle in ladders from a Christian worldview to climb out of the box.

Nagel: Darwin "Almost Certainly False"

Now let's eavesdrop on the other side of the debate—the people Gray calls humanists, who do not want to accept the inhumane consequences of reductionism. Thomas Nagel is the author of *Mind and Cosmos*, which bears the provocative subtitle *Why the Materialist Neo-Darwinian Conception of Nature Is Almost Certainly False*. He argues that Darwinist theory "is almost certainly false" precisely because it leads to reductionism. And reductionist theories fail to explain what we know about the world.

Consider the lowly pocket calculator. Tap in "5 + 3 =" and the number "8" appears in the screen. The figure-eight pattern of pixels may be explainable in purely physical terms, as the pulse of electrons traveling through microchip gates. But, Nagel argues, there is no reductionist explanation of how the calculator was programmed to produce the "8" in the first place. *That* requires "the intention of the designer."

Nagel is an atheist, so he is not alluding to a divine designer. He is arguing that Darwinist theory cannot explain even human designers: "Something more is needed to explain how there can be conscious, thinking creatures."[14] Humans exhibit a difference in kind, not merely in degree.

Something more is also needed to explain moral and scientific knowledge. Nagel argues that an evolutionary concept of the mind undercuts "our confidence in the objective truth of our moral beliefs," as well as "the objective truth of our mathematical or scientific reasoning." (To remind yourself why evolutionary epistemology undercuts human knowledge, turn back to Principle #4.) Yet, Nagel says, we cannot just give up our knowledge in these areas. Why not? Because that knowledge is "based ultimately on common sense and on what is plainly undeniable."[15]

Do you recognize the telltale phrases that indicate general revelation? Neo-Darwinism contradicts what is "based on common sense" and "what is plainly undeniable."

Nagel is trapped in cognitive dissonance. On one hand, he does not want to accept reductionism, which he criticizes as a "triumph of ideological theory over common sense." He praises critics of Darwinism, including Intelligent Design theorists—an act for which he has been viciously attacked.[16]

Nagel even grants that a theistic worldview would solve his problems—that the existence of God would explain the very things that Darwinism cannot explain, like mind and morality. Nevertheless, he rejects the theistic answer. Why? The reason is not so much intellectual as emotional: "I want atheism to be true ... I don't want there to be a God; I don't want the universe to be like that." He admits that his underlying motive is a "fear of religion itself," rooted ultimately in a "cosmic authority problem."[17]

Having rejected God, however, what alternative does Nagel propose? Nothing at all. "My aim is to present the problem rather than to propose a solution."[18]

Nagel is an eye-opening example of an atheist who is desperately trying to maintain both sides of a severe cognitive dissonance. On one hand, he maintains his atheism. On the other hand, he refuses to give up the "undeniable" facts of "common sense" that theism alone can explain.

Nagel is trying to retain the *benefits* of a Christian worldview while he rejects their basis in Christianity. He is free-loading.

Problems of a "Proud Atheist"

Another humanist suffering from severe cognitive dissonance is Raymond Tallis, a medical doctor and the author of *Aping Mankind*. Tallis boasts that he is "a proud atheist" and evolutionist. At the same time, he argues that "something rather important about us is left unexplained by evolutionary theory." Indeed, he lists several important things left unexplained:

- "Isn't there a problem in explaining how the blind forces of physics brought about (cognitively) sighted humans who are able to see, and identify, and comment on, the 'blind' forces of physics?" How did the forces of physics create beings who transcend those forces?
- Isn't there a problem in explaining how natural forces created humans who are able to turn around and use those forces "to engage with nature as if from the outside"? Why are humans able to rise above the forces that supposedly created them? Can a puppet gain control over the puppeteer?
- Isn't there a problem in explaining how the universe "brought us into being by mindless processes that are entirely without purpose"? How did a mindless process create beings with minds? How did a purposeless process create beings with purposes?

- Isn't there a problem in explaining how an undesigned process could produce "one species that is indeed a designer? *How did we humans get to be so different?*" How is it possible for humans to be "so different" from the forces that supposedly produced them? How can water rise above its source?[19]

A reductionist would resolve the dilemma simply by decreeing that humans are not so different after all—that what appear to be differences in kind are really only differences in degree. But Tallis rejects reductionism. Indeed, he is passionately concerned that a form of neurobiological reductionism is gaining a beachhead in virtually every field.

In the arts, neuroaesthetics claims that we are drawn to works of art because certain visual patterns stimulate the reward centers of the brain. In literature, neuroliterary critics try to explain why we love literature by scanning people's brains as they read Shakespeare. In legal theory, neurolaw seeks to establish guilt or innocence using magnetic resonance imaging (MRIs). In philosophy, neuroethics claims that "moral standards, practices, and policies reside in our neurobiology." Neuroeconomics uses brain imaging methods to determine how consumers' brains respond to brands and products.[20] Neuropolitics hopes to use brain science to guide people in making policy decisions. And neurotheology uses MRIs to find the "God spot," the part of the brain that supposedly leads people to conceive the idea of God and undergo mystical experiences.

These neurotheories are more faddish than factual, Tallis complains. Consider the attempt to explain Christianity by neurobiology: "What kinds of nerve impulses are capable of transcending their finite, local, transient condition in order to conceive of something that is infinite, ubiquitous, and eternal?" Tallis even invites theists to make "common cause" with atheists like himself against the "common enemy" of "neuro-evolutionary reductionism."

Yet though he seeks allies among Christians, Tallis emphatically rejects Christianity itself. So what answer does he propose to the reductionism he so passionately opposes? Nothing at all. "The truth is that I don't know."[21]

What do we learn by eavesdropping on atheists? First, many of them recognize the limitations and failures of their own worldview. In fact, a compelling case can be made against atheism *using their own words and arguments*. Second, many atheists find elements of a Christian worldview so appealing that they keep borrowing them. They are free-loaders.

When we realize how extensive free-loading is, we come to a greater appreciation of how attractive a biblical worldview really is. Otherwise, why is everyone trying to co-opt the parts they like best?

No wonder Paul says he is "not ashamed of the gospel" (Rom. 1:16). Recall that in Scripture, to be put to shame means to be disappointed or let down. Paul is saying that a Christian worldview will not let you down. It fulfills humanity's highest hopes and ideals. This is the good news that will attract people to the gospel who are jaded by the failure and inhumanity of reductionism.

Gimme That Old-Time Philosophy

Perhaps the most egregious example of free-loading is a movement to hijack the explicitly religious dimensions of Christianity. For example, there's a new field that uses philosophy to treat psychological problems. Labeled Philosophical Counseling, it is being touted as an alternative to the care provided by therapists, priests, and pastors.

These are atheists who want the psychological comfort of Christianity, while rejecting its content.

A book on the subject, titled *Plato, Not Prozac!*, became an international hit. You can even get certified to be a philosophical counselor. A *Washington Post* article says the counselors are "like intellectual life coaches. Very intellectual. They have in-depth knowledge of Jean-Paul Sartre's existentialist theories on the nature of life and can recite passages from Martin Heidegger's phenomenological explorations of the question of being. And they use them to help clients overcome their mother issues."[22]

Philosophical Counseling may be a new field, but the concept itself is not novel. Philosophies have never been merely academic enterprises. They begin with a God replacement and develop an entire worldview, exhorting people how to make sense of life and to prepare for death. The difference is that today some atheists are actively seeking to "hijack the religious spirit," as Terry Eagleton puts it.[23] They claim that secularism can nurture spirituality.

Luc Ferry diagnoses several "substitute religions" in *A Brief History of Thought*. Many atheist ideologies offer spirituality for secular people, he says: "If religions can be defined as 'doctrines of salvation', the great philosophies can also be defined as doctrines of salvation (but without the help of God)."[24]

An example is Pierre Hadot's *Philosophy as a Way of Life*. Hadot says accepting a philosophy is like a religious conversion: It involves "a total transformation of one's vision, life-style, and behavior." It "turns our entire life upside down."[25] You literally stake your life—and your eternity—on a set of ideas being true.

In the ancient world, when philosophy was still young, its life-transforming power was widely recognized. The philosopher was not regarded as an expert in an academic field but revered as a "spiritual guide," Hadot says. "He exhorted his charges to conversion, and then directed his new converts ... to the paths of wisdom."[26] Hadot is seeking to recover that spiritual role for secular philosophy.

So is philosopher Alain de Botton, author of *Religion for Atheists*. Botton is founder of a school in London where students study philosophy not to earn an academic degree but to ponder "the most serious questions of the soul." One class, titled Filling the God-Shaped Hole, helps people fill the vacuum in their lives when they abandon traditional religions.[27]

The common thread running through these examples is that they are all attempts to fill the God-shaped hole with something other than God. One book makes the claim frankly in its title: *The Little Book of Atheist Spirituality*.[28] Atheists are even founding their own churches. Britain now has its first atheist church. According to news reports, "Dozens of gatherings dubbed 'atheist megachurches' ... are springing up around the U.S."[29]

Atheists are free-loading the ceremonies of religious worship. They want to co-opt the rituals of Christianity, while rejecting its reality.

A Mass for Charles Darwin

Not all atheists are aware how much they hijack from Christianity. The most common pattern is to claim that atheism is based strictly on facts and science.

Yet even a commitment to science can function as an idol, an ultimate commitment. When science is treated as the sole source of truth, then it becomes scient*ism*. Philosopher Wilfrid Sellars expressed a commitment to scientism when he said, "Science is the measure of all things." Bertrand Russell tipped his hand in his remark, "What science cannot discover, mankind cannot know."[30]

The assumption is that whatever cannot be known by science is not real. But consider: Is that statement itself a fact discovered by science? Clearly not. It goes beyond anything science could possibly establish. It is a metaphysical assumption, an arbitrary definition of what counts as genuine knowledge.

Scientism remains one of today's most popular idols. Any claim that begins with "scientists now know" is likely to trump all competing claims. As John Gray writes, "Science hasn't enabled us to dispense with myths. Instead it has become a vehicle for myths—chief among them, the myth of salvation through science. Many of the people who scoff at religion are sublimely confident that, by using science, humanity can march onwards to a better world."[31]

A commitment to science has even been shown to have psychological effects similar to a religious commitment. The *New Scientist* reports on a study showing that under stress, atheists responded with a higher commitment to a "belief in science." The article concluded, "It's well known that religious faith can help believers cope with stress and anxiety, by providing them with a sense of meaning and control at times of uncertainty. It now seems that a 'belief' in science and a rationalistic outlook might do the same for the non-religious."[32]

Even the theory of evolution, often cited as support for atheism, can function as a substitute religion. In the 1965 introduction to Darwin's *Origin of Species*, W. R. Thompson observed that, for many biologists, the concept of organic evolution is "an object of genuinely religious devotion, because they regard it as a supreme integrative principle."[33]

More recently, Michael Ruse shocked his fellow atheists by pointing out that evolution often functions as a religion: "Evolution is promulgated as an ideology, a secular religion—a full-fledged alternative to Christianity, with meaning and morality."[34]

And with worship, we might add. A few years ago, a mass was composed titled "Missa Charles Darwin" (*missa* means mass). The piece is based on the five-movement structure of the traditional mass. It sounds very much like Renaissance church music, but the texts from Scripture have been replaced by excerpts from Darwin's writings, including *On the Origin of Species* and *The Descent of Man*.[35]

Evolutionary Religion

Darwinism is not the only version of evolution on the market. Yet most alternative theories are even more overtly religious. Biologist Stuart Kauffman is well known for his theory of self-organization. But he does not regard it as merely another scientific theory: It is "a new world view" with "a new view of God, not as transcendent, not as an agent, but as the very creativity of the universe itself." In other words, Kauffman treats *God* as a word for the ceaseless flux of the universe. That, he says, is "God enough for me."

Why retain the word *God* at all, which connotes a transcendent, caring, intelligent Person, when your theory really involves an immanent, non-caring, non-intelligent process? Precisely to smuggle in the emotional power connected to the term. Kauffman is open about his intentions: "What do we gain by using the God word? I suspect a great deal, for the word carries with it awe and reverence. If we can transfer that awe and reverence, not to the transcendental Abrahamic God of my Israelite tribe long ago, but to the stunning reality that confronts us, we will grant permission for a renewed spirituality, and awe, reverence and responsibility for all that lives, for the planet."[36]

In short, Kauffman hopes to inspire people to respond emotionally to a purely materialist universe *as if* it were the personal God of the Bible. He is another free-loader.[37]

Finally, there is economist and futurist Jeremy Rifkin, who promotes a quasi-pantheistic version of evolution. He envisions evolution as a process whereby an immanent "mind" evolves up the ladder of life, the great chain of being: "Evolution is no longer viewed as a mindless affair, quite the opposite. It is mind enlarging its domain up the chain of species." In those words we hear echoes of Hegel's concept of an Absolute Mind evolving upward through history. Rifkin goes on: "One eventually winds up with the idea of the universe as a mind that oversees, orchestrates, and gives order and structure to all things."

What are the implications of this pantheistic model of evolution? Most obviously, it eliminates a transcendent Creator—which Rifkin takes to be a good thing. For it means that "we no longer feel ourselves to be guests in someone else's home." Therefore we no longer feel "obliged to make our behavior conform with a set of pre-existing cosmic rules." Instead we are free to make up our own rules:

> It is our creation now. We make the rules. We establish the parameters of reality. We create the world, and because we do, we no longer feel beholden to outside forces. We no longer have to justify our behavior, for we are now the architects of the universe.

We create the world? *We* are the architects of the universe? Clearly, Rifkin is saying that if there is no transcendent God, then humans take his place. Humans become mini-gods. Rifkin ends with a hymn to evolved humanity: "We are responsible to nothing outside ourselves, for we are the kingdom, the power, and the glory forever and ever."[38]

If this is not a theological vision of evolution, I don't know what is.

Recognizing the religious nature of secular worldviews creates a level playing field. It undermines the pretensions of secularists to religious neutrality, which they use to claim superiority over religion. That is, they claim to be objective and fact-based, while discrediting religions as biased and "faith-based." Yet no worldview is neutral—not even atheism or secularism.

In relation to the biblical God, secular people may claim to be skeptics. But in relation to their own god substitutes, they are true believers. To adapt an observation from C. S. Lewis, their skepticism is only on the surface. It is for use on *other* people's beliefs. "They are not nearly skeptical enough" about their *own* beliefs.[39]

What drives religious variants of evolution is a sense that there must be more to reality than the flat, one-dimensional vision offered by materialism. Evolutionists are reaching out for higher dimensions to answer the human longing for greater meaning to life. Those longings are one more expression of general revelation. They are signposts to the biblical God.

Losing Faith, Finding God

One way to highlight Christianity's attractive features is to show where secularists borrow from it. Another way is to ask what you lose when you give it up. I first started to appreciate Christianity only after I had left it behind. As a young person growing up in a Christian home, I was like the proverbial fish that does not know what water is. Sometimes losing faith is the path to finding God.

Around the time I turned sixteen, I started asking basic questions: How do we know if Christianity is true? Are there any good reasons for holding it? None of the adults in my life seemed to have any answers. I once asked a university professor why he was a Christian. I hoped that such a highly educated person would offer a thoughtful response. But all he said was, "It works for me!" I thought, *It doesn't work for me.*

Later I had the opportunity to talk to a seminary dean. I hoped that a person highly trained in theology might have answers. But all he said was, "Don't worry, we all have doubts sometimes"—as though I were just going through a psychological stage. I thought, *Then why don't you have answers for my doubts?* Finally I concluded that this pragmatic, psychologized version of Christianity had no serious answers. I rejected it and embarked on an intentional search for truth.

The decision struck me as a matter of intellectual honesty: In principle, if you do not have good *reasons* for holding something, then how can you really say you believe it—whether Christianity or anything else?

Within a short time, I became a thorough-going relativist and skeptic. There may be "happy pagans" who don't know what they are missing, but I was acutely aware of what I had lost.

As a Christian, I had known that my life had a purpose: to live for God and "enjoy him forever" (in the words of the

Westminster Shorter Catechism). But if there is no God, and life is a chance product of blind material forces, what purpose does human life have? Is it just a chemical accident on a rock flying through the cold, empty reaches of space? While still in high school, I started cornering my friends and asking, "What do you think is the purpose of life?" Sadly, many of my classmates were not thinking much beyond the party that weekend.

As a Christian, I had known that my actions had a significance that would last into eternity. But if there is no God, then when we die, we rot. Eventually the universe itself will die a heat death and all human civilizations will turn to dust. The best and highest achievements of the human race will have no lasting significance.

As a Christian, I had known that the final reality behind all temporal realities is Love. The universe is the creation of a personal Agent, who thinks, feels, chooses, and acts. But if there is no personal God, then the final reality is blind mechanistic forces. There is no one "out there" who loves us or cares what happens to us. As Richard Dawkins writes, "There is, at bottom, no design, no purpose, no evil, no good, nothing but pitiless indifference."[40]

As a Christian, I had accepted the existence of an objective moral standard. When I made choices, I could be confident that I was building my life on eternally valid truths. But if there is no God, do transcendent moral truths even exist? Was there any way to know that I was constructing my life on things that really matter? I did not know the word *relativism*, but among my high school friends I was the one arguing that we cannot know if anything is genuinely right or wrong. I experienced what Sartre meant when he said we are "condemned to be free"—condemned to act in a moral vacuum, with no way to know if your choices will ultimately prove good or bad, beneficial or harmful.

My angst was intensified by having lived overseas as an adolescent. Our large family could not afford hotels, so we slept in campgrounds while traveling across Europe, gaining a close-up view of diverse cultures and customs. We once drove to Turkey, traversing then-Communist countries like Yugoslavia and Bulgaria. (I have never witnessed such extreme poverty as in rural Bulgaria.) The experience left me with an indelible awareness that many of the things Americans take for granted are culturally relative. I began to wonder: Is there any truth beyond all cultural traditions? Or are we trapped within limited, changing human perspectives?

Finally, as a Christian, I had known that God himself spoke to the human race through Scripture. Many people regard the Bible as a grab bag of works by human authors—a record of spiritual experiences or a set of ancient myths devised to convey moral lessons. But Scripture makes the striking claim that it is a record of communication from God, who acts and speaks into human history. In the Old Testament, the prophets claim to speak the word of God: "Thus says the Lord." In the New Testament, Paul calls Scripture "the oracles of God" (Rom. 3:2). Peter states that the Bible writers were inspired by the Holy Spirit (2 Pet. 1:21). Thus classic Christian theology regards Scripture as communication from a personal God. The heavens are open.

When I embraced agnosticism, however, the heavens were closed. I was locked in my own mind, limited to my own tiny slot in the immensity of time and space. It seemed obvious to me that, from that puny perspective, it was impossible to know any transcendent or timeless truths. Indeed, it might be impossible to know any truth at all. After all, I could not step outside my own head to gain an objective stance to verify my ideas. The logical conclusion is not just skepticism but solipsism, the idea that all we really know is the "inside" of our own experience.[41] In my high school English notebook, I began doodling cartoons of the entire universe as a thought bubble inside my head.

Bertrand Russell—My Role Model

The years I spent wrestling with moral and intellectual skepticism were a dark and difficult period of my life. When people's religious beliefs erode, they sometimes stay in the church for the friendships and social support. They retain the Bible's commitment to an objective morality (at least an objective morality for *other* people, so they won't rob or cheat you).

But my stance was that if Christianity was not true, then I did not want any of its benefits. I aspired to be like Bertrand Russell, who said atheists must build their lives on the "scaffolding ... of unyielding despair." Why despair? Because atheism holds that there is no higher purpose to life—"that man is the product of causes which had no prevision of the end they were achieving; that his origin, his growth, his hopes and fears, his loves and his beliefs, are but the outcome of accidental collocations of atoms."

If atheism was true, then I did not want to flinch from accepting its pessimistic implications—which Russell went on to describe with poetic gloom: that "all the labours of the ages, all the devotion, all the inspiration, all the noonday brightness of human genius, are destined to extinction in the vast death of the solar system, and that the whole temple of Man's achievement must inevitably be buried beneath the debris of a universe in ruins."[42]

William Provine, an evolutionary biologist at Cornell University, states the conclusion more bluntly: If no God exists, he says, then "no ultimate foundations for ethics exist, no ultimate meaning in life exists, and free will is merely a human myth."[43]

During my years as an agnostic, I was not just working through questions like these in my mind but living them out in my life. C. S. Lewis said he wrote *Pilgrim's Regress* to illustrate the impact of worldviews on lived experience. In the story, the main character encounters a variety of God substitutes, including rationalism, materialism, idealism, and Freudianism, on his journey to discover the true God. Lewis wrote that the book illustrated the "*lived* dialectic, and not the merely *argued* dialectic of my philosophical progress."[44]

I, too, was engaged in a "lived dialectic"—and every step of the way felt like a life-and-death struggle. While still in high school, I started walking to the library and pulling books off the philosophy shelf. If Christianity had no answers, I thought, maybe philosophy is the place where people discuss the big questions like, What is truth? What is the meaning of life? I was driven to study philosophy not by mere intellectual curiosity but by an anguished search for answers to life.

Later, while studying in Germany, I took a train to L'Abri, the ministry of Francis and Edith Schaeffer, nestled in a tiny village among the snowy peaks of the Swiss Alps. I intended only to meet up with family members who were visiting briefly. But the approach to Christianity that I encountered there took me completely by surprise. It was the first time I met Christians who could address my questions—who engaged with the wider intellectual and cultural world. It was so appealing that, paradoxical as it may sound, after only a month I left. To tell the truth, I fled: I was wary of being drawn in by the emotional attraction of L'Abri instead of acting from genuine intellectual conviction.

While there, however, I had discovered apologetics and I continued reading on my own. Eventually I was intellectually persuaded that Christianity is true. Or as I thought of it at the time, I admitted that God had won the argument. By then I had no connection to a church, so I reached out again to L'Abri. A year and a half later, I returned to Switzerland for several additional months of study to deepen my understanding of a Christian worldview.

What Is *Your* Answer?

The questions I had as a young person are not unique. Many teens and young adults struggle with intellectual questions, even if they are not intellectuals in a stereotypical sense. Just talk to those who have rejected Christianity.

Sociologist Bradley Wright at the University of Connecticut asked former Christians why they de-converted. The researchers expected to hear stories about people leaving the church because they had been hurt or emotionally wounded. To their surprise, the reason given most frequently by former Christians was that they could not get answers to their doubts and questions. In fact, they could not even get the church to treat their questions seriously. A former Southern Baptist (obviously still angry) said, "Christians always use the word 'faith' as their last word when they are too stupid to answer a question."[45]

Eventually, the doubters concluded that the church did not offer answers because there *are* no answers.

Churches have an obligation to equip their congregations to answer the questions that inevitably arise from living in a post-Christian society. Both young people and adults are subject to a constant barrage of secular and pagan ideas. Churches, schools, and families must take the responsibility for providing cogent and compelling answers.

One effective way of responding to doubters and skeptics is to help them face the real-world implications of their own views. I once had a conversation with a teenager who had been raised in a Presbyterian family. "I don't think I'm a Christian anymore," she told me.

"That's interesting," I said. "What have you accepted instead?"

"What?"

"If there is no God, what then? What *do* you think is true, and how would you support it?"

The teen was speechless. Her entire focus had been on reacting against her parents and church. It had not occurred to her that she now bore the responsibility to think through the options for herself and make an informed search for truth.

As she began to study the alternatives, she realized that giving up Christianity was not a matter of merely deleting a few files of doctrine from her mind. Christianity is an entire worldview that undergirds many of the great ideals of Western culture, from justice to equality to universal human rights—ideals that the teenager did not want to give up.

When people raise questions about Christianity, often the best response is not to shut them down, but precisely the opposite. Start by pressing them to take more seriously the implications of their own position. As a matter of intellectual integrity, they should stop free-loading and take a fearless inventory of the logical and practical conclusions of their own convictions.

The stakes are high. What God said to the ancient Hebrews is just as true today: "I have set before you life and death, blessing and curse. Therefore *choose life*, that you and your offspring may live" (Deut. 30:19). Christianity is either true or false, but it cannot be dismissed as inconsequential.

Lesson from *To Kill a Mockingbird*

What's the first step in equipping ourselves to press people to the logical conclusion of their worldview? Obviously, we must *know* their worldviews. We need to educate ourselves on the systems of thought widespread in our culture.

Think of it as missionary training. All Christians are called to be missionaries (Matt. 28:18–20). As every missionary, pastor, or teacher knows, a key to effective communication is "Know Your Audience." The more thoroughly we know our audience's worldview, the better prepared we will be to speak to their questions, objections, and hidden assumptions. As a character in *To Kill a Mockingbird* says, "You never really understand a person until you consider things from his point of view—until you climb into his skin and walk around in it."[46]

What would you think of a missionary in a Muslim country who refused to learn about Muslim culture? He would not be very effective in communicating a biblical message. Cultivating a missional mind-set means being willing to learn both the language and the thought patterns of our mission field.

When Paul said, "I have become all things to all people" (1 Cor. 9:22), he did not mean dressing like the locals. Nor was he embracing cultural relativism. Instead he was taking the assumptions of his audience into consideration in his language and approach. He tried to see the world through their eyes so he could communicate more persuasively. Ravi Zacharias, who grew up in India but came to the West as a young man, says, "Being able to speak in two languages from opposite ends of the world helps you to be sympathetic and, I believe, effective in not just hearing but *listening*; in responding not to the question but to the questioner."[47]

Learning to listen is especially important with young people. Cultural change occurs so rapidly today that children often absorb assumptions that are radically different from adult culture. One young woman wrote a blog lamenting that her family and church gave her no preparation for attending a secular university: "My parents had absolutely no idea what went on at university and therefore they had no idea how to help me prepare for it." They did not teach her how to argue persuasively for Christianity in a pluralistic context: "The most troubling thing was the amount of differing beliefs and worldviews I encountered, from professors and other students. At the time I thought they had much better arguments than I did for the validity of their views."[48]

This represents a striking failure on the part of the adults in this young woman's life—first of all, a failure of love. A central motivation for learning about worldviews should be to "love your neighbor" (Matt. 22:39). Christians are called to love people enough to listen to their questions and do the hard work of finding answers.

Scripture calls us to an exquisitely balanced approach: "speaking the truth in love" (Eph. 4:15). That balance is spelled out in the flagship verse for apologetics: "Always being prepared to make a defense to anyone who asks you for a reason for the hope that is in you"—there's the truth. "Yet do it with gentleness and respect"—there's the love (1 Pet. 3:15).

In the original Greek, the word Peter uses for defense is *apologia*, from which we get the word *apologetics*. But he is not talking about giving answers to intellectual questions only. The verse appears toward the end of a letter dealing largely with the theme of unjust suffering. Peter has just admonished Christians not to take their own revenge but to be willing to suffer for the sake of righteousness. Why does he speak of apologetics in *this* context? It seems that Peter is saying the goal of apologetics is not just to present better arguments but to exhibit a better character, especially when suffering hostility and opposition.

In Romans 1, Paul likewise sets his message in the context of suffering. That great ringing verse "The righteous shall live by faith" (Rom. 1:17) is a quotation from the book of Habakkuk, where the prophet asks God why evil always seems to win—why God allows his people to be attacked, oppressed, exploited, enslaved, and killed (Hab. 2:4). God's answer is that Habakkuk must "live by faith," confident that God is able to work good out of evil and injustice.

If we do not cultivate the same confidence, the danger is that Christians will tend toward defensiveness and anger. In today's grievance culture, it seems that some new group is always coming forward to complain that they are offended. It can be easy for Christians to pick up the same victim language. But our motivation for speaking out should not be only that we are offended. After all, we are called to share in the offense of the Cross. We are called to love the offender. Christians will be effective in reaching out to others only when they reflect biblical truth in their message, their method, and their manners.

A biblical practice of love can attract the unlikeliest of converts. Even a young man living a wild life of sex, drugs, and gangs, whose dramatic story we will unfold at the end of the next chapter.

PART THREE

·····

HOW CRITICAL THINKING SAVES FAITH

"Critical thinking?" the radio host burst out. "Most people on the conservative Christian Right would say that's one of the biggest dangers we have—this 'nonsensical' idea of critical thinking."

I was the guest on a radio program hosted by Barry Lynn, executive director of Americans United for the Separation of Church and State. This is an organization that works relentlessly to remove all expressions of Christianity from the public arena. On the air Lynn asked about my book *Saving Leonardo*: "Why did you write a book about worldviews? About philosophies?" I replied that my goal was to give people skills to understand the world they live in, to help them develop critical thinking.

That's when Lynn interrupted me. He seemed incredulous that Christians would care about cultivating the mind. Later when I wrote an article about the interview for *Christianity Today*, my husband (an editor) suggested the title "How Critical Thinking Saves Faith."[1]

Hostile radio hosts may not understand, but Scripture itself encourages humans to use their minds to examine truth claims: "Test everything; hold fast what is good" (1 Thess. 5:21). It turns out that you have to practice the first part of the verse—testing everything—in order to develop the wisdom to recognize and hold on to the good.

Today the need for critical thinking is greater than ever. We live in a technological age where information of every kind is available at the click of a mouse. There is no "safe" place where young people can avoid the challenge of contrary worldviews. Christians must become independent thinkers with the tools to think critically about diverse points of view—weighing the evidence and judging the validity of arguments. "The one who states his case first seems right, until the other comes and examines him" (Prov. 18:17). Christians must learn to examine both sides in order to develop "sales resistance" to the many dubious ideas hawked in the media, politics, education, entertainment, and yes, churches.

In today's pluralistic, multicultural world, no one can survive long on secondhand ideas.

Some Christians seem to think the way to avoid being "conformed to this world" (Rom. 12:2) is by avoiding "worldly" ideas. A better strategy is to learn the skills to critically evaluate them. G. K. Chesterton argued that ideas are actually *more* dangerous to the person who has not studied them. Because he has no mental filter, a new idea will "fly to his head like wine to the head of a teetotaler."[2] He is more likely to become intoxicated.

A Romans 1 strategy provides the basic tools to avoid being intoxicated. Its five principles will empower you to cut to the heart of any worldview and weigh its central tenets—to gain an "understanding of the times" in which we live (1 Chron. 12:32). With training in critical thinking, you will be prepared to interact with any point of view respectfully and intelligently.

In this chapter, we will survey several key applications to show how critical thinking can save *your* faith. We will end with the story of hip-hop artist Lecrae to discover why he is "not ashamed" of the gospel.

Churched but Not Prepared

Recently a mother told me with tears in her eyes that her son had lost his faith at a state university. The teen was a psychology major, and ever since Freud, most psychological theories have treated Christianity as a form of psychopathology, a symptom of neurosis, an infantile regression. Though the young man came from a strong Christian family and church, he was completely unprepared to critically evaluate the theories he was learning in the classroom. Within a semester, he had abandoned his religious upbringing altogether.

How can we help a psychology student respond to Freud's charge that religion is a symptom of emotional immaturity? An English student seeking to answer Foucault's charge that truth claims are merely power plays? A law student whose professor insists that law has no relation to morality? A unique feature of a Romans 1 strategy is that it can be applied universally. No more memorizing different arguments for each theory. We can be confident that Romans 1 applies to them all.

Let's remind ourselves of its key elements. Principle #1 is to identify the idol. Romans 1 says that if humans do not worship the Creator, they will make a deity out of something in the created order. Like the blind men and the elephant, they declare some part of created reality to be the ultimate reality.

Principle #2 is to identify the reductionism. When one part of creation is deified, the other parts will be denigrated. Why? Because a part is always too small to explain the whole. Something will always stick out of the box. That "something" will be suppressed—devalued, dismissed, or denied. Otherwise it would count as evidence to falsify the worldview.

Reductionism is always dehumanizing. It exchanges a high view of humanity made in the image of God for the image of something in the created order. Thus it will deny key attributes that make us distinctively human. And when reductionistic worldviews gain political power, the consequences are oppressive, coercive, and inhumane.

Principle #3 is to test the worldview against the facts of experience, the truths of general revelation. No matter how hard people try to suppress the evidence for God, the created order itself keeps challenging them—things they "can't help believing." Therefore every idol-based worldview will contradict the knowable facts of general revelation.

Principle #4 is to show that every reductionistic worldview is self-defeating. It commits suicide. That's because it reduces reason to something less than reason. Yet the only way a worldview can build its *own* case is by using reason. Thus it undercuts itself. It is self-refuting.

Principle #5 is to make the case for a Christian worldview. By identifying the points where non-Christians are free-loading, we can be confident that we are addressing areas where they sense a need for something more.

How can we use the five principles in conversations with non-Christians? Romans 1 describes the dynamics of persons struggling to avoid God, so we can start where it does: with general revelation, a body of knowledge available to everyone because it is part of universal human experience. The person before you has a profound experiential knowledge of being made in God's image—and that knowledge keeps breaking through even when his worldview tells him he is a machine made in the image of matter.

Then we use the same tests that are used universally to assess any worldview: Test it externally against the world; test it internally for logical consistency.

In short, the five principles draw on what everyone knows to be true and what everyone recognizes as good reasoning. Even the term *idols* is used by secular thinkers (ever since Nietzsche's famous essay "Twilight of the Idols"). What makes the Romans 1 strategy unique is that it explains *why* these tests work: The Romans 1 narrative, with its dramatic account of idols and suppression, is the larger framework that gives these arguments their theological rationale and weaves them into a dynamic unity.

Stealth Secularism

The philosophies discussed in this book form the backbone to all of Western thought. I've had students from many different disciplines, and they discover that the Romans 1 approach gives them tools to critique any theory, no matter what their field. An undergraduate recently wrote, "The method of critique you taught in this class has been incredibly helpful to me, not just in class but in my life—reading books and watching movies." A master's student wrote, "When watching television or movies with my family, I used to be afraid of secular ideas seeping into my psyche, but now I finally have the skills to identify and critique them. My kids are intrigued and delighted."

The point about books and movies is especially important. After all, this is how most people pick up their ideas about life. They don't think, *I need a personal philosophy* and sign up for a philosophy course at the local university. Instead they absorb their ideas about life through the books they read, the movies they watch, the music they listen to.

Worldviews do not typically come with a warning label attached to tell us what we're getting. They do not ask permission before invading our mental space. Instead there is what we might call a "stealth" secularism that uses images and stories to bypass people's critical grid and hook them emotionally, sometimes without their even knowing it. That's why it is imperative to learn the skill of deciphering worldviews when they come to us not in words, where they are easier to recognize, but in the idiom of picture, composition, plot line, and characterization.[3]

Take, for example, one of the most influential philosophies covered in earlier chapters: materialism or naturalism. In the nineteenth century, a movement arose that was actually called literary naturalism. Novels and plays began to appear that portrayed humans as merely products of nature, without free will, determined by their genes and the environment.

Virtually every student I have taught has read books by Jack London, like *Call of the Wild*. But what they *don't* know is that as a young man, London underwent what one historian calls "a conversion experience" to radical materialism by reading the works of Charles Darwin. He memorized long passages from Darwin and could even quote them by heart (like Christians who memorize Scripture). He wrote about dogs to soften the blow, but his real message was that *humans* are nothing but evolved organisms, with no free will, governed by natural selection and survival of the fittest.

In London's short story "The Law of Life," an old Eskimo is left behind by his family to die in the snow. As the wolves close in to devour him, the old man ponders that evolution assigns the individual only one task: to reproduce so the species will survive. "Nature did not care. To life she set one task, gave one law. To perpetuate was the task of life." After that, if the individual dies, "What did it matter after all? Was it not the law of life?"

The story pounds home the theme that humans have no higher purpose beyond sheer biological existence.

High culture filters down to pop culture, so materialist themes appear in movies and television as well. In a famous episode in

Star Trek, the characters debate whether the android Lieutenant Commander Data is a machine.

He is, of course, but Captain Picard retorts, "It is not relevant. We [humans], too, are machines, merely machines of a different type."

Naturalism tries to appeal by posing as tough and realistic. But, ironically, its main weakness is that it is not realistic enough. As we saw in Principle #3, it does not fit the real world. It holds that humans are essentially machines with no free will. But no one can live like a machine. We make choices every moment of the day.

Critics point out that the literary naturalists themselves did not live by their own philosophy. A Yale historian says they accepted "determinism as a theory but not something to live by." I would suggest that is because no one *can* live by it in practice. It is not true to life.

Philosophy in Paint

Not only literature but also the visual arts were deeply influenced by philosophy.

Impressionism

Everyone knows what an impressionist painting looks like, with its little dabs and dashes of color. But *why* did impressionists decide to break up images that way? Because they were influenced by the philosophy of empiricism, which claims that the ultimate foundation of knowledge is sensations. To reach that foundation, empiricism says, we must reach down to the level of sheer sensory input. We must not even interpret sensations in terms of discrete objects standing in three-dimensional space, but only as patches of color filling our field of vision.

That's why the great impressionist Claude Monet wrote, "When you go out to paint, try to forget what objects you have before you, a tree, a house, a field, or whatever. Merely think, here is a little square of blue, here an oblong of pink, here a streak of yellow." His goal was to cut through to the level of raw, immediate sense data. Spots. Streaks. Patches of color.

Recall that according to empiricism, humans mentally construct the world out of color patches (see Principle #1). Monet wanted to convey the same idea visually. Clearly, he was not interested just in painting pretty pictures. He was wrestling with the philosophical problem of knowledge (epistemology)—not in philosophical terms but in artistic terms.

For many of us, it is easier to grasp abstract ideas when they are fleshed out in visual form. After learning how empiricism was expressed visually, how would you respond to someone who is an empiricist—who says, "I can't accept Christianity because its central claims cannot be directly verified by empirical science"?

You might respond by asking: Why do you think *empiricism* should be the test for truth? After all, does anyone really think the ultimate basis for knowledge is color patches? Does anyone really reject everything *non*empirical, like love or justice? In practice, no one is a fully consistent empiricist. It fails the practical test.

Christianity respects the empirical dimension (see Principles #1 and #4), but as one thread in a rich fabric of truth.

Cubism

Take another example. Everyone knows what a cubist painting looks like, with its little squares and rectangles. But *why* did the cubists decide to break images up that way? Because these artists were influenced by the philosophy of rationalism. The apex of the scientific revolution was the development of mathematical physics. In Galileo's famous saying, the book of nature is written in the language of mathematics—"and its characters are triangles, circles, and other geometric figures."

Rationalism thus inspired a kind of geometric formalism. The intellectual springboard for cubism was a remark by Cézanne that artists should "interpret nature in terms of the cylinder, the sphere, the cone"—virtually a paraphrase of Galileo. The cubists' goal was to portray the underlying mathematical structure of the cosmos. They broke objects down into little squares and rectangles to reflect nature's hidden geometric blueprint.

These rationalist ideas did not stay locked inside art galleries. In architecture they inspired the International style—the glass-and-steel boxes that look like cubist buildings—which populate so many cities today. Architects began to think of themselves as social reformers who would lead the way in restructuring society according to a rational plan. They persuaded many cities to build huge housing projects, promising to solve a host of social problems in one fell swoop, from poverty to crime to drug abuse. The most influential was Le Corbusier, who called his buildings "machines to live in" because they had the functional efficiency of machines. Architects accepted the rationalist premise that humans are complex mechanisms whose problems can be fixed simply by slotting them into "machines to live in."

Many of the housing projects decayed into concrete prisons—dreary, depressing, seedbeds of crime and social pathology—until they were finally dynamited to the ground. As one social critic writes, the decaying housing projects still seen in cities around the world remain a visible expression of "the materialist and rationalist conception of human life."

When ideas come out of the university and into public policy, it is easier to identify their flaws. A "materialist and rationalist conception of human life" fails to take account of our full humanity; thus its consequences are inhumane. Because Christianity has a much richer view of human nature, its consequences are humane and life affirming.

Abstract Art

The art movement that the public finds perhaps most puzzling is abstract art. Why did some artists stop painting objects at all? Because they were influenced by pantheism. The first abstract painter was Kandinsky, who embraced a blend of Eastern and Western mysticism. He argued that the way to oppose philosophical material*ism* was to get rid of material *objects*. In his words, abstract art would liberate the mind from "the harsh tyranny of the materialistic philosophy," becoming "one of the most powerful agents of the spiritual life."

The purpose of an abstract painting, then, is to free the mind from its preoccupation with material objects and draw the viewer up to the spiritual realm. The goal is to impart a sense "of the Buddhist mystical state known as *sunyata*, the great void, or emptiness."[4]

Francis Schaeffer offered a fascinating phrase to describe this kind of content-free religious experience: He called it "mysticism with nobody there." It may lift us out of the ordinary, mundane world, but to connect with what? Not with a transcendent person who loves us and communicates with us, but with sheer emptiness. The void.

Mark Rothko painted several large, dark, monochromatic panels for the Rothko chapel in Houston. What was he saying with these somber, melancholy paintings? The person who commissioned the paintings said they express "the silence of God, the unbearable silence of God."

Shortly after finishing the paintings, before the chapel even opened, Rothko committed suicide. A mysticism with nobody there is not enough to give a sense of significance and meaning to life.

Postmodernism

What about postmodernism? How is it expressed in the arts? Recall that postmodernism is the claim that there is no "metanarrative" or universal story line valid for all people at all times. Each community has its own story line for making sense of the world. How would an artist give that idea visual expression?

By refusing to give a work of art any coherent overall design. This explains why deconstructionist artists favor the pastiche or collage—a patchwork of disconnected images that defy any attempt at interpretation.

For example, the famous collages by Robert Rauschenberg, says one art historian, "juxtaposed images in ways to suggest random incoherence, to which the artist—and viewer—can bring no meaningful order." What was Rauschenberg saying with these disconnected images? That "life's random occurrences ... cannot be made to fit in any inherent hierarchy of meaning."

Postmodern architecture has its own version of the pastiche or collage. As one journalist puts it, postmodernism "has brought us girders hanging unfinished out of the edges of buildings, archways cut off in space, and walls which don't meet walls." Ravi Zacharias describes seeing a building designed by a postmodern architect. "I had just one question," Zacharias says. "Did he do the same with the foundation?"[5] It was an apologetics argument put in artistic terms.

Whether in art or literature, education or psychology, mathematics or science, every theory or movement is inspired by an underlying philosophy. If you master the strategic principles in this book, they will equip you to identify and engage critically with the ideas that have shaped the Western world in every subject area.

What Wags Your Theology?

A Romans 1 approach will even help you sort out claims in theology. Robert Garcia is a philosophy professor, but as a teenager, he went to a Lutheran college to study theology. At the time, the vogue was neo-orthodoxy, a movement to "demythologize" the Bible, stripping it of its supposedly mythological elements. Initially the young freshman was puzzled. Why was the teaching in the classroom so different from what he had learned at home and church?

Garcia finally discovered that neo-orthodoxy was strongly influenced by the philosophy of existentialism. He realized that the best way to understand the *theology* was to walk down the hallway to the *philosophy* department and study the existentialism that had inspired it.

This was a crucial insight. Virtually every form of theology has been influenced to some degree by philosophy. Consider the leading schools of liberal theology. Classic nineteenth-century liberalism recast Christianity in terms of Hegelian idealism. It essentially identified the Holy Spirit with Hegel's quasi-pantheistic Absolute Spirit. Salvation was redefined as the gradual unfolding of the purposes of an immanent deity in and through the historical process. The process of salvation would be manifested in the progressive recognition of the universal Fatherhood of God and Brotherhood of Man—"the transformation of the world itself into a human Brotherhood," in the words of liberal churchman Lyman Abbott.[6]

More recently, liberation theology redefined Christianity in terms of Marxism. Gustavo Gutiérrez, who coined the term, writes, "Liberation theology categorizes people not as believers or unbelievers, but as oppressors or oppressed."[7]

Feminist theology recasts Christianity in terms borrowed from secular feminism. Elisabeth Schüssler Fiorenza says a feminist hermeneutic "does not appeal to the Bible as its primary source but begins with women's own experience and vision of liberation."[8]

A popular theology in many mainline seminaries is process theology, an offshoot of process philosophy. With roots in neo-Platonism (see Principle #2), it holds that God is in the world as the soul is in the body. Thus God is not infinite but finite. God is not omniscient (all-knowing) or omnipotent (all-powerful). This is process theology's answer to the problem of evil: God is doing the best he can. God does not have the power to foresee the future or to prevent evil from happening.[9]

The cutting edge today is postmodern theology, inspired obviously by postmodernism. Like secular postmodernism, it denies that humans have access to any timeless, universal truth, even in Scripture. In *The End of Apologetics*, Myron Penner writes, "We can, of course, say objectively 'true' things directly—like, for example, that it is –27°C outside this morning or that God was in Jesus Christ reconciling to himself the world. The point, however, is first that these sorts of objective 'facts' or statements are only approximately true and are made from a finite, contingent perspective."[10] By citing Scripture (2 Cor. 5:19), Penner is asserting that even *its* statements are "made from a finite, contingent perspective." For postmoderns, even Christians are trapped in Nietzsche's prison house of language. (See Principle #4.)

Postmodern Christians typically reject apologetics, claiming that if you use reasons and arguments to defend biblical truth, then you have capitulated to "Enlightenment modernism." Yet the line of reasoning you have learned in *Finding Truth* is informed by Scripture itself—which means its roots are *pre*modern, and its relevance is *trans*historical, applying to all cultures and historical periods.

In all the examples above, liberal schools of theology have redefined classic Christian theology in the shape of an idol-based philosophy. Yet they continue to use traditional theological terminology. Garcia told me, "My college professors insisted on using orthodox Christian terms and language, but vested with meanings imported from secular philosophies. That is what made their teaching so baffling and deceptive."

Moreover, liberal theologies are not taught objectively, as a way to gain a critical understanding of them. Instead, Garcia says, they are "taught in a triumphalistic spirit, as sources of enlightenment and liberation from your-parents'-naive-supernaturalist-Christianity." This goes a long way toward explaining why students who study theology at leading seminaries and universities often end up rejecting the orthodox Christianity they started out with.

In every field, Christians must learn critical thinking skills. Otherwise, we may simply absorb idol-based philosophies from the intellectual atmosphere.

When I was in my early twenties, working my way through Bible school in Los Angeles, I had a job as a teller at First Savings and Loan. We were carefully trained to discern the difference between genuine and counterfeit bills. By the same token, we must all train ourselves to discern the difference between worldviews, which are the currency of thought.

Critique and Create

At its best, apologetics includes not only the *critique* of idols but also the *creation* of life-giving alternatives. Christians often have a habit of defining themselves by what they are against. Yet to oppose what is wrong, it is most effective to offer something better—to "overcome evil with good" (Rom. 12:21).

If science is often used to bolster arguments for materialism and determinism, then Christians should make it their goal to do better, more accurate science. If literature is used to glamorize sin and brokenness, then Christians should fire up their imaginations to create higher quality, more inspiring works of fiction. If movies and music are vehicles for emotionally "hooking" people into Hollywood worldviews, then the best countermeasure is to create more compelling, more beautiful forms of art that express a biblical worldview. And if philosophy can lead to atheism, the solution is to craft more reasonable, more incisive, more truthful ways of thinking. As C. S. Lewis wrote, "Good philosophy must exist, if for no other reason, because bad philosophy needs to be answered."[11]

I've had philosophy majors in my classes whose parents and pastors warned them *not* to study the subject, quoting Paul's warning not to be taken "captive" by philosophy (Col. 2:8). But as Dallas Willard points out, when Scripture commands us to avoid "vain philosophy," it does not mean we should avoid *all* philosophy. After all, when Scripture commands us to avoid immodest clothing, it does not mean we should avoid *all* clothing.[12] In every area of life, our aim should be to counter the bad by cultivating the good.

A Total Book for Total Truth

A major barrier to cultivating the good in every area is that modern culture reduces Christianity to only one part of life—to a message of salvation, telling you how get to heaven. As a result, few think of Christianity as a worldview giving fundamental principles that apply to all of life.

Yet Scripture itself teaches that knowledge of God provides a universal framework. Consider these passages: "The fear of the LORD is the beginning of wisdom" (Ps. 111:10; Prov. 1:7; 9:10; 15:33). In Christ are "all the treasures of wisdom and knowledge" (Col. 2:3). Christianity is the key to "all that is good and right and true" (Eph. 5:9). Are these passages really teaching that the fear of the Lord is the foundation of *all* wisdom, the key to all that is true? That claim seems radical.

But now that we have learned about idols, the biblical claim is easier to understand. The Bible is simply describing how *every* system of thought works. Every system starts with something that is regarded as ultimate, unconditioned, divine—which in turn functions as the controlling motif for everything that follows. The fear of some "god" is the beginning of every proposed worldview. In this regard, Christianity is like every other answer to the riddle of the universe. Its starting assumptions provide the logical basis for everything that follows.

That's why Scripture insists that all truth begins with God. The Bible relates the plot line of universal, cosmic history. All true knowledge finds a place within its story line.

Allan Bloom, author of the bestselling book *The Closing of the American Mind*, says that through much of American history, the concept of a unified truth came from the Bible. It created a "common culture, one that united the simple and the sophisticated, rich and poor, young and old … as the very model for a vision of the order of the whole of things."

But as the Bible loses influence, the West is losing its sense of any unified truth. "The very idea of such a total book is disappearing," Bloom laments—and with it, the idea of total truth. Parents send their children to school to learn specialized skills so they can get a job. But they have lost the ideal of becoming a whole person living out an integrated vision of life. "Contrary to what is commonly thought, without the book even the idea of the whole is lost."[13]

Yet the idea of total truth is being regained today—often in unexpected places.

Crazy Crae: How Do We Break Free?

"God met me where I was at—baggy jeans and earrings." With those words, the celebrated hip-hop artist Lecrae Moore begins his story.[14] Growing up without a father, he experienced a childhood of abuse and neglect. He filled his life with drugs, theft, alcohol, sex, and gang activity. He was so wild that his friends nicknamed him "Crazy Crae."[15] He was a poster child for every stereotype of urban subculture.

What it took to bring him to Christianity was someone who was not afraid of that subculture—who knew that the real problem for Lecrae was not his culture but his sin and brokenness. A white man named Joe loved the black teenager enough to enter into his culture and speak his language. Today Lecrae is the president and co-founder of Reach Records, and is the winner of several Dove Awards and a Grammy Award. His album *Anomaly* was the first album ever to top both the Gospel Albums and the Billboard 200 chart.

In a conference presentation, Lecrae said a key turning point in his life was when he grasped what comes after conversion—when he understood that "Christianity is not just religious truth, it is Total Truth."[16] In other words, the real transformation came when he realized that Christians are called to roll up their sleeves and work out the implications of a biblical worldview for justice and politics, for science and scholarship, for art and music—and all the rest of life.

"We've limited Christianity to salvation and sanctification," he said. But "Christianity is the truth about everything. If you say you have a Christian worldview, that means you see the world through that lens—not just how people get saved and what to stay away from."[17]

Lecrae's message is that we do not need to be afraid of cultural differences because Christianity has the resources to speak to every culture. Quoting from my book *Total Truth*, Lecrae says the reason Christians hold back from being salt and light in the world is that they are trapped in the sacred/secular divide. "We live fractured and fragmented lives. Church and family rarely speak to our work and public life. We navigate between two separate worlds."[18]

"Most religions tell you not only how to be right with God but how to interpret the world we live in," Lecrae explains. "Historically, Christians have been good at the first function, 'saving souls,' but not at helping people interpret the world around them. We limit spirituality to salvation and sanctification."

Salvation is the crucial first step in the Christian life, of course. "But how do we deal with politics, science, economics, bioethics, TV, music, and art? Typically, we leave people to their own devices. We usually don't operate out of a biblical worldview." Instead, "we tend to have bifocals, half seeing things as spiritual and half seeing things as secular."

Where did the sacred/secular split come from? Not from the Bible. It came from the Greeks. And the reason is that they thought matter was eternal. "A great divide was born when the Greek philosophers argued that matter was pre-existing and eternal—that matter contained the ability to resist the Creator," Lecrae explains. "As Christians, we refute that claim with the doctrine that only God is pre-existing and eternal, ex nihilo. He is the source of all creation." The implication is that no part of creation is inherently bad or evil. "Everything created by God is good, and nothing is to be rejected if it is received with thanksgiving" (1 Tim. 4:4).

Most evil consists of "a perversion of good things," Lecrae explains. "God gave us the ingenuity and tools to make a butcher knife, so we can use it to murder or serve food to the homeless."[19]

How can we heal the sacred/secular split, which marginalizes and disempowers Christians? "How do we break free of this split that robs the gospel of its power to redeem every aspect of our lives?" Lecrae asks. The answer is to understand that "Christianity is saving truth and it's sanctifying truth, but we believe that it's Total Truth. It is the truth about every aspect of life from economics to masculinity to marriage. God has the right view on all of these things."[20]

This is not just pious talk for Lecrae. He has worked hard to understand how the principle of total truth applies to his own work. In contrast to some Christians, who might be prone to write off hip-hop music as evil, he is determined to cultivate the genre's creativity and artistry. Lecrae once told me that discovering total truth has enriched his art—that it "liberated" him to address all areas of life in his lyrics. Christian music is music that addresses any subject area from a biblical perspective.

Christians are called to be ambassadors for Christ (2 Cor. 5:20)—and that means we need to prepare ourselves as thoroughly as any professional working in international relations. When I lived in the Washington, DC, area, I often met graduate students preparing to be ambassadors and diplomats, and I discovered that they were very familiar with the concept of worldview—not because they were reading Christian books on the subject but because it was the focus of their secular graduate studies. Their courses taught that the critical factor in engaging a foreign culture is not learning the language but the worldview.

"Most people are intimidated by worldviews that they don't understand," Lecrae says. To overcome our fears, we need to be driven by compassion for those who are suffering under the tyranny of false idols. In a rap titled "Truth," Lecrae talks about people in the grip of "idols in their heart." His music aims to release people from the power of false gods by counterposing the power of truth.

In recent years Lecrae has spearheaded the Unashamed movement, which takes its lead from Romans 1:16. The hip-hop artists associated with Lecrae and Reach Records even call themselves the "116 clique." (Lecrae has the number 116 tattooed on his right arm.) The Unashamed movement aims to inspire people to live out biblical truth with confidence in every area of life.

No area is off limits. No area is too "scary" because you might lose your grip on your Christian convictions. Let me end with a final quote from Lecrae: "What we need to realize is that

Christianity is total truth not just religious truth. Because it is total truth, it is relevant and applicable to all areas of life."[21]

The five strategic principles in *Finding Truth* can help you live an unashamed life, whether at work, at school, or with your family and friends. They will provide you with the tools to recognize what's right and what's wrong with any worldview—and then to craft a biblically informed perspective that is both true and humane.

NOTES

PART I—"I Lost My Faith at an Evangelical College"

1. David Kinnaman writes, "The significant spiritual and technological changes over the last 50 years make the dropout problem more urgent. Young people are dropping out earlier, staying away longer, and if they come back are less likely to see the church as a long-term part of their life." Cited in "Five Myths about Young Adult Church Dropouts," Barna Group, November 16, 2011, www.barna.org/teens-next-gen-articles/534-five-myths-about-young-adult-church-dropouts.
2. Cited in Allen C. Guelzo, "The Return of the Will," in *Edwards in Our Time: Jonathan Edwards and the Shaping of American Religion*, ed. Sang Hyun Lee and Allen C. Guelzo (Grand Rapids, MI: Eerdmans, 1999), 133. The problem is that although God is knowable through general revelation, humans suppress that knowledge and are therefore in need of redemption—which is why we also need the Bible, or special revelation, with its message of redemption.
3. See Robin Collins, "The Teleological Argument: An Exploration of the Fine-Tuning of the Universe," in *The Blackwell Companion to Natural Theology*, ed. William Lane Craig and J. P. Moreland (Oxford: Blackwell, 2012).
4. Dennis Overbye, "Zillions of Universes? Or Did Ours Get Lucky?," *New York Times*, October 28, 2003. To counter the implications of fine-tuning, some cosmologists propose that there are multiple universes besides our own (the Many Worlds hypothesis). Most of those universes would be dark, lifeless places, but a few might possibly have the right conditions for life—and ours just happens to be one of them. This is sheer speculation, of course, since it is impossible to know if any other universes actually exist. "The multiverse theory requires as much suspension of disbelief as any religion," comments Gregg Easterbrook. "Join the church that believes in the existence of invisible objects 50 billion galaxies wide!" The only reason for proposing such a

far-fetched idea is that it makes our own universe seem a little less like a freak improbability. Gregg Easterbrook, "The New Convergence," *Wired*, December 2002.
5. George Greenstein, *The Symbiotic Universe: Life and Mind in the Cosmos* (New York: William Morrow, 1988), 85–90; and Paul Davies, "A Brief History of the Multiverse," *New York Times*, April 12, 2003. Elsewhere Davies writes that "the seemingly miraculous concurrence of numerical values" for nature's fundamental constants is "the most compelling evidence for an element of cosmic design." *God and the New Physics* (New York: Simon & Schuster, 1983), 189. For more on fine-tuning, see Guillermo Gonzalez and Jay Richards, *The Privileged Planet: How Our Place in the Cosmos Is Designed for Discovery* (Washington, DC: Regnery, 2004) and my book *Total Truth: Liberating Christianity from Its Cultural Captivity* (Wheaton, IL: Crossway, 2004), 188–91.
6. Paul Davies, "The Secret of Life Won't Be Cooked Up in a Chemistry Lab," *Guardian*, January 13, 2013. Earlier Davies wrote, "Trying to make life by mixing chemicals in a test tube is like soldering switches and wires in an attempt to produce Windows 98. It won't work because it addresses the problem at the wrong conceptual level." "How We Could Create Life: The Key to Existence Will Be Found Not in Primordial Sludge, but in the Nanotechnology of the Living Cell," *Guardian*, December 11, 2002.
7. See Stephen C. Meyer, *Signature in the Cell: DNA and the Evidence for Intelligent Design* (New York: HarperCollins, 2010).
8. Cicero, *On the Nature of the Gods*, bk. II, chap. XXXVII; and "The Tusculan Disputations," trans. C. D. Yonge (New York: Harper, 1877), 39.
9. See my treatment in *The Soul of Science*, coauthored by Charles Thaxton (Wheaton, IL: Crossway, 1994), especially chapter 10; *Total Truth*, especially chapters 5 and 6; and *How Now Shall We Live?*, coauthored by Chuck Colson and Harold Fickett (Wheaton, IL: Tyndale, 1999), chapters 6 through 10. On the broader outworkings of Darwinian thought in philosophy and culture, see *Total Truth*, chapters 7 and 8, and *Saving Leonardo* (Nashville: B&H, 2010), chapters 3 and 6.
10. With the Judeo-Christian religion "a new way of thinking is introduced into the Western world." Its God "is very different from the divinities of earlier philosophies. He is a personal God, not an abstract principle." C. H. Perlman, *An Historical Introduction to Philosophical Thinking*, trans. Kenneth Brown (New York: Random, 1965), 96–97. "To Greco-Oriental thought, whether mystical or philosophical, the ultimate reality is some primal impersonal force … some ineffable, immutable, impassive divine substance that pervades the

universe or rather is the universe." By contrast, in biblical thought, "God is neither a metaphysical principle nor an impersonal force.... Hebraic religion affirms God as a transcendent Person." Will Herberg, *Judaism and Modern Man: An Interpretation of Jewish Religion* (New York: Boucher, 2007), 48.
11. Étienne Gilson, *God and Philosophy* (New Haven, CT: Yale University Press, 1941), 19–20, 37, 42.
12. Paul Bloom, "Religion Is Natural," *Developmental Science* 10, no. 1 (2007): 147–51.
13. Cited in Martin Beckford, "Children Are Born Believers in God, Academic Claims," *Telegraph*, November 24, 2008.
14. C. S. Lewis, *Miracles* (New York: HarperCollins, 1974), 150.
15. Around the 1930s, a new field called the sociology of knowledge began to investigate how even scholars and scientists fail to fit the ideal of objectivity, but are influenced (often unconsciously) by their prior expectations and assumptions. The sociology of knowledge was founded by philosopher Max Scheler and sociologist Karl Mannheim.
16. See Thomas K. Johnson, *The First Step in Missions Training: How Our Neighbors Are Wrestling with God's General Revelation* (Bonn: Verlag für Kultur und Wissenschaft, 2014), 23–24.
17. See Margaret Heffernan, *Willful Blindness: Why We Ignore the Obvious at Our Peril* (New York: Walker, 2011).
18. Johnson, *First Step*, 23.
19. David Powlison, "Idols of the Heart and 'Vanity Fair,'" *Journal of Biblical Counseling*, October 16, 2009.
20. Similarly, in Paul's letter to the Colossians, he warns against "sexual immorality, impurity, passion, evil desire, and covetousness, which is idolatry" (Col. 3:5). Again, idolatry is the sin driving the other sins.
21. *The Larger Catechism of Martin Luther*, trans. Robert H. Fischer (Philadelphia: Fortress, 1959), 9.
22. Cited in Pericles Lewis, *Religious Experience and the Modernist Novel* (Cambridge: Cambridge University Press, 2010), 36. For a fuller discussion of the trend to treat art as a religion, which started with Romanticism, see *Saving Leonardo*, chapters 7 and 8.
23. John Calvin, *Institutes of the Christian Religion*, 1536 ed. (Grand Rapids, MI: Eerdmans, 1995), 4.17.36.
24. "In the ancient world there was no banking system as we know it today, and no paper money. All money was made from metal, heated until liquid, poured into moulds and allowed to cool. When the coins were cooled, it was necessary to smooth off the uneven edges. The coins were comparatively

soft, and of course many people shaved them closely. In one century, more than eighty laws were passed in Athens to stop the practice of whittling down the coins then in circulation." This money, which was less than full weight, was described as "debased." Donald Grey Barnhouse, *Romans: God's Glory* (Philadelphia: Evangelical Foundation, 1964), 18, cited at Blue Letter Bible, s.v. "*dokimos*," www.blbclassic.org/lang/lexicon/lexicon.cfm?Strongs=G1384&t=NASB.

25. In using the term *exchanged*, Paul is echoing a verse from the Old Testament: "They made a calf in Horeb and worshiped a metal image. They exchanged the glory of God for the image of an ox that eats grass" (Ps. 106:19–20). An echo goes back even further to Genesis 1:26, where the cultural mandate gives humans stewardship over the rest of creation. "God created human beings for 'dominion' over these creatures, but fallen human idolaters now bow before the likenesses of animals." Richard B. Hays, *Echoes of Scripture in the Letters of Paul* (New Haven, CT: Yale University Press, 1989), 211, n. 26.

26. Richard B. Hays, *The Moral Vision of the New Testament: A Contemporary Introduction to New Testament Ethics* (New York: HarperOne, 1996), 387. Sarah Ruden, a scholar of Greco-Roman culture, says the main form of homosexual behavior that Paul was most likely to observe in his day was pederasty, most frequently the sexual abuse of young male slaves by their masters, although freeborn boys were vulnerable to being raped as well. Among the Greeks and Romans, the active partner was praised as virile and masculine, even when they were cruel and vicious, while the passive partner (the victim) was regarded as weak and disgusting. But Paul treats the active partner as equally guilty and degraded, and in fact condemns homosexuality as a form of injustice (the word for "unrighteousness" in Romans 1:18 is often translated "injustice"). Because pederasty was accepted in Roman culture, and the perpetrators even admired, "Paul's Roman audience ... would have been surprised to hear that justice applied to homosexuality, of all things." "No Closet, No Monsters? Paul and Homosexuality," chap. 3 in *Paul among the People: The Apostle Reinterpreted and Reimagined in His Own Time* (New York: Image Books, 2010).

27. Cited in *Soul of Science*, 184–85.

28. Roy Clouser, *The Myth of Religious Neutrality: An Essay on the Hidden Role of Religious Belief in Theories*, rev. ed. (Notre Dame, IN: University of Notre Dame Press, 2005), 104.

29. Not all forms of reductionism are problematic. In some cases, a good understanding of a system's components enables one to predict all the important properties of a system as a whole. That is to say, some things really

are merely the sum of their parts. Take, for example, the kinetic theory of gases. As John Polkinghorne writes, we can use "the kinetic theory of gases to reduce the concept of temperature (originating in the thermodynamics of bulk matter) to exact equivalence to the average kinetic energy of the molecules of the gas." *Interdisciplinary Encyclopedia of Religion and Science*, s.v. "Reductionism," ed. G. Tanzella-Nitti and A. Strumia, 2002, http://inters.org/reductionism.

30. Herman Dooyeweerd describes how absolutization leads to reductionism: Those who look for ultimate reality within creation "will be inclined to present one aspect of reality ... as reality in its completeness. They will then reduce all the others to the point where all of them become different manifestations of the absolutized aspect.... Think of modern materialism, which reduces all of temporal reality to particles of matter in motion. Consider the modern naturalistic philosophy of life, which sees everything one-sidedly in terms of the development of organic life.... [Humans tend] to absolutize the relative and deify the creature." *Roots of Western Culture: Pagan, Secular, and Christian Options* (Grand Rapids, MI: Paideia Press, 2012), 42.

31. John Horgan, "More Than Good Intentions: Holding Fast to Faith in Free Will," *New York Times*, December 31, 2002. Francis Schaeffer offered this analogy: When a person's worldview is too "small," it's like trying to stuff a person into a garbage can—an arm or a leg will always stick out. *True Spirituality* in *The Complete Works of Francis A. Schaeffer* (Westchester, IL: Crossway, 1982), vol. 3, 172–73.

32. John Searle, interview by Jeffrey Mishlove, *Thinking Allowed: Conversations on the Leading Edge of Knowledge and Discovery*, 1998, www.williamjames.com/transcripts/searle.htm (italics added).

33. The book was Gene Edward Veith, *Postmodern Times: A Christian Guide to Contemporary Thought and Culture* (Wheaton, IL: Crossway, 1994).

PART 2—PRINCIPLE #1: Twilight of the Gods

1. Albert M. Wolters, *Creation Regained: Biblical Basics for a Reformational Worldview* (Grand Rapids, MI: Eerdmans, 1985), 4.
2. Christian Smith and Melinda Lundquist Denton, *Soul Searching: The Religious and Spiritual Lives of American Teenagers* (Oxford: Oxford University Press, 2005), 89.
3. David Kinnaman, *You Lost Me: Why Young Christians Are Leaving Church ... and Rethinking Faith* (Grand Rapids, MI: Baker Books, 2011), 190. A study by Fuller Seminary found that the single most important factor in whether teens hold on to their Christian convictions in college is whether they found

answers to their questions while still in high school: "The more college students felt that they had the opportunity to express their doubt while they were in high school, the higher [their] levels of faith maturity and spiritual maturity." Lillian Kwon, "Survey: High School Seniors 'Graduating from God,'" *Christian Post*, August 10, 2006.
4. Bradley Wright, "If People Leave the Faith, When Do They Do It?," Patheos, January 28, 2012, www.patheos.com/blogs/blackwhiteandgray/2012/01/if-people-leave-the-faith-when-do-they-do-it/. Wright cites a study showing that those most likely to leave are ages seventeen to twenty. The next most likely to leave are a year or two younger (ages fifteen to sixteen). After age twenty, the numbers decline somewhat, then finally drop off after age twenty-six.
5. Christian Smith, director of the Center for the Study of Youth and Religion at the University of Notre Dame, reports that teenagers today often define faith primarily in terms of "meeting emotional needs." Their one-dimensional understanding is the product of "an overwhelmingly relativistic and privatized cultural climate," as well as "youth leaders who have not challenged that climate." Cited in Chris Norton, "Apologetics Makes a Comeback among Youth," *Christianity Today*, August 31, 2011.
6. Norton, "Apologetics." See also Troy Anderson, "A New Day for Apologetics: People Young and Old Are Flocking to Hear—and Be Changed by— Winsome Arguments for the Christian Faith," *Christianity Today*, July 2, 2008.
7. An idol may also be something mistakenly thought to be in creation— something unreal or imaginary, such as space aliens. The point is that *if it were real*, it would be something less than God, something within the cosmic order.
8. Terry Eagleton, *Culture and the Death of God* (New Haven, CT: Yale University Press, 2014), 119. See also Andrew Brown, "Religion without a Church? Humanism Almost Qualifies," *Guardian*, August 12, 2014. Herman Dooyeweerd notes that idols result from a "deification of the creature" and "the absolutizing of the relative" *New Critique of Theoretical Thought* (Ontario, Canada: Paideia, 1984), I:58, 61, 176 and II:322, 572. For example, the mechanistic materialism of the Enlightenment resulted from "an absolutization of the mechanical phenomena." *Roots*, 172–73. Reinhold Niebuhr defined idolatry as the tendency to lift "some finite and contingent element of existence into the eminence of the divine," treating it "as the ultimate principle of coherence and meaning." *The Nature and Destiny of Man*, vol. 1 (Louisville: Westminster John Knox, 1996), 164–65. H. Richard Niebuhr also warned of "the absolutizing of what is relative." *Christ and Culture* (New

York: HarperCollins, 1951), 145. George Steiner notes that many modern philosophies function as "surrogate theologies." They are propounded by "secular messiahs" and express a "nostalgia for the absolute." *Nostalgia for the Absolute* (Toronto: House of Anansi, 1974), 49. Chapter 1 is titled "The Secular Messiahs."

9. Timothy Keller, "Talking about Idolatry in a Postmodern Age," Gospel Coalition, April 2007, http://old.westerfunk.net/archives/theology/Talking%20About%20Idolatry%20in%20a%20Postmodern%20Age/.

10. That's why philosopher David Naugle describes worldviews as "visions of the heart." *Worldview: The History of a Concept* (Grand Rapids, MI: Eerdmans, 2002), 268ff.

11. "Atheistic religions ... include eastern religions like Theravedic Buddhism, Jainism, Taoism, and Confucianism." Eric Steinhart, "On Atheistic Religion," Patheos, January 8, 2012, www.patheos.com/blogs/camelswithhammers/2012/01/on-atheistic-religion-2/. However, "godless faiths are sustained only by small intellectual elites, and the popular forms of Buddhism, Confucianism, and Taoism abound in Gods." Rodney Stark, "Why Gods Should Matter in Social Science," *Chronicle of Higher Education* 49, no. 39 (June 6, 2003). In the Supreme Court decision *Torcaso v. Watkins* (1961), Justice Hugo Black stated that "among religions in this country which do not teach what would generally be considered a belief in the existence of God are Buddhism, Taoism, Ethical Culture, Secular Humanism and others"; and André Comte-Sponville, *The Little Book of Atheist Spirituality* (New York: Penguin, 2006), 2.

12. Hermann Hesse, *Siddhartha*, trans. Hilda Rosner (New York: Bantam, 1951), 144. At the same time, many of these religions do have moral teachings, however difficult that may be to square with their metaphysics. In Hinduism the concept of karma involves a concept of justice—good actions cause good karma and bad actions cause bad karma; what you reap is what you sow. It is a near-mechanical rule, almost like a law in physics (e.g., for every action, there is an equal and opposite reaction).

13. Journalist Arthur Koestler observes that the Eastern view leads to the "denial of a universal moral law" and finally to "passive complicity" with evil. He illustrates the Eastern view with lines from one of the oldest of Zen poems: "Be not concerned with right and wrong / The conflict between right and wrong / Is the sickness of the mind." *The Lotus and the Robot* (New York: Macmillan, 1960), 272, 270.

14. Cited in Stark, "Why Gods Should Matter." Stark offers a great deal of additional evidence: "The founder of British anthropology, Edward Burnett Tylor, and the founder of British sociology, Herbert Spencer, both took

pains to point out that only some kinds of religions have moral implications. 'Savage animism [religion] is almost devoid of that ethical element which to the educated modern mind is the very mainspring of practical religion,' Tylor reported. 'The lower animism is not immoral, it is unmoral.' Spencer also noted that many religions ignore morality, and he went even further by suggesting that some religions actively encourage crime and immorality: 'At the present time in India, we have freebooters like the Domras, among whom a successful theft is always celebrated by a sacrifice to their chief god Gandak.' ... In his distinguished study of the Manus of New Guinea, Reo Franklin Fortune contrasted the moral aspects of their religion with that of the typical tribe, agreeing that 'Tylor is entirely correct in stating that in most primitive regions of the world, religion and morality maintain themselves independently.' Ruth Benedict also argued that to generalize the link between religion and morality 'is to misconceive' the 'history of religions.' She suggested that the linkage probably is typical only of 'the higher ethical religions.' Ralph Barton reported that the Ifugaos impute their own unscrupulous exchange practices to their Gods and seize every opportunity to cheat them. Peter Lawrence found that the Garia of New Guinea have no conception whatever of 'sin,' and 'no idea of rewards in the next world for good works.'"
15. Xenophanes, cited in Adam Drozdek, *Greek Philosophers as Theologians: The Divine Arche* (Burlington, VT: Ashgate, 2007), 15; and Augustine, *City of God*, bk. 3, chap. 3.
16. The city-state of ancient Carthage was a Phoenician colony located in what is now Tunisia. Phoenician colonies in Sicily, Sardinia, and Malta also practiced child sacrifice, as did ancient Israel, where it was ringingly denounced by several Old Testament prophets (Lev. 20:2–5; Deut. 12:31; 18:10; Jer. 7:31; 19:4–5; 32:35; Ezek. 16:20–21; 20:26, 31; 23:37).

    Revisionists (mostly from Tunisia) have denied that Carthage practiced child sacrifice, but a new study seems to have laid that theory to rest. Sarah Griffiths, "Ancient Greek Stories of Ritual Child Sacrifice in Carthage Are True, Study Claims," *Daily Mail*, January 23, 2014; and Maev Kennedy, "Carthaginians Sacrificed Own Children, Archaeologists Say," *Guardian*, January 21, 2014.
17. Clouser, *Myth*, chap. 2. Even a creator god may not be the ultimate reality. Gnosticism taught that within the cosmic order are several levels of spiritual beings from the highest deity down to the lowest deity or sub-god (usually translated as demiurge). It was this subordinate deity who created the material world where humans live. Because this world is the realm of death, decay, and destruction, the demiurge who created it was even said to be evil. To be

precise, the demiurge was not even a true creator but merely an architect, because matter was thought to be eternal. He merely gave form to unformed matter.

18. There is evidence that many ancient cultures held monotheism prior to becoming polytheistic, which supports Paul's statement in Romans 1 that people reject worship of the Creator and substitute worship of creation. For a recent study, see Winfried Corduan, *In the Beginning: A Fresh Look at the Case for Original Monotheism* (Nashville: B&H, 2013). Some scholars believe that the ancient Chinese worshipped a monotheistic divinity before the rise of Confucianism, Taoism, and Buddhism. See Chan Kei Thong and Charlene L. Fu, *Finding God in Ancient China: How the Ancient Chinese Worshiped the God of the Bible* (Grand Rapids, MI: Zondervan, 2009). John S. Mbiti studied some three hundred peoples of Africa, concluding, "In all these societies, without a single exception, people have a notion of God" as the Supreme Being and Creator. *African Religions and Philosophy*, 2nd ed. (New York: Praeger, 1969), 29. Geoffrey Parrinder also argues that the indigenous African culture was monotheistic. *African Mythology* (New York: Peter Bedrick Books, 1991). However, even when teaching that one supreme God exists, most traditional religions also teach that there are lower-level spirits or divinities. Often these religions teach that the Supreme God was alienated from his people and withdrew from them, which is why they now have to placate the lower-level spirits.

    The finding that many cultures held an original monotheism has discredited the nineteenth-century Hegelian-inspired view that religions evolve from simple to complex (from animism through polytheism, to henotheism, to monotheism). See Gleason L. Archer, *A Survey of Old Testament Introduction* (Chicago, IL: Moody Press, 1975). On the implications for missions, see Don Richardson, *Eternity in Their Hearts: Startling Evidence of Belief in the One True God in Hundreds of Cultures throughout the World*, 2nd ed. (Venture, CA: Regal, 1984).

19. Jonathan Petre, "And after Double Maths It Will Be … Paganism: Schools Told to Put Witchcraft and Druids on RE Syllabus," *Daily Mail*, April 14, 2012.

20. "A Definition of Wicca," Church and School of Wicca, www.wicca.org/Church/define.html. Another website states, "Wiccans believe that the spirit of the One, Goddess and God, exist in all things … [and] that we must treat all things of the Earth as aspects of the divine." Herne, "What Is Wicca?," Celtic Connection, http://wicca.com/celtic/wicca/wicca.htm. There are also people today who consider themselves pagans but are completely secular, treating the

gods as psychological symbols or Jungian archetypes. They might view the goddess, for example, as a symbol of female empowerment.
21. G. S. Kirk, J. E. Raven, M. Schofield, *The Presocratic Philosophers: A Critical History*, 2nd ed. (Cambridge, UK: Cambridge University Press, 1983), 150ff.; and Eric Temple Bell, *The Magic of Numbers* (New York: Dover, 1946), 85.
22. See *Total Truth*, appendix 3, "The Long War between Materialism and Christianity."
23. Aristotle, *Metaphysics*, bk. XI, pt. 7; and Plato, *Republic*, bks. VI and VII. In the *Timaeus*, Plato attributes the origin of the material world to a personal deity, but it is a low-level god or sub-deity or demiurge (as in Gnosticism). This low-level deity did not create from nothing; he merely injected reason (rational forms) into reasonless matter. As Reijer Hooykaas writes, this is a creator whose hands are tied in two respects: "He had to follow not his own design but the model of the eternal Ideas [Forms]; and second, he had to put the stamp of the Ideas on a chaotic, recalcitrant matter which he had not created himself." *Religion and the Rise of Modern Science* (Grand Rapids. MI: Eerdmans, 1972), 3–4.
24. Brian J. Shanley in Thomas Aquinas, *The Treatise on the Divine Nature*, trans. Brian J. Shanley (Indianapolis: Hackett, 2006), 244 (italics added). Irving Singer says, "Aristotle's ladder of existence starts with *pure matter* and culminates in *pure form*." *The Nature of Love: Plato to Luther*, 2nd ed. (Chicago: University of Chicago Press, 2009), 108 (italics in original). Romano Guardini says the ancients never attained to the Christian understanding of transcendence: "To the man of the ancient world, however, the universe itself was the whole of reality." Even the philosophers "did not transcend the universe." "The absolute essences [Forms] of ancient philosophy were enmeshed forever within the totality of being to which they gave stability and eternity." For example, Plato's concept of the Good "was not severed from the world; it remained immanent to it as its very eternity, as a 'beyond' within the final whole." Likewise, "the Unmoved Mover of Aristotle, itself immobile, brought about all the change in the world. In the final analysis, it only had meaning when related to the whole of the eternally changing universe itself." *The End of the Modern World* (Wilmington, DE: ISI Books, 1998), 1–3, 8. Dooyeweerd calls Aristotle's deity an "idol." *New Critique*, I:122.
25. E. O. Wilson, *Consilience: The Unity of Knowledge* (New York: Vintage Books, 1998), 291. Wilson also writes on page 60, "Nature is organized by simple universal laws of physics to which all other laws and principles can eventually be reduced"; and Jerry Coyne, "Philosopher Thomas Nagel Goes the Way of Alvin Plantinga, Disses Evolution," *Why Evolution Is True* (blog), October 13,

2012, http://whyevolutionistrue.wordpress.com/2012/10/13/philosopher-thomas-nagel-goes-the-way-of-alvin-plantinga-disses-evolution/.
26. John R. Searle, *Mind: A Brief Introduction* (Oxford: Oxford University Press, 2004), 48; and Gordy Slack, "What Neo-Creationists Get Right," *The Scientist*, June 20, 2008, 26. Dallas Willard, "What Significance Has 'Postmodernism' for Christian Faith?," www.dwillard.org/articles/artview.asp?artID=70.
27. "Tysonism," Facebook, https://www.facebook.com/Tysonism.
28. In Marx's terms, economic relations form the base, while all other dimensions of society are merely superstructure. See my chapter on Marxism, "Does It Liberate?," in *How Now Shall We Live?* (Wheaton, IL: Tyndale, 1999), chap. 24.
29. David Hume, *Inquiry Concerning Human Understanding*, ed. Charles Hendel (Pearson, 1995), 80.
30. A report of the survey can be found in Anthony Gottlieb, "What Do Philosophers Believe?," *Intelligent Life*, spring 2010.
31. See Donald T. Williams, "Kahless and Christ: On Faith, Fictional and Factual," *While We're Paused* (blog), June 11, 2012. Worf is expressing the fact/value split, which is a major theme throughout *Total Truth*.
32. "There is simply no way to show that humans can gain knowledge of extra-mental realities if we are only directly aware of mental realities. Neither reason nor experience will allow us to bridge the chasm between our minds and the external world that looms if representationalism is true." C. Stephen Evans, *Natural Signs and Knowledge of God: A New Look at Theistic Arguments* (Oxford: Oxford University Press, 2010), 28.
33. *The Collected Works of John Stuart Mill*, ed. John M. Robson, vol. 9 (Toronto: University of Toronto Press, 1963–91), 183. See Clouser, *Myth*, 144, 336.
34. In philosophy, this is often dubbed the brain-in-a-vat problem: How do you know that you're not really just a brain in a vat that is being stimulated by electrical impulses administered by a mad scientist to make you *think* that you have a body and that you live in a real world of people and objects?
35. David Hume, *A Treatise of Human Nature* (CreateSpace Independent Publishing Platform, 2012), 37.
36. Ernst Mach, *The Analysis of Sensations*, in John T. Blackmore, *Ernst Mach: His Life, Work, and Influence* (Berkeley, CA: University of California Press, 1972), 327n14. See the discussion of Mach in Clouser, *Myth*, 149–50.
37. To read about the impact of empiricism and rationalism on art and literature, see *Saving Leonardo*, chaps. 5 and 6.
38. See Richard H. Popkin, *History of Skepticism: From Erasmus to Spinoza* (Los Angeles: University of California Press, 1979); Harris Harbison, "The

Struggle for Power," chap. 3 in *The Age of Reformation* (Ithaca, NY: Cornell University Press, 1955).

39. Jeffrey Stout writes, "The crisis of authority made an absolutely radical break with the past seem necessary. Methodical doubt therefore sought complete transcendence of situation. It tried to make the inheritance of tradition irrelevant, to start over again from scratch, to escape history." *The Flight from Authority: Religion, Morality, and the Quest for Autonomy* (Notre Dame, IN: University of Notre Dame Press, 1981), 67. See *Total Truth*, appendix 1, "How American Politics Became Secularized"; *Saving Leonardo*, 137–40; and my lecture, "The Creation Myth of Modern Political Philosophy" (respondent to the Sixth Annual Kuyper Lecture, Washington, DC, 2000).

40. Cited in Michael Oakeshott, *Rationalism in Politics and Other Essays* (Indianapolis: Liberty, 1991), 15. See also A. W. Ward and A. R. Waller, ed., *The Cambridge History of English Literature* (New York: G. P. Putnam's Sons, 1919), 329.

41. Bacon is known for his pithy saying that a little philosophy inclines a person toward atheism, but "depth in philosophy" brings a person to religion. *The Essays of Lord Bacon* (London: Longman and Green, 1875), 64. Descartes, a devout Catholic, was so certain that God had revealed to him the irrefutable logic of the cogito that he vowed to make a pilgrimage to the shrine of Our Lady of Loreto in Italy, which he did. See *Total Truth*, 39.

42. Robert C. Solomon, *Continental Philosophy Since 1750: The Rise and Fall of the Self* (Oxford: Oxford University Press, 1988), 5–6. In one sense, of course, everyone must start with conscious experience—with what we know. But there is a difference between an experiential starting point and a logical starting point. We all begin the search for knowledge from within our own experience. But a logical starting point refers to what we consider most ultimate and foundational—the basis for explaining all of reality.

43. Karl Popper, *Conjectures and Refutations: The Growth of Scientific Knowledge* (New York: Routledge, 1963, 2002), 20–21 (italics in original).

44. Randall adds, "Their ideal was still a *system of revelation*, though they had abandoned the *method* of revelation." John Herman Randall, *The Making of the Modern Mind* (New York: Columbia University Press, 1940), 267 (italics in original). Similarly, Stout writes that the early modern philosophers who gave up traditional authority "merely substituted one class of privileged claims for another.... They were not disputing the epistemological necessity for *something like* sacred authority." Stout, *Flight*, 75 (italics in original).

45. Cited in *Saving Leonardo*, 95. For additional background, see *Soul of Science*, 139–40.

46. Alvin Plantinga, "How to Be an Anti-Realist," *Proceedings and Addresses of the American Philosophical Association* 56, no. 1. (September 1982): 48. For more on Kant's Copernican revolution, see *Saving Leonardo*, 181–83.
47. Immanuel Kant, *Philosophical Correspondence 1759–1799*, ed. and trans. Arnulf Zweig (Chicago: University of Chicago Press, 1967), 254.
48. Anthony Kenny, *An Illustrated Brief History of Western Philosophy* (Malden, MA: Blackwell, 2006), 377. As Dooyeweerd says, empiricism leads to "epistemological nihilism." *New Critique*, II:332.
49. Alan Jacobs, "Psychological Criticism: From the Imagination to Freud and Beyond," *Contemporary Literary Theory: A Christian Appraisal*, ed. Clarence Walhout and Leland Ryken (Grand Rapids, MI: Eerdmans, 1991), 99, 119, 98.
50. Ernest Lee Tuveson, *The Imagination as a Means of Grace* (Los Angeles: University of California Press, 1960). For sources for the quotations in this section by Coleridge, Herder, Wordsworth, and Yeats, see *Saving Leonardo*, 183.
51. Herman Dooyeweerd, *A New Critique of Theoretical Thought* (Ontario: Paideia, 1984), I:46.
52. B. R. Hergenhahn and Tracy B. Henley, *An Introduction to the History of Psychology* (Belmont, CA: Wadsworth, 2014). Every educational theory is likewise the application of a philosophy: See George R. Knight, *Philosophy and Education: An Introduction in Christian Perspective*, 4th ed. (Berrien Springs, MI: Andrews University Press, 2006). Even mathematics, supposedly the most objective field of all, has been deeply influenced by philosophy: See *Soul of Science*, chapters 6 and 7; Clouser, *Myth,* chap. 7, and "Is There a Christian View of Everything, from Soup to Nuts?," *Pro Rege*, June 2003.
53. C. S. Lewis, *The Screwtape Letters* (New York: HarperCollins, 1996), 2.
54. From the 1984 edition.
55. See Richard Bauckham, *Jesus and the Eyewitnesses: The Gospels as Eyewitness Testimony* (Grand Rapids, MI: Wm. B. Eerdmans, 2008). The Old Testament likewise contains events that were public and open to empirical investigation. In Moses's confrontation with the Egyptian priests, his ability to perform miracles was the authentication that he spoke for the true God. In Elijah's confrontation with the prophets of Baal on Mount Carmel, a highly visible miracle constituted evidence for the true God. See also 2 Peter 1:16–17; Acts 1:21–22; 3:15; 4:20.

    In our own day, empirical evidence continues to provide some of the most persuasive arguments for God's existence, such as the argument from design, arguments for the historicity of the Resurrection, and evidence for the reliability of Scripture from archaeology and the study of ancient manuscripts.

56. The first quotation comes from Justin Martyr, *Second Apology*, chap. 13. His actual wording was "Whatever things were rightly [or truly] said among all men, are the property of us Christians." Yet the fullest truth, he said, is found in Christ. The second quotation was coined by Jerome. See E. K. Rand, *The Founders of the Middle Ages* (New York: Dover, 1928), 64.

PRINCIPLE #2: How Nietzsche Wins

1. The following account is from a personal interview with John R. Erickson, along with an article by Erickson titled "Mugged by Nietzsche" (unpublished) and his memoir, *Small Town Author* (unpublished).
2. Leil Lowndes, "How Neuroscience Can Help Us Find True Love," *Wall Street Journal*, February 14, 2013. See also Helen Fisher, *Why We Love: The Nature and Chemistry of Romantic Love* (New York: Henry Holt, 2004).
3. Richard Rorty, "Thugs and Theorists," *Political Theory* 15, no. 4 (November 1987): 564–80.
4. They also stole more than participants who were assigned to a neutral condition with control statements such as "Sugar cane and sugar beets are grown in 112 countries." Jesse Bering, "Scientists Say Free Will Probably Doesn't Exist, but Urge: 'Don't Stop Believing!,'" *Scientific American*, April 6, 2010. Another experiment is reported here: "The commonest criticism of reductionism—the idea that we are a pack of neurons and nothing more—is that it will lead us to treat our fellow human beings as if ... well, as if they were a pack of neurons and nothing more. John Evans, a sociologist of religion at University of California, San Diego, has set about testing whether the criticism has any merit.... He asked a series of questions designed to elicit their attitudes toward behavior. Were they in favor of allowing experiments on prisoners without their consent? Selling human organs for profit? Allowing suicide in the case of people who wanted to save money? Intervening to stop genocide? Sure enough, he found that people who hold the reductionist view—who deny the special status of the human species in nature, who believe behavior is determined by physical processes alone—were far more likely to agree with the maltreatment of humans. Evans can't draw conclusions about whether determinism causes those views. But the correlations between them, he said, are unmistakable." Andrew Ferguson, "The End of Neurononsense," *Weekly Standard*, October 20, 2014.
5. Note that these findings actually offer evidence that free will is real. If I encouraged you to believe that you could fly, you still could not fly. Believing that you have the ability does not make it any easier to fly. By contrast, as these studies show, believing that you have the power not to cheat *does* make

it easier not to cheat. Conclusion: Belief makes no difference when you do not have the power to do something anyway. But it does seem to help you exercise a power that you do have. Thus these findings support the reality of free will. (Thanks to Angus Menuge for this insight.)

6. Francis Schaeffer analyzed the history of Western thought as a series of dualisms. See *Escape from Reason* and *The God Who Is There*. Schaeffer's analysis was inspired by Herman Dooyeweerd, who identified three major dualisms in Western thought: the Greek matter/form dualism, the medieval nature/grace dualism, and the Kantian nature/freedom dualism. (Kant defined nature in terms of a mechanistic, material machine while defining freedom in terms of moral norms that humans choose for themselves.) See Dooyeweerd's *Roots* and *New Critique*, passim, and *In the Twilight of Western Thought*, chapter 2 (Grand Rapids, MI: Paideia, 2012).

7. Nicholas Humphrey, "Consciousness: The Achilles Heel of Darwinism? Thank God, Not Quite," in John Brockman, ed., *Intelligent Thought: Science versus the Intelligent Design Movement* (New York: Vintage, 2006), 58.

8. Colin McGinn, "All Machine and No Ghost?," *New Statesman*, February 20, 2012.

9. Francis Crick, *The Astonishing Hypothesis: The Scientific Search for the Soul* (New York: Touchstone, 1994), 3; and Daniel Wegner, *The Illusion of Conscious Will* (Cambridge, MA: Massachusetts Institute of Technology, 2002). The interview with Wegner is by Dennis Overbye, "Free Will: Now You Have It, Now You Don't," *New York Times*, January 2, 2007.

10. Steven Pinker, *How the Mind Works* (New York: Norton, 2009), 24, passim; and "Is Science Killing the Soul?," Edge.org, April 7, 1999, www.edge.org/3rd_culture/dawkins_pinker/debate_p9.html.

11. The example is from Teed Rockwell, *Dictionary of Philosophy of Mind*, s.v. "Eliminativism," http://philosophy.uwaterloo.ca/MindDict/eliminativism.html.

12. Emergentism can be thought of as the opposite of reductionism. Instead of claiming that higher-level phenomena can be reduced to lower, less complex levels, it claims that lower levels can give rise to higher, more complex levels. Scientists identify two types of emergence: weak and strong. An example of weak emergence is water. At room temperature, hydrogen and oxygen are gases. If that were all we knew, we might not expect the product of their chemical reaction to be a liquid (H_2O). Yet the result is completely determined by ordinary laws of nature acting on the initial physical conditions.

By contrast, strong emergence is a claim regarding phenomena that cannot be explained by the ordinary laws of nature, including mind and consciousness. As philosopher David Chalmers writes, strong emergence would involve "phenomena whose existence is not deducible from the facts about the exact distribution of particles and fields throughout space and time (along with the laws of physics)." This "suggests that new fundamental laws of nature are needed to explain these phenomena." However, no one has discovered those "new fundamental laws of nature." ("Strong and Weak Emergence," http://consc.net/papers/emergence.pdf.)

13. See J. P. Moreland, "The Argument from Consciousness," in *Debating Christian Theism*, ed. J. P. Moreland, Chad Meister, and Khaldoun A. Sweis (Oxford: Oxford University Press, 2013); and Douglas Groothuis, *Christian Apologetics: A Comprehensive Case for Biblical Faith* (Downers Grove, IL: InterVarsity, 2011), chap. 17.

14. Evan Fales, "Naturalism and Physicalism," in *The Cambridge Companion to Atheism*, ed. Michael Martin (Cambridge: Cambridge University Press, 2007), 120. Fales tries to solve the mystery by simply decreeing that consciousness *must* be natural: "Since such processes evidently *have* produced consciousness, ... consciousness is evidently a natural phenomenon" (italics in original).

15. Colin McGinn, *The Problem of Consciousness* (Oxford: Basil Blackwell, 1993), 45; and *The Mysterious Flame* (New York: Basic Books, 1999), 13–14.

16. Mark A. Bedau, "Weak Emergence," in J. Tomberlin, ed., *Philosophical Perspectives: Mind, Causation, and World*, vol. 11 (Malden, MA: Blackwell, 1997), 375–99. For a detailed discussion of various versions of emergentism, see J. P. Moreland, *Consciousness and the Existence of God: A Theistic Argument* (New York: Routledge, 2008).

17. Galen Strawson, *Real Materialism and Other Essays* (Oxford: Oxford University Press, 2008), 6 (italics added).

18. Thomas Reid, *An Inquiry into the Human Mind*, ed. Derek R. Brookes (University Park, PA: Pennsylvania State University Press, 1997), 215–16.

19. Philosopher Jaegwon Kim spells out the problem. On one hand, many philosophers who embrace materialism or naturalism deny that consciousness is real, holding that mental states are fictions. On the other hand, Kim writes, "contrast this lowly status of consciousness in science and metaphysics with its lofty standing in moral philosophy and value theory." When philosophers discuss what is intrinsically good, what makes life worth living, most of the time the answer is happiness or love or significance or even simply pleasure. But these are all aspects of conscious experience. "It is an ironic fact that the felt qualities of conscious experience, perhaps the only things that ultimately matter to us, are often relegated in the rest of philosophy to the status of 'secondary qualities,' in the shadowy zone between the real and the unreal, or

even jettisoned outright." *Physicalism, or Something Near Enough* (Princeton, NJ: Princeton University Press, 2005), 10–12.

20. Arthur Schopenhauer, *The World as Will and Representation*, vol. 2 (Mineola, NY: Dover, 1958), 13. Similarly, Catholic novelist Walker Percy writes, "The Self since the time of Descartes has been stranded, split off from everything else in the Cosmos, a mind which professes to understand bodies and galaxies but is … marooned in the Cosmos, with which it has no connection." *Lost in the Cosmos: The Last Self-Help Book* (New York: Picador, 1983), 47.

21. Ian Barbour, *Issues in Science and Religion* (New York: Harper & Row, 1972), 67. For more detail on Romantic pantheism, see M. H. Abrams, *Natural Supernaturalism: Tradition and Revolution in Romantic Literature* (New York: Norton, 1971). Seeking scientific support, the Romantics fastened on the work of Leibniz, a contemporary of Newton. For Newton, everything was composed of atoms, tiny hard particles of matter. For Leibniz, everything was composed of monads, tiny centers of spiritual or mental energy. The term *monad* derives from neo-Platonism, and Leibniz employed it to say that nature is a vast organism imbued with a soul or spirit. "The whole nature of bodies is not exhausted in their extension, that is to say their size, figure, and motion," he wrote. Instead "we must recognize something that corresponds to soul." See *Soul of Science*, 84.

22. Randall, *Making*, 419.

23. Walker Percy, *Signposts in a Strange Land* (New York: Picador, 1991), 278. The former pope John Paul II was a trained philosopher. "He points out that the radical separation between the two great currents in the Western philosophy [realism versus idealism] originated in the absolutization of one of the two aspects of human experience"—either outer experience (absolutizing the material world) or inner experience (absolutizing consciousness). Jaroslaw Kupczak, *Destined for Liberty: The Human Person in the Philosophy of Karol Wojtyla/John Paul II* (Washington, DC: Catholic University Press, 2000), 76. See also Rocco Buttiglione, *Karol Wojtyla: The Thought of the Man Who Became Pope John Paul II* (Grand Rapids, MI: Eerdmans, 1997), 68, 72. For a fuller discussion, see my chapter "*Evangelium Vitae*: John Paul II Meets Francis Schaeffer," in *The Legacy of John Paul II: An Evangelical Assessment*, ed. Tim Perry (Downers Grove, IL: InterVarsity, 2007).

24. For a fuller treatment of these two philosophical traditions, tracing their expression through the arts and humanities, see *Saving Leonardo*, chapters 4–9.

25. Arthur Lovejoy writes that a conspicuous aspect of Romanticism was "a revival of the direct influence of neo-Platonism." *The Great Chain of Being: A Study of the History of an Idea* (Cambridge, MA: Harvard University Press, 1964),

297. Paul Reiff writes: "If we are to speak of anyone at all as a 'key' to the understanding of Romanticism, one man only merits the term, Plotinus," the founder of neo-Platonism. Cited in Abrams, *Natural Supernaturalism*, 428.

Neo-Platonism, which was founded by Plotinus, was the main avenue by which Greek thought influenced Christian theologians all through the Middle Ages (including Augustine, Origen, Pseudo-Dionysius, John Scotus Eriugena, and the Cappadocian fathers). Even other philosophies, such as Aristotelianism, were typically read through a neo-Platonic lens, until additional writings by Aristotle became available in the form of Arabic translations (twelfth century) and Greek copies from Constantinople (thirteenth century). Neo-Platonism was also at the heart of the Platonic Academy in Florence that did so much to launch the Renaissance. At the birth of modern science, neo-Platonism influenced such diverse figures as the early chemists Paracelsus and Van Helmont, the astronomers Copernicus and Kepler, and both Leibniz and Newton. (See *Soul of Science*.) So it is not surprising that the Romantics still considered neo-Platonism a viable intellectual option.

Lloyd Gerson summarizes: "In the writings of the Italian Renaissance philosophers, the 15th and 16th century humanists John Colet, Erasmus of Rotterdam, and Thomas More, the 17th century Cambridge Platonists, and German idealists, especially Hegel, Plotinus' thought was the (sometimes unacknowledged) basis for opposition to the competing and increasingly influential tradition of scientific philosophy." "Plotinus," *The Stanford Encyclopedia of Philosophy*, ed. Edward N. Zalta, summer 2014 ed., http://plato.stanford.edu/archives/sum2014/entries/plotinus/.

26. See Lovejoy, *Great Chain*. Technically, neo-Platonism is not pantheism but pan*en*theism. What's the difference? In classic pantheism, the material world is an illusion. In panentheism, the material world is real, but it is a concretization of the divine and imbued with spirit. As an illustration, think of a cascading fountain in the winter when the top layer freezes: the ice is a solidification of the water itself, while the water continues to run below the surface.

How does a non-personal essence create the world, since it cannot consciously will or act? Neo-Platonism answered that the One was so "full" of being that it simply emanated other beings automatically, from necessity, without any conscious intention, like the sun radiating light or a fountain gushing water. Some of these ideas were in the cultural air when the New Testament was being written, especially in early Gnosticism. In Colossians, when Paul speaks of "thrones, dominions, principalities, and authorities," he is referring to the spiritual entities (the higher levels) that emanate from the One out of the "fullness" of its being. In fact, "fullness" was a technical term (Greek: *pleroma*) describing the sum of these higher spiritual levels. So when Paul says that in Christ, "the whole fullness [*pleroma*] of the Deity dwells bodily" (Col. 2:9), he is appropriating that term from Gnosticism, proclaiming that the full range of divinity does not reside in multiple spiritual emanations from the One but rather resides solely in Christ.

27. Eagleton, *Culture and the Death of God*, 96; and Ralph Waldo Emerson, "The Over-Soul," in *Self-Reliance, the Over-Soul and Other Essays* (Claremont, CA: Coyote Canyon, 2010), 56.

28. See Lovejoy, "The Temporalizing of the Chain of Being," chap. 9 in *Great Chain*, 242–87. The escalator metaphor comes from Mary Midgley, *Evolution as a Religion* (London: Methuen, 1985). In chapters that I contributed to *How Now Shall We Live?*, I show that several modern ideologies are variations on the Escalator Myth, notably Marxism and the many liberation movements that are its offshoots. See chapters 23–29.

29. Friedrich Nietzsche, *The Gay Science*, bk. 5, aphorism 357. Because of Hegel, many Europeans were already thinking in evolutionary categories prior to Darwin, and were just waiting for someone to fill in the biological piece of the puzzle; and Georg Wilhelm Friedrich Hegel, *Philosophy Works (3 in 1)*, trans. William Wallace (Oxford: Clarendon Press, 1894), *Philosophy of Right*, sect. 342. The word "Mind" is the German word *Geist*, which is a cognate of the English *ghost* and is translated as either spirit or mind.

30. John Herman Randall, *Philosophy after Darwin* (New York: Columbia University Press, 1977), 8.

31. "Just as the classical science ideal absolutized the aspect of mechanical motion, so the historical science ideal absolutized the aspect of history." Dooyeweerd, *Roots*, 183. For precursors to Hegel's historicism, see John Passmore, "Progress by Natural Development: From Joachim to Marx," chap. 11 in *The Perfectibility of Man*, 3rd ed. (Indianapolis: Liberty Fund, 2000).

32. Passmore, *Perfectibility*, 369.

33. Steven Pinker, "The Trouble with Harvard," *New Republic*, September 4, 2014.

34. Solomon, *Continental Philosophy*, 57. For example, for Hegel, morality was not "a matter of rational principle, but part of a life of shared values, feelings, and customs" within particular communities (70); and Hegel, *Philosophy of Right*, sect. 344. "Hegel's idealism saw history as an unfolding of absolute spirit through a necessary dialectical process, and this framework left little room for the freedom or significance of individual persons." Thomas Williams and Jan

Olof Bengtsson, "Personalism," in *The Stanford Encyclopedia of Philosophy*, November 12, 2009.

35. The secularization of Hegel's thought was partly the work of his followers, several of whom were materialists, such as Marx. (Marx liked to say he "turned Hegel on his head" by proposing that material forces shape ideas instead of the other way around.) Others progressively cut the Absolute Mind down to size. First it became human consciousness: phenomenology absolutized human consciousness (Husserl spoke of consciousness as "absolute being"). Then it became individual consciousness: existentialism treated the self as absolute (Merleau-Ponty wrote, "I am the absolute source"). See Solomon, *Continental Philosophy*, chaps. 9, 12.

36. For Hegel, "the individual can only exist as such within particular communities. The individual is a product rather than a premise of the social order." David West, *Introduction to Continental Philosophy*, 2nd ed. (Malden, MA: Polity, 2010), 40. For Hegel, even Christianity is merely a mythological way of talking about the evolution of consciousness: the real meaning of the narrative sequence of Jesus's death and resurrection "is that it represents the negation of individual consciousness (death) and … the passage of individual consciousness into the general spirit which is the community-consciousness (resurrection)." Hans Frei, *The Eclipse of Biblical Narrative: A Study in Eighteenth and Nineteenth Century Hermeneutics* (New Haven, CT: Yale University Press, 1974), 318.

37. Dooyeweerd, *Roots*, 179. Dooyeweerd was writing before the rise of postmodernism, but he saw clearly that the same trends were already evident in Romanticism: "Romanticism replaced the gospel of the autonomous and nondescript *individual* [from the Enlightenment] with the gospel of the autonomous and individual *community*." *Roots*, 178–79.

38. Stanley J. Grenz, *A Primer on Postmodernism* (Grand Rapids, MI: Eerdmans, 199), 8. Terry Eagleton says in postmodernism, culture "operates as a kind of absolute." He adds that in this regard postmodernism shows itself to be a successor to idealism, for whom "culture is a secular name for God." *Culture and the Death of God*, 191, 77. Rorty, "Solidarity or Objectivity," in *Objectivity, Relativism, and Truth* (Cambridge: Cambridge University Press, 1991), 23.

39. Don Cupitt, *Is Nothing Sacred? The Non-Realist Philosophy of Religion* (New York: Fordham University Press, 2002), 34. According to J. P. Moreland and William Lane Craig, the two main streams of Western thought are "Enlightenment naturalism and postmodern anti-realism." *Philosophical*

Foundations for a Christian Worldview (Downers Grove, IL: InterVarsity, 2003), 1.
40. Nietzsche, "On Truth and Lie in a Nonmoral Sense" (1873), *Philosophy and Truth: Selections from Nietzsche's Notebooks of the Early 1870s*, trans. and ed. Daniel Breazeale (Atlantic Highlands, NJ: Humanities, 1979), 88.
41. Philosopher Roger Scruton writes, "The assumption that there is first-person certainty, which provides a starting-point for philosophical enquiry ... has finally been removed from the centre of philosophy." *A Short History of Modern Philosophy: From Descartes to Wittgenstein* (New York: Taylor & Francis, 2002), 292. See the discussion by Roger Lundin, "Interpreting Orphans: Hermeneutics in the Cartesian Tradition," in *The Promise of Hermeneutics* (Grand Rapids, MI: Eerdmans, 1999).
42. Katherine Timpf, "Harvard Plans 'Mandatory Power and Privilege Training' for Poli-Sci Students," *Campus Reform*, May 13, 2014.
43. "One would hope that any young person precocious enough to read Kant would have the ability to recognize historical context and to approach critically statements that sound unethical, bigoted, or scientifically dated to her modern ears. One would hope parents buying Kant for their kids could do the same without chiding from publishers." Josh Jones, "Publisher Places a Politically Correct Warning Label on Kant's *Critiques*," *Open Culture*, March 20, 2014.
44. Dallas Willard, "What Significance Has 'Postmodernism' for Christian Faith?," www.dwillard.org/articles/artview.asp?artID=70.
45. Richard Rorty, *Contingency, Irony, and Solidarity* (Cambridge: University of Cambridge Press, 1999), 22.
46. Rorty, *Contingency*, 21.
47. Dooyeweerd, *New Critique*, I:58, n. 3.
48. Nirvana "is a state beyond and without desire or personal, individual existence." "Despite the considerable differences between these two religions (and the pluralism within each religion), the enlightenment experience of both nirvana (Buddhism) and moksha (Hinduism) requires the negation of individuality, personality." The individual's personal existence "is dissolved into the impersonal divine." Groothuis, *Christian Apologetics*, 385–87.
49. Ivan Granger, "Li Po—The Birds Have Vanished into the Sky [the title of the poem]," *Poetry Chaikhana Blog*, March 18, 2013, www.poetry-chaikhana.com/blog/2013/03/18/li-po-the-birds-have-vanished-into-the-sky-2/. Granger continues: "The 'mountain' is finally recognized as your true Self, your only self, eternal." That is, your individual self dissolves into the pantheistic deity.

50. Lit-sen Chang, *Zen-Existentialism: The Spiritual Decline of the West*, cited in Walter R. Martin, *Kingdom of the Cults*, revised, updated, and expanded (Grand Rapids, MI: Bethany, 2003), 309.
51. A philosophical movement called personalism pointed out that both Enlightenment and Romantic worldviews dehumanize the person: "Personalism ... emerged only in the context of the broad critical reaction against what can be called the various *impersonalistic* philosophies which came to dominate the Enlightenment and Romanticism in the form of rationalistic and romantic forms of pantheism and idealism.... Personalism thus arose as a reaction to impersonalist modes of thought which were perceived as dehumanizing. The impersonal dynamic of modern pantheism and monism in both their rationalistic and Romantic forms underlie many of the modern philosophies that personalism turns against, idealistic as well as materialistic.... Certain distinctive characteristics can be discerned that generally hold for personalism as such. These include an insistence on the radical difference between persons and non-persons and on the irreducibility of the person to impersonal spiritual or material factors." Williams and Bengtsson, "Personalism," *Stanford Encyclopedia of Philosophy*.
52. In the Koran, the angel Gabriel is portrayed as claiming that he is "confirming previous scriptures" (Sura 2:97). Those previous scriptures are the Hebrew Torah, the psalms of David, and the Gospels of Jesus Christ (Sura 4:163; 5:44–48).
53. Sura 4:171.
54. Seyyed Hossein Nasr, *Islam: Religion, History, and Civilization* (New York: HarperOne, 2002), 3, 6; and see *Total Truth*, appendix 2. The French philosopher René Guénon (who converted to Islam) argued that the concept of the divine as a non-personal Absolute is a common core uniting neo-Platonism in the West, Hinduism in the East, and Islam in the Middle East. See Parviz Morewedge, ed., *Neoplatonism and Islamic Thought: Studies in Neoplatonism, Ancient and Modern*, vol. 5 (New York: SUNY, 1992); Majid Fakhry, *Al-Farabi, Founder of Islamic Neoplatonism: His Life, Works, and Influence* (Rockport, MA: Oneworld, 2002); and Ian Richard Netton, *Muslim Neoplatonists: An Introduction to the Thought of the Brethren of Purity* (Ikhwan Al-Safa') (New York: Routledge, 2003). A helpful summary by Netton can be found in "Neoplatonism in Islamic Philosophy," Islamic Philosophy Online, www.muslimphilosophy.com/ip/rep/H003.htm.
55. C. S. Lewis, *Mere Christianity* (New York: HarperOne, 2000), 174. The same intellectual weakness besets unitarianism and deism, which have functioned

for many people in the West as temporary stepping-stones from full-blooded Christian theism to outright atheism.

56. Robert Letham, *The Holy Trinity: In Scripture, History, Theology, and Worship* (Phillipsburg, NJ: P&R, 2004), 444–46. Similarly, theologian Peter Toon writes, "the Christian understanding of personhood flows from the Christian doctrine of the three persons who are God.... If God is simply a monad then he cannot be or know personality. To be personal, otherness must be present together with oneness, the one must be in relation to others." *Our Triune God: A Biblical Portrayal of the Trinity* (Vancouver: Regent College Publishing, 1996), 241. See also Anthony Thiselton, "Further Issues on 'Interpreting God': Christology and Trinity," chap. 23 in *Interpreting God and the Postmodern Self: On Meaning, Manipulation and Promise* (Grand Rapids, MI: Eerdmans, 1995). Henri Blocher comments: "If God is caught in the perennial dipolarity of the One and the Many ... he cannot claim real independence, absolute primacy and ultimacy. He is defined by reference to another principle than himself, he is included together with the plural world in a broader totality—he is *correlative*. In order for God to be autarkic, self-sufficient, 'self-contained' ... he needs to be the foundation of both unity and diversity, holding them eternally within himself." That is, God must be a Trinity. "Immanence and Transcendence in Trinitarian Theology," in *The Trinity in a Pluralistic Age: Theological Essays on Culture and Religion*, ed. Kevin J. Vanhoozer (Grand Rapids, MI: Eerdmans, 1997).
57. Williams and Bengtsson, "Personalism," *The Stanford Encyclopedia of Philosophy*. This explains why many Islamic philosophers have adopted neo-Platonism, with its non-personal concept of the divine One.
58. Udo W. Middelmann, "The Islamization of Christianity," Francis A. Schaeffer Foundation, www.theschaefferfoundation.com/footnote4_1.php.
59. "No one thought it important for children to understand the meaning of the Koran—after all, even adults, even great theologians, understand only snippets of its total significance. What was important in education was memorization of the Word of God. The actual, spoken words should be learned by rote such that their recitation becomes second nature.... It was always recognized that the most essential formal learning was memorization of the divine Word, whether or not its meaning was understood." Sachiko Murata and William C. Chittick, *The Vision of Islam* (New York: Paragon, 1994), xvi, xviii, xxxvii–xxxviii.

Sociologists tell us that a focus on mechanical ritual is typical of religions that have a less personal conception of God. These religions tend to stress precision in the performance of rituals and sacred formulas. (Placating the gods

becomes similar to magic, which involves manipulating forces, not interacting with a personal being.) By contrast, religions with a highly personal God worry less about ritual precision because a personal Being with knowledge of the worshipper's inner intentions will respond to impromptu supplication and spontaneous prayer. See Stark, "Why Gods Should Matter in Social Science." See also Justin L. Barrett, "Smart Gods, Dumb Gods, and the Role of Social Cognition in Structuring Ritual Intuitions," *Journal of Cognition and Culture* 2, no. 3 (2002): 183–93.
60. Richard Schweder, "Atheists Agonistes," *New York Times*, November 27, 2006.
61. See Stéphane Courtois, Nicolas Werth, Jean-Louis Panné, Andrzej Paczkowski, Karei Bartošek, Jean-Louis Margolin, *The Black Book of Communism* (Cambridge, MA: Harvard University Press, 1990). See also R. J. Rummel, *Death by Government* (New Brunswick, NJ: Transaction 1996); and Jung Chang and John Halliday, *Mao: The Unknown Story* (New York: Random, 2006).
62. Gilson, *God and Philosophy*, 136.
63. Aldous Huxley, *The Devils of Loudun* (New York: HarperCollins, 1952), 123.
64. John Gray, "The Atheist Delusion," *Guardian*, March 14, 2008.
65. Those enslaving yokes may even be demonic. The Bible often treats idols as fronts for spiritual forces. In the Old Testament, the psalmist says the Israelites sacrificed their children to demons: "They sacrificed their sons and their daughters to the demons ... whom they sacrificed to the idols of Canaan" (Ps. 106:37–38). In the New Testament, Paul warns that pagan sacrifices are "offered to demons" (1 Cor. 10:19–20). What does this frankly supernatural language mean? Many philosophies treat evil as merely the privation of good, as dark is the absence of light. But those who have suffered under oppressive, bloodthirsty regimes often speak of experiencing evil as an active malevolent force. The Romanian pastor Richard Wurmbrand, who was imprisoned by Communist authorities for fourteen years, reports that the guards would torture inmates, screaming, "We are the devil." Richard Wurmbrand, *Tortured for Christ* (Basingstoke, UK: Marshall Pickering, 1983), 35. In short, good and evil are not merely abstractions. Just as goodness has its source in a personal Being, so, too, much of the evil in the world is connected to powerful personal beings.
66. Isaiah Berlin, *The Roots of Romanticism* (Princeton, NJ: Princeton University Press, 1999), 3.
67. G. K. Chesterton, *Orthodoxy* (Rockville, MD: Serenity, 2009), 54.
68. Johnson, *First Step*, 33.
69. See Hays, *Echoes*, 38.

PRINCIPLE #3: Secular Leaps of Faith

1. Deborah Mitchell blogs under the name TXBlue08. "Why I Raise My Children without God," CNN iReport, January 14, 2013, http://ireport.cnn.com/docs/DOC-910282. Mitchell is the author of *Growing Up Godless: A Parent's Guide to Raising Kids without Religion* (New York: Sterling Ethos, 2014).
2. The CNN author's argument from evil fails logically as well. If my argument against God is that the world has too much injustice and cruelty, that presumes a moral standard by which we can identify injustice. But a purely material universe does not generate moral standards. It tells us only what *is*, not what *ought* to be. Therefore materialism does not give a basis for saying the world is unjust. Moreover, if humans are nothing but complex biochemical machines, then to call their actions evil is illogical. Machines do not have the capacity to choose good or evil, nor do we hold them accountable for their actions.
3. The phenomenologist Edmund Husserl is the origin of most of these phrases. See Richard Kearney, *Modern Movements in European Philosophy*, 2nd ed. (Manchester: Manchester University Press, 1994), 13–15. Dooyeweerd uses the terms "pre-theoretical experience" or "naïve experience." This is not the same as "naïve realism" or a copy theory of knowledge; rather it refers to a "pre-theoretical datum, corresponding with the integral structure" of experience. *Twilight*, 14. Reformed epistemology gets at roughly the same idea in its concept of "properly basic" knowledge—what we know immediately, not as a result of logical inference or discursive argument. Reformed epistemology was in turn inspired in part by Thomas Reid's common-sense realism. Reid argued that there are truths "which the constitution of our nature leads us to believe, and of which we are under a necessity to take for granted in the common concerns of life, without being able to give a reason for them." *Inquiry*, 33. For more detail, see *Total Truth*, chapter 11.
4. Dooyeweerd, *New Critique*, I:83 and *Twilight*, 14. Through pre-theoretical, concrete experience, humans have access to "undeniable states of affairs" in the "cosmic order"—undeniable because they "force themselves on everybody." And "it is the common task of all philosophical schools and trends to account for them." *New Critique*, I:115–16; II:71–73.
5. J. P. Moreland, *The Recalcitrant* Imago Dei: *Human Persons and the Failure of Naturalism* (London: SCM, 2009), 4.
6. Alvin Plantinga writes: "Some people think of John Calvin himself, that *fons et origo* of Reformedom, as accepting determinism. But this is far from clear. Calvin did, of course, endorse predestination: but determinism doesn't follow. Predestination, as Calvin thinks of it, has to do with salvation; it implies

nothing about whether I can freely choose to take a walk this afternoon." Plantinga, "Bait and Switch," *Books and Culture*, January/February 2013. Likewise with Luther. He wrote *The Bondage of the Will* arguing that humans can do nothing to contribute to their salvation. But he did not mean we cannot choose what to wear today.

7. Sean Carroll, "Free Will Is as Real as Baseball," *Cosmic Variance* (blog), *Discover*, July 13, 2011, http://blogs.discovermagazine.com/cosmicvariance/2011/07/13/free-will-is-as-real-as-baseball/#.VHSb7r4ULyx. Carroll is paraphrasing from John Searle, *Freedom and Neurobiology: Reflections on Free Will, Language, and Political Power* (New York: Columbia University Press, 2004), 11.

8. C. S. Lewis invokes the same argument in his argument from morality in *Mere Christianity*. His argument rests on the fact that humans unavoidably, irresistibly make moral judgments—and therefore we had better find a philosophy that accounts for this behavior: In his words, "We are *forced* to believe in a real Right and Wrong" (7). Morality is among those "things we are *bound* to think" (14). "Whether we like it or not, we believe in the Law of Nature" (8). "We *can not get rid of* the idea [of the Moral Law], and most of the things we say and think about men would be reduced to nonsense if we did" (20). For example, if we do not acknowledge a real right and wrong, then "all the things we said about the war [i.e., the evils of Nazism] were nonsense" (5). (All italics added.) Lewis's argument (though he does not explicitly state it) is that there are certain ways of thinking and acting that are intrinsic to human nature, and that this bedrock human experience should inform our philosophy. In short, we had better find a philosophy that makes sense of how humans unavoidably behave.

9. Cited in Saul Smilansky, *Free Will and Illusion* (Oxford: Clarendon, 2000), 169. Fundamentally, the power of choice is simply the ability to redirect the course of events. The entire world of human artifacts—cities and buildings, technology and computers, books and films—gives eloquent testimony to the human ability to use natural forces to create things that nature acting on its own would not create. Dooyeweerd notes that the concept of human culture "means essentially the free forming of matter." *Roots*, 21.

10. Smilansky, *Free Will*, 284, 166.

11. Rick Lewis says, "The nature of consciousness is a philosophical problem which has come to centre stage mainly in the last few years." "Consciousness," *Philosophy Now*, July/August 2014. A third position, which is common among philosophers, is called compatibilism. It accepts determinism while claiming that humans nevertheless have free will. What kind of free will? The compatibilists' definition of a free action is one that is driven from within by

one's own desires and reasons, with no external constraints. But those internal desires and reasons are themselves held to be determined. All of our mental states arise from other states outside of our minds and thus outside of our control. This is not what ordinary people mean by free will. For example, in discussing the compatibilism of Daniel Dennett, Michael Norwitz writes, "There is a sacrifice in that he loses track of our ordinary, common-sense views of what mind and free will are. Dennett claims he is doing ordinary language philosophy but I suspect he has been an academic so long he has forgotten what 'ordinary people' are concerned with." Dennett's compatibilism comes "at the cost of not really approaching what we worry about when we worry whether we have free will, or responsibility." "Free Will and Determinism," *Philosophy Now*, July/August 2014.

12. Galen Strawson, interview by Tamler Sommers, "You Cannot Make Yourself the Way You Are," *The Believer*, March 2003. By "radical free will," Strawson says he means the ordinary use of the term: "I mean what nearly everyone means. Almost all human beings believe that they are free to choose what to do in such a way that they can be truly, genuinely responsible for their actions in the strongest possible sense ... and so ultimately morally responsible when moral matters are at issue."

13. Galen Strawson, "On Free Will," *Richmond Journal of Philosophy* 4, summer, 2003.

14. Johnson, *First Step*, 11.

15. Edward Slingerland, *What Science Offers the Humanities: Integrating Body and Culture* (New York: Cambridge University Press, 2008), 6, 218, 289–95 (italics in original).

16. The term *dualism* is sometimes used to describe the biblical teaching of body and soul, but the crucial difference is that in the biblical view these two things are complementary, not contradictory. In Paul's words, the body is the "outer self," the means by which we interact with the material world, while the soul is the "inner self" (2 Cor. 4:16). At death humans do undergo a temporary splitting of body and soul, but that's why death is called "the last enemy" (1 Cor. 15:26)—because it separates what God intended to be unified. And in the new creation, they will be reunified, eternally.

17. Julie Reuben, *The Making of the Modern University: Intellectual Transformation and the Marginalization of Morality* (Chicago: University of Chicago Press, 1996), 17.

18. Marvin Minsky, *The Society of Mind* (New York: Simon & Schuster, 1986), 307 (italics in original in the first part of the quote, italics added in the last part of the quote).

19. An "existentialist leap" means holding that, on rational grounds, life has no meaning, yet asserting—without rational grounds—that it does. "On the one hand, the existentialist seeks to remain true to his original vision of the meaninglessness and futility of everything ...; on the other hand, his stark personal reality is that he finds himself unable to appropriate the truth of nihilism existentially, unable to affirm it as his personal truth,...: it is at this point that he clutches at the artifice of commitment, hoping to save himself from nihilistic despair by a desperate leap towards a faith that will restore purpose and meaning to his shattered world." R. W. K. Paterson, *The Nihilistic Egoist: Max Stirner* (Oxford: 1971), 238.
20. Smilansky, *Free Will*, 6, 145, 187. For what Smilansky means by "morally necessary," see 7–8, 153, 158, 278. We "cannot live" on the basis of determinism: 154, 170, 246, 296. We "ought" to foster the illusion of free will: 187–88 (italics in original).
21. The review is by Tom Clark, "The Viability of Naturalism," Naturalism. org, www.naturalism.org/resource.htm. Similarly, Matt Ridley writes in his bestselling book *Genome*, "Full responsibility for one's actions is a necessary fiction without which the law would flounder, but it is a fiction all the same." *Genome: The Autobiography of a Species in 23 Chapters* (New York: HarperCollins, 1999), 309.
22. Richard Dawkins, "Let's All Stop Beating Basil's Car," *Edge,* http://edge.org/response-detail/11416.
23. Dawkins's remarks were made in a question-and-answer session at a bookstore in the Washington, DC, area. They are described in *Saving Leonardo*, 152–53. Of course, even the concept of a machine malfunctioning has no place in Dawkins's materialist philosophy because it implies teleology—that something has a purpose or standard that it is failing to meet. Dawkins is trying to avoid the moral language of good and evil, but the concept of malfunctioning requires some standard of right functioning.
24. Cited in Walter Isaacson, *Einstein: His Life and Universe* (New York: Simon & Schuster, 2007), 391, 392 (italics added). What Einstein overlooked is that even his scientific work depends on free will: "If Einstein did not have free will in some meaningful sense, then he could not have been responsible for the theory of relativity—it would have been a product of lower level processes but not of an intelligent mind choosing between possible options." George Ellis, interview by John Horgan, "Physicist George Ellis Knocks Physicists for Knocking Philosophy, Falsification, Free Will," *Scientific American*, July 22, 2014.

25. Immanuel Kant, *Critique of Pure Reason*, trans. Werner Pluhar (Indianapolis: Hackett, 1996), A811. Additional examples of Kant's *as if* reasoning: In theology, we can never know whether God is the cause of the world, but we can view "all objects *as if* they drew their origin from such an archetype" (*CPR* A673/B701). In cosmology, we can never know whether the world has a beginning or an end, but we are able to function "*as if* it had an absolute beginning, through an intelligible cause" (*CPR* A685/B713). We cannot know whether there is a Creator, but we can "consider every connection in the world according to principles of a systematic unity, hence *as if* they had all arisen from one single all-encompassing being, as supreme and all-sufficient cause" (*CPR* A686/B714). In psychology, we can not explain the soul or the self, but we can "connect all the appearances, all the actions and receptivity of our mind, *as if* the mind were a simple substance which persists with personal identity" (*CPR* A672/B700). See Howard Caygill, ed., *A Kant Dictionary*, s.v. "As-if" (Oxford: Blackwell Publishing, 1995), 86. Kant labels *as if* reasoning "regulative principles."

Chemist and philosopher Michael Polanyi denounces *as if* thinking as a form of prevarication—the "modern intellectual prevarication first systematized by Kant in his regulative principles." He explains why: "Knowledge that we hold to be true and also vital to us, is made light of, because we cannot account for its acceptance in terms of a critical philosophy. We then feel entitled to continue using that knowledge, even while flattering our sense of intellectual superiority by disparaging it. And we actually go on, firmly relying on this despised knowledge to guide and lend meaning to our more exact enquiries, while pretending that these alone come up to our standards of scientific stringency." *Personal Knowledge: Towards a Post-Critical Philosophy* (New York: Routledge, 1962), 354.

26. Eric Baum, *What Is Thought?* (Cambridge, MA: MIT Press, 2004), 433–34. "Not even wrong" is a phrase coined by physicist Wolfgang Pauli. Once when reading a paper by a young physicist, Pauli remarked, "This paper is so bad, it's not even wrong." In other words, it is not even in the ballpark of possible answers.
27. McGinn, "All Machine and No Ghost?" (italics added).
28. Francis Schaeffer, *The God Who Is There*, in the *Francis A. Schaeffer Trilogy* (Wheaton, IL: Crossway, 1990), sect. 2, chaps. 2–4.
29. Slingerland, *What Science Offers*, 255, 289. Slingerland, "Mind-Body Dualism and the Two Cultures," in *Creating Consilience: Integrating the Sciences and the Humanities*, ed. Edward Slingerland and Mark Collard (Oxford: Oxford University Press, 2012), 83, 84.
30. Rodney Brooks, *Flesh and Machines: How Robots Will Change Us* (New York: Pantheon, 2002), 174. For more on the themes in this chapter,

see *Total Truth*, study guide edition, and my article "Intelligent Design and the Defense of Reason," in *Darwin's Nemesis: Phillip Johnson and the Intelligent Design Movement*, ed. William A. Dembski (Downers Grove, IL: InterVarsity, 2006).

31. On the way idols lead to dualisms and disharmonies, Dooyeweerd says, "The cosmic order passes an internal judgment on the theoretical absolutizations" of idol-based philosophies. "The Divine world-order ... avenges itself on every deification" of the temporal creation. *New Critique*, II:334, 363. That is, as God gives people up to their idols, their philosophies increasingly contradict the cosmic order itself.
32. G. K. Chesterton, *The Everlasting Man* (San Francisco: Ignatius, 1993), 143, 141. Yet, ironically, these same secularists claim to be "free thinkers." Nonsense, Chesterton responds. We must vigorously protest when secularists "close all the doors of the cosmic prison on us with a clang of eternal iron, tell us that our emancipation is a dream and our dungeon a necessity; and then calmly turn round and tell us they have a freer thought."
33. Schopenhauer, *The World as Will and Representation*, 421.
34. Rorty, *Contingency, Irony, and Solidarity*, 3.
35. Dallas Willard, "Truth in the Fire," presented at the C. S. Lewis Centennial, Oxford, July 21, 1998, www.dwillard.org/articles/artview.asp?artID=68.
36. Rorty, *Contingency*, 5.
37. William Lane Craig, "God Is Not Dead Yet," *Christianity Today*, July 3, 2008 (italics in original). Explaining this dichotomy between facts and values is a major theme of *Total Truth*.
38. Ernest Gellner, *Legitimation of Belief* (New York: Cambridge University Press, 1974), 193–95.
39. "Seeking Christian Interiority: An Interview with Louis Dupré," *Christian Century*, July 16–23, 1997.
40. Derek Parfit, "Reductionism and Personal Identity," in *Philosophy of Mind: Classical and Contemporary Readings*, ed. David J. Chalmers (Oxford: Oxford University Press, 2002), 661 (italics added).
41. Karsten Harries, "The Theory of Double Truth Revisited," in *Politics of Practical Reasoning: Integrating Action, Discourse, and Argument*, ed. Ricca Edmondson and Karlheinz Hülser (Lanham, MD: Lexington, 2012), (italics added).
42. Francis Crick, interview by Roger Highfield, "Do Our Genes Reveal the Hand of God?," *Telegraph*, March 20, 2003.
43. Francis Schaeffer called this strategy "taking the roof off"—removing the shield of denial that people erect to protect themselves from the dangerous

and unsettling implications of their own worldview. See *The God Who Is There*, 140–42.

PRINCIPLE #4: Why Worldviews Commit Suicide

1. The following account is from a personal interview with Michael Egnor, along with an article by Egnor, "A Neurosurgeon, Not a Darwinist," *Forbes*, Feb 5, 2009.
2. Michael Ruse, *Darwin and Design: Does Evolution Have a Purpose?* (Harvard: Harvard University Press, 2003), 268 (italics added).
3. Darwin proposed the mechanism of variation plus natural selection as the means by which material forces might mimic the effects of design. As historian Neal C. Gillespie writes, Darwin hoped to show "how blind and gradual adaptation could counterfeit the apparently purposeful design" of living things, which on the surface seem so obviously "a function of mind." *Charles Darwin and the Problem of Creation* (Chicago: University of Chicago Press, 1979), 83–85.
4. Czesław Miłosz, "The Discreet Charm of Nihilism," *New York Review of Books*, November 19, 1998 (italics added).
5. Greg Koukl, "Suicide: Views That Self-Destruct," chap. 7 in *Tactics: A Game Plan for Discussing Your Christian Convictions* (Grand Rapids, MI: Zondervan, 2009).
6. There is one exception. Idol analysis tells us that every worldview deifies one part of creation and denigrates the rest. Therefore the single worldview that does not denigrate reason is the one that deifies it—namely, rationalism. Of course, rationalism has other problems (e.g., it cannot explain where reason comes from), but it does not self-destruct because it does not reduce reason to something less than reason.
7. Logical positivism is also called verificationism. Craig continues: "Its downfall meant that philosophers were free once again to tackle traditional problems of philosophy that verificationism had suppressed. Accompanying this resurgence of interest in traditional philosophical questions came something altogether unanticipated: a renaissance of Christian philosophy." Craig, "God Is Not Dead Yet."
8. See the section on Marxism in *Total Truth*, 134–37, and my chapter on Marxism in *How Now Shall We Live?*, chapter 24. Though Marxism has been discredited in the economic realm, neo-Marxist knockoffs are endemic, especially on the university campus. Radical liberation movements of many stripes apply Marxist categories of analysis.

9. "The origin of the holy lie is the *will to power*." Friedrich Nietzsche, *The Will to Power*, trans. Walter Kaufmann and R. J. Hollingdale (New York: Random House, 1967), sect. 142.
10. Skinner rejected the very concept of "conscious intelligence" on the grounds that "evolutionary theorists ... have never shown how a *nonphysical* variation could arise to be selected by *physical* contingencies of survival." "Can Psychology Be a Science of Mind?," *American Psychologist*, November 1990 (italics added).
11. Paul Ricoeur dubbed the triumvirate of Marx, Nietzsche, and Freud "the masters of suspicion," and the phrase has stuck. These thinkers practiced a "hermeneutics of suspicion" that treated ordinary statements as expressions of "false consciousness." See *Freud and Philosophy*, trans. D. Savage (New Haven, CT: Yale University Press, 1970).
12. Alvin Plantinga, *Where the Conflict Really Lies: Science, Religion, and Naturalism* (Oxford: Oxford University Press, 2011), 271.
13. Slingerland, *What Science Offers*, 257.
14. C. S. Lewis, "Is Theology Poetry?" in *The Weight of Glory* (New York: HarperCollins, 1976), 139; and *Case for Christianity*, 32. See also Victor Reppert, *C. S. Lewis's Dangerous Idea: In Defense of the Argument from Reason* (Downers Grove, IL: InterVarsity, 2003); and Stewart Goetz and Charles Taliaferro, "The Argument from Reason," appendix in *Naturalism* (Grand Rapids, MI: Eerdmans, 2008).
15. Lewis, *Miracles*, 36. The phrase "angelic observer" is from Charles Taylor, *Hegel* (Cambridge: Cambridge University Press, 1975), 564.
16. John Gray, *Straw Dogs: Thoughts on Humans and Other Animals* (New York: Farrar, Straus, and Giroux, 2003), 26. Similarly, Edward O. Wilson writes, "All that has been learned empirically about evolution ... suggests that the brain is a machine assembled not to understand itself, but to survive." *Consilience: The Unity of Knowledge* (New York: Vintage, 1998), 105. More recently, John Gray has finally recognized the problem: "If the human mind has evolved in obedience to the imperatives of survival, what reason is there for thinking that it can acquire knowledge of reality, when all that is required in order to reproduce the species is that its errors and illusions are not fatal? A purely naturalistic philosophy cannot account for the knowledge that we believe we possess." Gray even quotes Arthur Balfour, whom C. S. Lewis credited as a source of his own critique of naturalism as self-defeating. "Balfour's solution was that naturalism is self-defeating: humans can gain access to the truth only because the human mind has been shaped by a divine mind. Similar arguments can be found in a number of contemporary philosophers, most notably Alvin Plantinga. Again,

one does not need to accept Balfour's theistic solution to see the force of his argument. A rigorously naturalistic account of the human mind entails a much more skeptical view of human knowledge than is commonly acknowledged." "The Closed Mind of Richard Dawkins," *New Republic*, October 2, 2014.

17. Francis Crick, *The Astonishing Hypothesis: The Scientific Search for the Soul* (New York: Touchstone, 1994), 262. This idea is not new. Back in 1903, philosopher F. C. S. Schiller wrote that human reason is nothing but "a weapon in the struggle for existence and a means of achieving adaptation." "The Ethical Basis of Metaphysics," in *Humanism: Philosophical Essays* (London: Macmillan, 1903), 7–8.

18. Baum, *What Is Thought?*, 226. Steven Pinker, *How the Mind Works* (New York: W. W. Norton, 1997), 305. Again, this idea is not new. Philosopher Charles Peirce wrote, "It is probably of more advantage to the animal to have his mind filled with pleasing and encouraging visions, independently of their truth; and thus ... natural selection might occasion a fallacious tendency of thought." "The Fixation of Belief," *Popular Science Monthly* 12 (November 1877).

19. Leon Wieseltier, "The God Genome," *New York Times*, February 19, 2006. Alvin Plantinga writes that "what evolution guarantees is (at most) that we behave in certain ways—in such ways as to promote survival.... It does not guarantee mostly true or verisimilitudinous beliefs." *Warrant and Proper Function* (New York: Oxford University Press, 1993), 218. Philosopher Roger Trigg writes: For evolution, "it does not matter if a belief is true or false, as long as it is useful, from a genetic point of view." *Philosophy Matters* (Oxford: Blackwell, 2002), 83. See also Angus Menuge, *Agents under Fire: Materialism and the Rationality of Science* (New York: Rowman & Littlefield, 2004).

20. Thomas Nagel, *The Last Word* (Oxford: Oxford University Press, 1997), 135–36 (italics in original). See also Douglas Groothuis, "Thomas Nagel's 'Last Word' on the Metaphysics and Rationality of Morality," *Philosophia Christi* (series 2) 1, no. 1 (1999).

21. The context of Darwin's remarks clearly reveals the selective nature of his skepticism. From a personal letter: "Nevertheless you have expressed my inward conviction, though far more vividly and clearly than I could have done, that the Universe is not the result of chance. But then with me the horrid doubt always arises whether the convictions of man's mind, which has been developed from the mind of the lower animals, are of any value or at all trustworthy. Would any one trust in the convictions of a monkey's mind, if there are any convictions in such a mind?" C. R. Darwin to William Graham, July 3, 1881, Darwin Correspondence Project, www.darwinproject.ac.uk/letter/entry-13230.

From Darwin's *Autobiography*: "Another source of conviction in the existence of God, connected with the reason and not with the feelings, impresses me as having much more weight. This follows from the extreme difficulty or rather impossibility of conceiving this immense and wonderful universe, including man with his capacity of looking far backwards and far into futurity, as the result of blind chance or necessity. When thus reflecting I feel compelled to look to a First Cause having an intelligent mind in some degree analogous to that of man; and I deserve to be called a Theist.

"This conclusion was strong in my mind about the time, as far as I can remember, when I wrote the *Origin of Species*; and it is since that time that it has very gradually with many fluctuations become weaker. But then arises the doubt—can the mind of man, which has, as I fully believe, been developed from a mind as low as that possessed by the lowest animal, be trusted when it draws such grand conclusions? May not these be the result of the connection between cause and effect which strikes us as a necessary one, but probably depends merely on inherited experience? Nor must we overlook the probability of the constant inculcation in a belief in God on the minds of children producing so strong and perhaps an inherited effect on their brains not yet fully developed, that it would be as difficult for them to throw off their belief in God, as for a monkey to throw off its instinctive fear and hatred of a snake." "Recollections of the Development of My Mind and Character," Darwin Online, http://darwin-online.org.uk/content/frameset?pageseq=116&itemID=CUL-DAR26.1-121&viewtype=side.

22. Stephen Jay Gould, *Ever Since Darwin: Reflections in Natural History* (New York: Norton, 1977), 12–13.
23. Kenan Malik, "In Defense of Human Agency," in *Consciousness, Genetics, and Society* (Stockholm: Ax:son Johnson Foundation, 2002).
24. Cited in Victoria Gill, "Big Bang: Is There Room for God?," *BBC News*, October 19, 2012. C. S. Lewis described evolution as a "Great Myth" and said, "The Myth asks me to believe that reason is simply the unforeseen and unintended by-product of a mindless process at one stage of its endless and aimless becoming. The content of the Myth thus knocks from under me the only ground on which I could possibly believe the Myth to be true. If my own mind is a product of the irrational—if what seem my clearest reasonings are only the way in which a creature conditioned as I am is bound to feel—how shall I trust my mind when it tells me about Evolution?" "The Funeral of a Great Myth" in *Christian Reflections* (Grand Rapids: MI: Eerdmans, 1967), 89. Elsewhere Lewis writes that those who describe human thought "as an evolutionary phenomenon"

always have to make "a tacit exception" for their own thinking—at least, at the moment they are making the claim. *Miracles*, 36.
25. Phillip E. Johnson writes, "We still see the reductionists complacently describing religious belief either as a meme or as the product of a 'God module' in the brain without realizing that they are sawing off the limb on which they themselves are sitting. If unthinking matter causes the thoughts the materialists *don't* like, then what causes the thoughts they *do* like?" *The Wedge of Truth: Splitting the Foundations of Naturalism* (Downers Grove, IL: InterVarsity, 2000), 149 (italics in original).
26. Richard Cohen, "Alternative Interpretations of the History of Science," in *The Validation of Scientific Theories*, ed. Philipp G. Frank (Boston: Beacon, 1956), 227; and Christopher Kaiser, *Creation and the History of Science* (Grand Rapids, MI: Eerdmans, 1991), 10.
27. Here's how Johannes Kepler expressed the idea: The same God who founded the world according to mathematical norms "also has endowed man with a mind which can comprehend these norms." Why? "God wanted us to perceive [those mathematical laws] when he created us in his image in order that we may take part in his own thoughts." Cited in Robert Nadeau, *Readings from the New Book on Nature* (Amherst, MA: University of Massachusetts Press, 1981), 28. See also *The Soul of Science*, chapters 3 and 6.
28. Eugene Wigner, "The Unreasonable Effectiveness of Mathematics in the Natural Sciences," in *Mathematics: People, Problems, Results*, vol. 3, ed. Douglas M. Campbell and John C. Higgins (Belmont, CA: Wadsworth International, Brigham Young University, 1984). See my discussion in *The Soul of Science*, 159.
29. Morris Kline, *Mathematics: The Loss of Certainty* (New York: Oxford University Press, 1980), 35.
30. The quote is from Hans-Georg Gadamer, *Truth and Method* (New York: Continuum, 1989), 459. Similarly, Roland Barthes writes, "For us, too, it is language which speaks, not the author." "The Death of the Author," in *Image—Music—Text* (New York: Hill and Wang, 1977). Martin Heidegger writes, "Language speaks.... Man acts as though he were the shaper and master of language, while in fact language remains the master of man." *Poetry, Language, Thought* (New York: HarperCollins, 1971), 194, 144. It was Wittgenstein who redefined questions in philosophy as questions in language, "transforming Kantian questions about reason into ones about language." Solomon, *Continental Philosophy*, 148.
31. Jean-François Lyotard, *The Postmodern Condition: A Report on Knowledge*, trans. Geoff Bennington and Brian Massumi (Minneapolis: University of

Minnesota Press, 1984, originally published in French in 1979), 36. Lyotard borrows the term *language games* from Wittgenstein and says: "What he means by this term is that each of the various categories of utterance can be defined in terms of rules specifying their properties and the uses to which they can be put—in exactly the same way as the game of chess is defined by a set of rules determining the properties of each of the pieces, in other words, the proper way to move them" (10).

32. The charge that postmodernism "gets caught in a performative contradiction" was made by Jürgen Habermas, *Philosophical Discourse of Modernity* (Cambridge, MA: MIT Press, 1987).
33. Barthes, "Death of the Author"; and Derrida, cited in Solomon, *Continental Philosophy*, 201.
34. Barthes, "Death of the Author."
35. Alan Jacobs, "Deconstruction," *Contemporary Literary Theory: A Christian Appraisal*, ed. Clarence Walhout and Leland Ryken (Grand Rapids, MI: Eerdmans, 1991), 192.
36. In the words of literature professor John Ellis, "the race-gender-class scholar's commitment to his or her truths ... is as rigid as anything could be." *Literature Lost: Social Agendas and the Corruption of the Humanities* (New Haven, CT: Yale University Press, 1997), 191.
37. Mark C. Taylor, *Disfiguring: Art, Architecture, Religion* (Chicago: University of Chicago Press, 1992), 261. Taylor is referring specifically to architecture, though he generalizes to the other arts: "Inasmuch as the author-architect is made in the image of God, the death of God implies the disappearance of the author-architect."
38. Lyotard, *Postmodern Condition*, 81–82; and Eagleton, *Culture and the Death of God*, 192.
39. West, *Introduction to Continental Philosophy*, 40.
40. Jacobs, "Deconstruction," 190.
41. *Chronicle of Higher Education*, June 27, 1997, B13, cited in Carl P. E. Springer, "The Hermeneutics of Innocence: Literary Criticism from a Christian Perspective," Leadership U, www.leaderu.com/aip/docs/springer.html#ref6.
42. Frank Lentricchia, "Last Will and Testament of an Ex-Literary Critic," *Lingua Franca*, September/October 1996, 64.
43. Bruno Latour, "Why Has Critique Run Out of Steam? From Matters of Fact to Matters of Concern," *Critical Inquiry*, 30 (winter 2004): 237–39. As Latour remarks, "One thing is clear, not one of us readers would like to see *our* own most cherished objects treated in this way" (italics in original).

44. Karen Swallow Prior, "'Empathetically Correct' Is the New Politically Correct," *Atlantic*, May 23, 2014.
45. Jean-Paul Sartre, "Existentialism and Humanism," in *The Modern Tradition: Backgrounds of Modern Literature*, ed. Richard Ellmann and Charles Fiedelson Jr. (New York: Oxford University Press, 1965), 828.
46. Michel Foucault, "Nietzsche, Genealogy, History," in *The Foucault Reader*, ed. Paul Rabinow (New York, Pantheon, 1984), 81, 94. The philosopher is John McCumber, *Time and Philosophy: A History of Continental Thought* (Montreal: McGill-Queen's University Press, 2011), 323. An example might be helpful: Judith Butler illustrates both the dissolution of the subject and the idea that the self is a product of group identity. She argues that a person has no core gender identity—in fact, there is no "stable subject" to "have" a gender. Instead gender is continually being created through the very acts by which it is expressed: "Gender is always a doing.... There is no gender identity behind the expressions of gender; ... identity is performatively constituted by the very 'expressions' that are said to be its result." Moreover, "gender intersects with racial, class, ethnic, sexual, and regional modalities of discursively constituted identities." *Gender Trouble: Feminism and the Subversion of Identity* (New York: Routledge, 1990), 25, 3.
47. See *Total Truth*, 132–33, 138, and 408, n. 17.
48. From the 1984 edition.
49. The first part of the quote is from an interview with Slavoj Žižek in *The Believer*, July 2004. The second part of the quote is from Slavoj Žižek, *The Fragile Absolute, or Why Is the Christian Legacy Worth Fighting For?* (London: Verso, 2002), 129.
50. See Dennis Hollinger, "The Church as Apologetic: A Sociology of Knowledge Perspective," in *Christian Apologetics in a Postmodern World*, ed. Timothy R. Phillips and Dennis L. Okholm (Downers Grove, IL: InterVarsity, 1995), 183.
51. Francis Schaeffer, *The Mark of the Christian*, 2nd ed. (Downers Grove, IL: InterVarsity, 2006), passim.
52. Materialism's low view of the material world has powerful real-world implications for issues such as abortion and homosexuality. See *Saving Leonardo*, chapter 3, and "Transgender Politics vs. the Facts of Life," The Pearcey Report, www.pearceyreport.com/archives/2013/07/nancy_pearcey_transgender_politics_vs_facts_of_life.php.
53. Alvin Plantinga, *Warrant and Proper Function* (New York: Oxford University Press, 1993), esp. chap. 5, "Perception."
54. See *The Soul of Science*, chap. 1.

PRINCIPLE #5: Free-Loading Atheists

1. "Barna Survey Examines Changes in Worldview among Christians over the Past 13 Years," March 6, 2009, www.barna.org/barna-update/21-transformation/252-barna-survey-examines-changes-in-worldview-among-christians-over-the-past-13-years#.VC1nu_ldWSo. Only one question in the survey addresses a genuinely worldview issue: belief "that absolute moral truth exists."
2. Hume, *Inquiry*, 77. Hume consistently pits reason (philosophy) against nature ("instinct or natural impulse"), complaining that nature keeps us from following our thoughts to their logical conclusions. See *Treatise of Human Nature*, 101.
3. Johnson, *First Step*, 25. This section draws on a lecture of mine titled "Sexual Identity in a Secular Age," presented August 5, 2013, Houston Baptist University, Summer in the City lecture series.
4. Alexis de Tocqueville, *Democracy in America: Historical-Critical Edition of "De la démocratie en Amérique,"* vol. 3, ed. Eduardo Nolla, trans. James T. Schleifer (Indianapolis: Liberty Fund, 2010), 733.
5. Friedrich Nietzsche, *The Will to Power*, sect. 765.
6. Luc Ferry, *A Brief History of Thought: A Philosophical Guide to Living* (New York: Harper Perennial, 2011), 77 (italics in original).
7. Richard Rorty, "Moral Universalism and Economic Triage," presented at the Second UNESCO Philosophy Forum, Paris, 1996. Reprinted in *Diogenes*, vol. 44, issue 173 (1996).
8. Richard Rorty, "Postmodernist Bourgeois Liberalism," *Journal of Philosophy* 80, no. 10 (October 1983): 583–89. "Free-loading" is what I called "philosophical cheating" in *Total Truth*, 319–21. Francis Schaeffer calls it "intellectual 'cheating'" in "A Review of A Review," *The Bible Today*, October, 1948, 7–9.

  Robert Kraynak, professor of political science, notes that the number of people who are free-loading is increasing: "What is so strange about our age is that demands for respecting human rights and human dignity are *increasing* even as the foundations for those demands are disappearing. In particular, beliefs in man as a creature made in the image of God ... are being replaced by a scientific materialism that undermines what is noble and special about man, and by doctrines of relativism that deny the objective morality required to undergird human dignity." "Justice without Foundations," *New Atlantis*, www.thenewatlantis.com/publications/justice-without-foundations. Kraynak adds: "Post-modern relativists like Rorty and Darwinians like Dennett and Pinker have commitments to social justice, understood as democracy, human rights, and respect for human dignity, that are completely inconsistent with their philosophical and scientific views. Darwinian evolution does not support democracy and human rights or the inherent dignity of the individual—if it supports any kind of moral code, it would be a code of the strong dominating the weak" (http://darwinianconservatism.blogspot.com/2012/01/kraynaks-nietzschean-attack-on.html).

9. A. R. Hall, *The Scientific Revolution, 1500–1800: The Formation of the Modern Scientific Attitude* (Boston: Beacon, 1954), 171–72. Moreover, the concept of laws in nature was not considered metaphorical, a mere figure of speech, but literally true. As historian John Randall explains, "Natural laws were regarded as real laws or commands, decrees of the Almighty, literally obeyed without a single act of rebellion." John Herman Randall, *The Making of the Modern Mind* (New York: Columbia University Press, 1940), 274. See also Stephen F. Mason, *A History of the Sciences*, originally published under the title *Main Currents of Scientific Thought* (New York: Collier Books, 1962), 173, 182.

10. Mary Midgley, "Does Science Make Belief in God Obsolete? Of Course Not," John Templeton Foundation, www.templeton.org/belief/.

11. Paul Davies, "Physics and the Mind of God: The Templeton Prize Address," *First Things* 55 (August/September 1995): 31–35.

12. Many people mistakenly think science arose only after the Enlightenment had liberated Europe from its former Christian influence—that science is therefore a product of secularism. Not so. Sociologist of religion Rodney Stark goes so far as to say, "The 'Enlightenment' [was] conceived initially as a propaganda ploy by militant atheists and humanists who attempted to claim credit for the rise of science." *For the Glory of God: How Monotheism Led to Reformations, Science, Witch-Hunts, and the End of Slavery* (Princeton, NJ: Princeton University Press, 2003), 123.

13. John Gray, *Straw Dogs* (Farrar, Straus and Giroux, 2007), xi–xii, xiii, 4, 49. Gray argues that the whole of Western liberalism is actually parasitic on Christianity. He maintains, for example, that liberalism's high view of the human person is derived directly from Christianity: "Liberal humanism inherits several key Christian beliefs—above all, the belief that humans are categorically different from all other animals." No other religion has given rise to the conviction that humans have a unique dignity. Think of it this way: If Darwin had announced his theory of evolution in India, China, or Japan, it would hardly have made a stir. "If—along with hundreds of millions of Hindus and Buddhists—you have never believed that humans differ from everything else in the natural world in having an immortal soul, you will find it hard to get worked up by a theory that shows how much we have in common with other animals." The West's high view of human dignity and

human rights is borrowed directly from Christianity. "The secular world-view is simply the Christian take on the world with God left out," Gray concludes. "Humanism is not an alternative to religious belief, but rather a degenerate and unwitting version of it." John Gray, "Exposing the Myth of Secularism," *Australian Financial Review*, January 3, 2003.

In another article, Gray writes, "The idea of free will that informs liberal notions of personal autonomy is Biblical in origin (think of the Genesis story). The belief that exercising free will is part of being human is a legacy of faith." Thus virtually every variety of atheism today "is a derivative of Christianity." Gray, "The Atheist Delusion," *Guardian*, March 14, 2008. To read more, see *Total Truth*, 320.

14. Thomas Nagel, *Mind and Cosmos: Why the Materialist Neo-Darwinian Conception of Nature Is Almost Certainly False* (Oxford: Oxford University Press, 2012), 48–52.
15. Nagel, *Mind and Cosmos*, 18–19. Nagel writes that we need an alternative view of the cosmos that makes "mind, meaning, and value as fundamental as matter and space-time in an account of what there is" (20). See also Thomas Nagel, "The Core of 'Mind and Cosmos,'" *New York Times*, August 18, 2013.
16. Nagel, *Mind and Cosmos*, 128. "Nagel was immediately set on and (symbolically) beaten to death by all the leading punks, bullies, and hangers-on of the philosophical underworld. Attacking Darwin is the sin against the Holy Ghost that pious scientists are taught never to forgive." David Gelernter, "The Closing of the Scientific Mind," *Commentary*, January 1, 2014.
17. Thomas Nagel, *The Last Word* (Oxford: Oxford University Press, 1997), 130–31. Nagel proposes that the same cosmic authority problem "is responsible for much of the scientism and reductionism of our time."
18. Nagel, *Mind and Cosmos*, 15. My goal is "not to offer an alternative" but merely to show why an alternative is needed (12). "All that can be done at this stage in the history of science is to argue for recognition of the problem, not to offer solutions" (33). Nagel hopes to find an explanation that involves some kind of teleology (purpose) immanent in the material cosmos, to avoid the need for a transcendent Purposer. He writes of his "ungrounded intellectual preference" for an immanent teleology, or what he calls a "naturalistic teleology." "My preference for an immanent natural explanation is congruent with my atheism" (12, 26, 93). He admits that he is not confident that the concept of "teleology without intention makes sense" (93), and his hunch is correct: it does not.

One philosophy that Nagel considers—but does not embrace—is the idea of a mind permeating the universe from within. This view is called panpsychism.

It is the neo-Platonic notion that everything is permeated by a rudimentary form of mind or consciousness. Panpsychism is being revived today especially among proponents of process thought and process theology. They argue that life and consciousness could not emerge from sheer matter. Therefore there must be some rudimentary form of life and consciousness even at the lowest levels of matter. Read this description by an adherent: "The type of panpsychism I find compelling is that developed into a comprehensive system by Alfred North Whitehead, Henri Bergson, Charles Hartshorne, David Ray Griffin, and many others during the 20th Century. It is growing in popularity, but still a minority view. The basic idea is that all components of the universe have at least some rudimentary type of consciousness or experience, which are just different words for subjectivity or awareness.... No modern panpsychist that I know of argues that a chair or a rock is conscious. Rather, the molecules that comprise the chair or rock presumably have a very rudimentary type of consciousness." Tam Hunt, "The C Word—Consciousness—and Emergence," *Santa Barbara Independent*, January 8, 2011. In the recent book *Consciousness and Its Place in Nature*, British philosopher Galen Strawson defends panpsychism, and it has also been supported by Australian philosopher David Chalmers and Oxford physicist Roger Penrose.
19. Raymond Tallis, *Aping Mankind: Neuromania, Darwinitis, and the Misrepresentation of Humanity* (Durham: Acumen, 2011), 212–13 (italics in original).
20. Tallis, *Aping Mankind*, 317. On neuroethics, Tallis is quoting Paula Churchland in *Neurophilosophy*. On neuroeconomics, see, for example, Dan Monk, "Nielson (NLSN) clients use neuroscience to craft better commercials," WPCO Cincinnati. Copyright 2013 Scripps Media.
21. Tallis, *Aping Mankind*, 332; 59–71 and chap. 8; and 348.
22. Emily Wax, "Thinking Man's Therapy," *Washington Post*, August 22, 2011.
23. Eagleton, *Culture and the Death of God*, 204.
24. Luc Ferry, *A Brief History of Thought: A Philosophical Guide to Living* (New York: Harper, 2011), 6.
25. Pierre Hadot, *Philosophy as a Way of Life* (Oxford: Blackwell, 1995), 103, 83.
26. Pierre Hadot, *Plotinus, or the Simplicity of Vision* (Chicago: University of Chicago Press, 1993, originally published in French in 1989), 75–76.
27. Alain de Botton, "Can Tolstoy Save Your Marriage?," *Wall Street Journal*, December 18, 2010; Samuel Muston, "Too Cool for Night School?," *Independent*, January 9, 2014. For a review of Botton's book, see Douglas Groothuis, "Religion for Atheists: A Nonbeliever's Guide to the Uses of Religion," *Denver Journal*, 16 (January 24, 2013).

28. André Comte-Sponville, *The Little Book of Atheist Spirituality*, trans. Nancy Huston (New York: Penguin, 2006).
29. "Britain's First Atheist Church," *Huffington Post UK*, July 1, 2013; and "Atheist 'Mega-churches' Take Root across US, World," *Newsmax*, November 10, 2013.
30. Wilfrid Sellars, *Science, Perception, and Reality* (Atascadero, CA: Ridgeview, 1991), 173; and Bertrand Russell, *Science and Religion* (Oxford: Oxford University Press, 1935), 235.
31. John Gray, "A Point of View: Can Religion Tell Us More Than Science?," *BBC News*, September 16, 2011.
32. Michael Bond, "Atheists Turn to Science during Times of Stress," *New Scientist*, June 7, 2013.
33. W. R. Thompson, "Introduction," in Charles Darwin, *Origin of Species* (New York: Dent, 1956), 12.
34. "Evolution, akin to religion, involves making certain a priori or metaphysical assumptions, which at some level cannot be proven empirically." Michael Ruse, "Nonliteralist Antievolution," AAAS Symposium: "The New Antievolutionism," February 13, 1993, Boston, www.leaderu.com/orgs/arn/orpages/or151/mr93tran.htm. Cf. Tom Woodward, "Ruse Gives Away the Store," http://simpleapologetics.com/tomwoodward.html.
35. The piece was composed by Gregory Brown. Watch a performance here: www.gregorywbrown.com/missa-charles-darwin/.
36. Stuart Kauffman, "Beyond Reductionism: Reinventing the Sacred," *Edge*, November 12, 2006. Kauffman goes on: "This God brings with it a sense of oneness, unity, with all of life, and our planet—it expands our consciousness and naturally seems to lead to an enhanced potential global ethic of wonder, awe, responsibility within the bounded limits of our capacity, for all of life and its home, the Earth, and beyond as we explore the Solar System.... Shall we use the God word? It is our choice. Mine is a tentative 'yes.' I want God to mean the vast ceaseless creativity of the only universe we know of, ours." Francis Schaeffer warned that undefined religious words like "God" can be used for their connotations to manipulate people emotionally. See *The God Who Is There* and *Escape from Reason*.
37. Views like Kauffman's are sometimes labeled religious naturalism. Examples of religious naturalism include Jerome A. Stone, *Religious Naturalism Today* (New York: State U. of New York Press, 2008); Chet Raymo, *When God Is Gone, Everything Is Holy: Making of a Religious Naturalist* (Notre Dame, IN: Sorin Books, 2008); Loyal Rue, *Religion Is Not about God* (Piscataway, NJ: Rutgers University Press, 2006).

38. Jeremy Rifkin, *Algeny* (New York: Viking, 1983), 188, 195, 244.
39. C. S. Lewis, *The Abolition of Man* (New York: HarperCollins, 1947), 29.
40. Richard Dawkins, *River Out of Eden: A Darwinian View of Life* (London: Orion, 1995), 155.
41. On solipsism, see Principle #1 in this book. Philosopher Stephen Thornton notes that much of modern philosophy would lead to solipsism, if followed out to its logical conclusion: "While no great philosopher has explicitly espoused solipsism, this can be attributed to the inconsistency of much philosophical reasoning. Many philosophers have failed to accept the logical consequences of their own most fundamental commitments and preconceptions. The foundations of solipsism lie at the heart of the view that the individual gets his own psychological concepts (thinking, willing, perceiving, and so forth.) from 'his own cases,' that is by abstraction from 'inner experience.'

    "This view, or some variant of it, has been held by a great many, if not the majority of philosophers since Descartes made the egocentric search for truth the primary goal of the critical study of the nature and limits of knowledge. In this sense, solipsism is implicit in many philosophies of knowledge and mind since Descartes and any theory of knowledge that adopts the Cartesian egocentric approach as its basic frame of reference is inherently solipsistic." "Solipsism and the Problem of Other Minds," *The Internet Encyclopedia of Philosophy*, www.iep.utm.edu/solipsis/.
42. Bertrand Russell, "A Free Man's Worship," 1903, in *Mysticism and Logic* (New York: Routledge, 1986).
43. From a debate between William B. Provine and Phillip E. Johnson at Stanford University, April 30, 1994, titled "Darwinism: Science or Naturalistic Philosophy?," www.cjas.org/~leng/provine.txt.
44. Lewis adds that the hunger for truth will "force you not to propound, but to *live through*, a sort of ontological proof" for God's existence. Lewis, *The Pilgrim's Regress: An Allegorical Apology for Christianity, Reason and Romanticism*, (Grand Rapids, MI: Eerdmans, 1981), 204–5 (italics added).
45. Bradley Wright, "Why Do Christians Leave the Faith? The Fundamental Importance of Apologetics," *Patheos*, November 17, 2011; "Why Do Christians Leave the Faith? The Problem of Responding Badly to Doubt," *Patheos*, December 1, 2011; and "Why Do Christians Leave the Faith? The Relative Unimportance of Non-Christians," *Patheos*, December 8, 2011. See also Larry Taunton, "Listening to Young Atheists," *Atlantic*, June 6, 2013.
46. Harper Lee, *To Kill a Mockingbird* (New York: Grand Central, 1960), 39.
47. Ravi Zacharias and R. S. B. Sawyer, *Walking from East to West* (Grand Rapids, MI: Zondervan, 2006), 36.

48. "What I Wish I'd Known before I Went to University," *Beyond Teachable Moments* (blog), June 25, 2014, http://beyondtm.wordpress.com/2014/06/25 /what-i-wish-id-known-before-i-went-to-university/?utm_content=bufferb7f07 &utm_medium=social&utm_source=twitter.com&utm_campaign=buffer.

PART 3—How Critical Thinking Saves Faith

1. Nancy Pearcey, "How Critical Thinking Saves Faith," *The Pearcey Report*, December 22, 2010. When *Christianity Today* published the article, the editors changed the title to "How to Respond to Doubt," www.christianitytoday.com/women /2010/december/nancy-pearcey-how-to-respond-to-doubt.html?paging=off.
2. G. K. Chesterton, *Heretics* (Radford, VA: Wilder, 2007 [1905]), 115.
3. For more detail, along with sources, for the art movements described in the following section, see *Saving Leonardo*, chapters 4–9.
4. These words are from a description of all-black paintings by Ad Reinhardt. Walter Smith, "Ad Reinhardt's Oriental Aesthetic," *Smithsonian Studies in American Art* 4, no. 3/4 (summer-autumn 1990). See also Jack Flam, "Ad Reinhardt's Black Paintings, the Void, and Chinese Painting," *Brooklyn Rail*, January 16, 2014.
5. Ravi Zacharias, *Can Man Live without God?* (Nashville: Thomas Nelson, 1994), 21.
6. Cited in Richard M. Gamble, *The War for Righteousness: Progressive Christianity, the Great War, and the Rise of the Messianic Nation* (Wilmington, DE: Intercollegiate Studies Institute, 2003), 30.
7. Gustavo Gutiérrez, "Two Theological Perspectives: Liberation Theology and Progressivist Theology," *The Emergent Gospel: Theology from the Developing World*, eds. Sergio Torres and Virginia Fabella (London: Geoffrey Chapman, 1978), *Papers from the Ecumenical Dialogue of Third World Theologians*, Dar es Salaam, Tanzania, August 5–12, 1976, 227–55, quote 241.
8. Elisabeth Schüssler Fiorenza, *Bread Not Stone: The Challenge of Feminist Biblical Interpretation* (Boston: Beacon, 1984), 145.
9. See William Hasker, "The Problem of Evil in Process Theism and Classical Free Will Theism," *Process Studies* 29, no. 2 (fall-winter 2000).
10. Myron Penner, *The End of Apologetics: Christian Witness in a Postmodern Context* (Grand Rapids, MI: Baker, 2013), 99. Penner does offer some qualifications: The fact that human knowledge is "finite, fallible, and contingent" does not mean that the gospel truths "are therefore *false* or *relative* in any absolute and final way" (120, italics in original). However, throughout the book, Penner endorses postmodern thinkers and concepts in an uncritical manner that makes it problematic to explain how (as he tentatively writes) "it may just be possible after all to speak about Christian truth" (40).

11. C. S. Lewis, "On Learning in Wartime," in *The Weight of Glory* (New York: Macmillan, 1980), 28.
12. Dallas Willard, "The Redemption of Reason" (speech, Biola University, La Mirada, CA, February 28, 1998), www.dwillard.org/articles/artview.asp?artID=118.
13. Allan Bloom, *The Closing of the American Mind* (New York: Touchstone, 1987), 58.
14. Lecrae, interviewed by Dustin Stout, "Lecrae on Engaging Culture for Jesus: #R12," ChurchMag, October 24, 2012, http://churchm.ag/r12-lecrae-engaging-culture/.
15. "Interview: Lecrae Talks about Going from 'Crazy Crae' to Christian Rapper," *Complex*, June 8, 2012.
16. Lecrae Moore, "Because Jesus Lives, We Engage Culture," Resurgence Conference, October 9–10, 2012, http://cdn.theresurgence.com/files/R12_Newsprint_web.pdf. For additional places where Lecrae quotes *Total Truth*, see the Liberty University Convocation, March 22, 2013, www.youtube.com/watch?v=aCVBUA8SMTs; Matt Perman, "Lecrae and the Doctrine of Vocation," *What's Best Next*, October 6, 2013, http://whatsbestnext.com/2013/10/lecrae-doctrine-vocation/.
17. Cited in Emma Green, "Lecrae: 'Christians Have Prostituted Art to Give Answers,'" *Atlantic*, October 6, 2014.
18. To read the context of the quotes in this section, see *Total Truth*, 35, 75–76, 83–84.
19. Cited in Andrew Greer, "Lecrae: Defying Gravity," *Today's Christian Music*, September 1, 2012.
20. Cited in Chad Bonham, "A Conversation with Christian Hip-Hop Artist Lecrae," Beliefnet, http://features.beliefnet.com/wholenotes/2012/06/a-conversation-with-christian-hip-hop-artist-lecrae.html#ixzz2IjfeLe91.
21. Lecrae, interview, "We Engage Culture for Jesus," Encouragements through the Word, March 4, 2013, http://encouragementsthroughtheword.wordpress.com/2013/03/04/we-engage-culture-for-jesus-an-interview-of-christian-artist-lecrae/.

APPENDIX

Romans 1:1–2:16

1 Paul, a servant of Christ Jesus, called to be an apostle, set apart for the gospel of God, 2 which he promised beforehand through his prophets in the holy Scriptures, 3 concerning his Son, who was descended from David according to the flesh 4 and was declared to be the Son of God in power according to the Spirit of holiness by his resurrection from the dead, Jesus Christ our Lord, 5 through whom we have received grace and apostleship to bring about the obedience of faith for the sake of his name among all the nations, 6 including you who are called to belong to Jesus Christ,

7 To all those in Rome who are loved by God and called to be saints:

Grace to you and peace from God our Father and the Lord Jesus Christ.

8 First, I thank my God through Jesus Christ for all of you, because your faith is proclaimed in all the world. 9 For God is my witness, whom I serve with my spirit in the gospel of his Son, that without ceasing I mention you 10 always in my prayers, asking

that somehow by God's will I may now at last succeed in coming to you. 11 For I long to see you, that I may impart to you some spiritual gift to strengthen you— 12 that is, that we may be mutually encouraged by each other's faith, both yours and mine. 13 I do not want you to be unaware, brothers, that I have often intended to come to you (but thus far have been prevented), in order that I may reap some harvest among you as well as among the rest of the Gentiles. 14 I am under obligation both to Greeks and to barbarians, both to the wise and to the foolish. 15 So I am eager to preach the gospel to you also who are in Rome.

16 For I am not ashamed of the gospel, for it is the power of God for salvation to everyone who believes, to the Jew first and also to the Greek. 17 For in it the righteousness of God is revealed from faith for faith, as it is written, "The righteous shall live by faith."

18 For the wrath of God is revealed from heaven against all ungodliness and unrighteousness of men, who by their unrighteousness suppress the truth. 19 For what can be known about God is plain to them, because God has shown it to them. 20 For his invisible attributes, namely, his eternal power and divine nature, have been clearly perceived, ever since the creation of the world, in the things that have been made. So they are without excuse. 21 For although they knew God, they did not honor him as God or give thanks to him, but they became futile in their thinking, and their foolish hearts were darkened. 22 Claiming to be wise, they became fools, 23 and exchanged the glory of the immortal God for images resembling mortal man and birds and animals and creeping things.

24 Therefore God gave them up in the lusts of their hearts to impurity, to the dishonoring of their bodies among themselves, 25 because they exchanged the truth about God for a lie and worshiped and served the creature rather than the Creator, who is blessed forever! Amen.

26 For this reason God gave them up to dishonorable passions. For their women exchanged natural relations for those that are contrary to nature; 27 and the men likewise gave up natural relations with women and were consumed with passion for one another, men committing shameless acts with men and receiving in themselves the due penalty for their error.

28 And since they did not see fit to acknowledge God, God gave them up to a debased mind to do what ought not to be done. 29 They were filled with all manner of unrighteousness, evil, covetousness, malice. They are full of envy, murder, strife, deceit, maliciousness. They are gossips, 30 slanderers, haters of God, insolent, haughty, boastful, inventors of evil, disobedient to parents, 31 foolish, faithless, heartless, ruthless. 32 Though they know God's righteous decree that those who practice such things deserve to die, they not only do them but give approval to those who practice them.

1 Therefore you have no excuse, O man, every one of you who judges. For in passing judgment on another you condemn yourself, because you, the judge, practice the very same things. 2 We know that the judgment of God rightly falls on those who practice such things. 3 Do you suppose, O man—you who judge those who practice such

things and yet do them yourself—that you will escape the judgment of God? 4 Or do you presume on the riches of his kindness and forbearance and patience, not knowing that God's kindness is meant to lead you to repentance? 5 But because of your hard and impenitent heart you are storing up wrath for yourself on the day of wrath when God's righteous judgment will be revealed.

6 He will render to each one according to his works: 7 to those who by patience in well-doing seek for glory and honor and immortality, he will give eternal life; 8 but for those who are self-seeking and do not obey the truth, but obey unrighteousness, there will be wrath and fury. 9 There will be tribulation and distress for every human being who does evil, the Jew first and also the Greek, 10 but glory and honor and peace for everyone who does good, the Jew first and also the Greek. 11 For God shows no partiality.

12 For all who have sinned without the law will also perish without the law, and all who have sinned under the law will be judged by the law. 13 For it is not the hearers of the law who are righteous before God, but the doers of the law who will be justified. 14 For when Gentiles, who do not have the law, by nature do what the law requires, they are a law to themselves, even though they do not have the law. 15 They show that the work of the law is written on their hearts, while their conscience also bears witness, and their conflicting thoughts accuse or even excuse them 16 on that day when, according to my gospel, God judges the secrets of men by Christ Jesus.

ACKNOWLEDGMENTS

The parents of a college freshman were close to tears. Their sweet-natured daughter had signed up for classes at a local Christian college. But after only one semester, Alexandra (not her real name) was just a hair's-breadth from turning her back on her entire Christian upbringing.

In class after class, the professors had presented the latest secular theories, lightly baptizing them by assuring students that God was somehow behind it all. What stuck in Alexandra's mind, however, was the secular view of the world communicated by the theories. Although she lived at home with her parents, she quickly became estranged from them. When they invited her to discuss the secular theories she was learning, she angrily let them know she considered them unqualified to respond to what her professors were teaching in the classroom. After all, *they* had PhDs; *they* were the experts.

Fortunately, this young woman signed up for a course that my husband, Rick, and I were co-teaching. There she discovered that Christianity does have the intellectual resources to answer the challenges posed by secular theories. It is more than capable of holding its own in the intellectual marketplace. I dedicate this book to "Alexandra" and to all the other young people who are struggling, as I once did, to learn how to challenge the idols of our day.

It is an honor to acknowledge the friends, family members, and colleagues who gave of their time and expertise to read *Finding Truth* in manuscript form and to offer incisive insights on the text: Jonas Erne, Douglas Groothuis, Ron Kubsch, Angus Menuge, J. P. Moreland, David Naugle, Roderich Nolte, Dorothy Randolph, June Randolph, Dieter Pearcey, Michael Pearcey, Jenna Wichterman, Albert Wolters.

In addition, I want to thank my students who worked through earlier drafts of the book; a local chapter of Reasonable Faith, hosted by David Tong, whose members spent several weeks engaging in lively discussions of the manuscript; the students in a summer school course based on the manuscript hosted by Schola, a homeschool group run by Kathy Hart and Patricia Samuelson; Southern Adventist University where I conducted a faculty seminar on the material in the book; New Orleans Baptist Theological Seminary, where I delivered a conference presentation; and several churches, universities, and seminaries where I was invited to give presentations on the material. Finally, thanks to Paul Shockley, who invited me to lecture on the material in the book several times in his classes at the College of Biblical Studies in Houston and also organized a reading group to discuss the manuscript. The feedback from these audiences was invaluable in shaping the message.

Special thanks to my husband, Rick, whose editorial expertise improved the manuscript in countless ways.

I want to express my gratitude to Houston Baptist University, and especially to President Robert Sloan and Provost John Mark Reynolds, for a position as professor and scholar in residence that gave me time to write *Finding Truth*.

Many thanks to the team at David C Cook, especially associate publisher Tim Peterson, for their support and expertise in publishing and marketing the book.

It was a blessing to work with Steve Laube as my literary agent, who supported the project with unflagging competence and enthusiasm.

Finally, I owe a debt of gratitude to my family, who joined in spirited discussions as I hammered out the ideas for *Finding Truth*. They have supported me with both love and insight. I have dedicated earlier books to them; otherwise I would do it again.

STUDY GUIDE

The purpose of this study guide is to help you interact more deeply with the ideas in *Finding Truth*. As you paraphrase what you have read, searching for your own words to restate the ideas, you will process the material more fully. You will also connect the new ideas you are learning to the store of knowledge you already have, which gives the new material greater sticking power.

The key to making the best use of a study guide, then, is not simply to state your own views and opinions. When you do that, you are repeating what you already know instead of learning something new. Our thinking is stretched and deepened by grappling with unfamiliar ideas. The most effective strategy is to start each answer by referring to the text. First summarize what you have read. Then feel free to offer your own thoughts. (Some questions specifically ask for your views.)

The goal of apologetics is to learn how to communicate your Christian convictions more clearly and persuasively. As you fill out the study guide, then, do not think only of getting the "right answers." Think of how you would explain the idea to someone who does not accept Christianity. Use the study guide as practice for real conversations you will soon be having.

Questions: For each question, write a short paragraph answer. Subheads are given to indicate which section you should refer to in answering each question. Some questions include multiple parts. Be sure your answer addresses all the parts.

Dialogues: Many assignments ask you to compose sample dialogues. This is the same training used by professional apologists like Greg Koukl. In a real conversation, you cannot simply dump an entire paragraph on someone; you have to unfold your ideas bit by bit, in response to the other person's questions and objections. So strive to make your dialogues as realistic as possible to prepare yourself for real conversations with real people. Dialogues do not need to be long (about four comments by each character), but they should reflect a plausible conversation.

Each dialogue should start with a hypothetical person stating an objection based on the topic in the assignment. You think of an answer that keeps the discussion going. Have fun by giving your characters creative names. The dialogues will help you bridge the gap between *knowing* something and knowing how to explain it to others.

In a classroom or discussion group, participants should bring two copies of each dialogue and read them aloud dramatically with a partner. (Depending on the time, you may decide that each participant will choose only one dialogue to present, while answering the other dialogues as ordinary questions.)

PART ONE

"I Lost My Faith at an Evangelical College"

Give Me Evidence / Evidence from Life

1. The atheist philosopher Bertrand Russell was once asked what he would say if he died, stood before God, and God asked him, "Why didn't you believe in Me?" Russell replied, "I would say, 'Not enough evidence, God! Not enough evidence!'" Summarize the evidence from physical nature described in the text:

> Origin of the universe:
> Origin of life:

Do you find this evidence persuasive? Why or why not?

Evidence from Personhood

2. What are the philosophical meanings of the terms *personal* and *non-personal*? How does the fact that humans are personal beings function as evidence for God? Do you find that evidence persuasive? Why or why not?

Atheists' Children and Their God

3. Explain the concept of common grace. What are the implications for apologetics?

Tug of War

4. What is an "epistemological sin"? Do you agree that at the heart of the human condition is an epistemological sin (i.e., sin related to knowledge)? Why or why not?

How Humans Hide

5. "An atheist professor once told me that the Bible teaches polytheism because the first commandment speaks of 'other gods.'" This claim is made frequently on atheist Internet sites. Practice explaining what the first commandment really means to someone who claims that it teaches polytheism.

6. The text says that the easy-to-diagnose, surface-level sins are often driven by the more hidden sin of idolatry. Think of examples in your own life. Discuss if you feel comfortable doing so.

When Good Gifts Are False Gods

7. How can even good things become idols? Describe something good that you have been tempted to turn into an idol. Discuss if you feel comfortable doing so.

Idols Have Consequences

8. What does the Greek word *nous* mean? How does that give richer meaning to scriptural verses such as these: "God gave them up to a debased mind" (Rom. 1:28); "Be transformed by the renewal of your mind" (Rom. 12:2)? Add your own examples.

9. In debates over moral issues such as homosexuality, most people today use the word *nature* to mean behavior patterns observed among organisms in the natural world. What is the older meaning of the word *nature*, as in the phrase "human nature"? How is this traditional meaning expressed in Romans 1?

Five Strategic Principles

Principle #1: *Identify the Idol*

10. The text says that every nonbiblical religion or worldview starts with an idol. It must locate an eternal, uncaused cause within the created order. Explain why, and list some examples. Can you think of any exceptions to this principle?

Principle #2: *Identify the Idol's Reductionism*

11. Define reductionism. In what way is reductionism like trying to stuff the entire universe into a box? Give an example.

12. How does reductionism affect one's view of human nature? In your answer, explain this principle: "Every concept of humanity is created in the image of *some* god." Use materialism as an example.

Principle #3: *Test the Idol: Does It Contradict What We Know about the World?*

13. "We can be confident that every idol-based worldview *will* fail." It will be unable to account for what is knowable by general revelation. Explain why. Illustrate by using materialism as an example.

14. Explain how every idol-based worldview leads people to cognitive dissonance—a gap between what their worldview tells them and what they know from general revelation.

15. Explain how reductionism is a strategy of suppression. How is it used to suppress the evidence for God from general revelation?

Principle #4: *Test the Idol: Does It Contradict Itself?*

16. Define self-referential absurdity. Give an example of how the argument works.

17. Explain why idol-based worldviews refute themselves. The text says that adherents of reductionist worldviews "have to borrow Christianity's high view of reason in order to give reasons for their view." Explain what that means.

Principle #5: *Replace the Idol: Make the Case for Christianity*

18. "What a powerful image of people caught in cognitive dissonance, reaching out to grab on to truths that their own worldviews deny—truths that only a biblical worldview logically supports." Unpack this sentence. Explain how secular thinkers are trying to hold on to truths that are logically supported only by Christianity.

Liberated Minds

19. Dialogue: When *Finding Truth* was in manuscript form, I taught a class using it as a text. One student, a father of pre-teens, said, "Your book is convicting me that I brush off my kids when they have questions about Christianity. I have made a commitment

that from now on, I will listen to my children and treat their questions seriously."

But another student, a young woman from El Salvador, rejected the very idea of apologetics. In her view, the use of reason to defend Christianity is a matter of "pride" and "the flesh." "Christians should rely on the Holy Spirit," she said, quoting Paul: "Has not God made foolish the wisdom of the world?" and "I decided to know nothing among you except Jesus Christ and him crucified" (1 Cor. 1:20; 2:2).

Write a dialogue as if you are speaking with the young woman from El Salvador. How would you persuade this woman that it is valid for Christians to defend their convictions?

PART TWO

PRINCIPLE #1
·····
Twilight of the Gods

Leaving Teens Vulnerable
1. Summarize the sociological research on young people who report having doubts or questions. Do you know anyone with doubts who is struggling to find answers? Are you struggling yourself?

Principle #1: *Identify the Idol*
2. How is the biblical word *heart* often misunderstood? What is its correct meaning?

3. "Atheism is not a belief. Atheism is merely the lack of a belief in God or gods." Because this is a common line among atheists today, you should know how to respond. Based on the text, what could you say?

4. What are the two advantages of using the biblical term *idols* for both secular and religious worldviews? (The second one is under the next subhead.)

Religion without God
5. As you read through the rest of this chapter, make a diagram like the one presented here. On the left side, write the features that most people associate with religion. On the right side, explain why that feature is not a necessary part of the definition of religion. Give examples.

Common Definitions of Religion	Why Isn't That Definition Adequate?

6. Why are Buddhism, Taoism, and Confucianism described as atheistic religions?

Religion without Morality

7. Give examples of amoral and even immoral religions.

Search for the Divine

8. What is the one thing that characterizes all religions as well as all secular philosophies? Can you think of any exceptions?

Philosophers and Their Gods

9. As you read through the rest of this chapter, make a diagram like the one presented here. On the left side, write the name of each ism discussed. On the right side, identify its idol. Go back and start with the section titled "Search for the Divine."

Philosophy	What Is Its Idol?

10. What does the Greek word *arché* mean? Do you agree that the early Greek philosophies qualify as idols under the definition in Romans 1? Give your reasons.

The Church of Physics: Idol of Matter

11. Dialogue: I once had a Facebook discussion with a young fan of Richard Dawkins, who was outraged that I would suggest secularism had *anything* in common with religion. To this young man, religion represented blind faith while science stood for reason and facts. Imagine yourself in a conversation with a young man like that. Write a dialogue in which you level the playing field by showing that all belief systems share the same basic structure.

12. Explain the logical steps that lead from materialism to Marxism's economic determinism.

Hume Meets the Klingons: Idol of the Senses

13. Like Data in *Star Trek*, atheists often charge that Christianity is "irrational" simply because it accepts the existence of a realm beyond the empirical world. Based on the text, how could you answer that charge?

Inside the Matrix

14. Dialogue: Explain to an empiricist how his or her philosophy involves a divinity belief.

Sensational Bacon, Dubious Descartes

15. One philosopher says that Enlightenment epistemologies set up "the first-person standpoint" as the only path to certainty. They turned the self into "the locus and arbiter of knowledge." Explain what that means and what the end result was.

Signposts or Dead Ends

16. Philosophers like Karl Popper and John Herman Randall pointed out the "religious character" of Enlightenment epistemologies. Explain what they meant.

Kant's Mental Prison: Idol of the Mind

17. What was Kant's "Copernican revolution"? What was his God substitute? Define solipsism, and explain why philosophies that start within the human mind end in solipsism.

The Artist as God: Idol of the Imagination

18. Describe the evidence showing that, for the Romantics, the imagination was their God substitute, and art was their substitute religion.

Cure for Blind Philosophers

19. Read "The Blind Men and the Elephant" by John Godfrey Saxe on the following pages. How does it illustrate the origin of idols?

"The Blind Men and the Elephant"

It was six men of Indostan
To learning much inclined,
Who went to see the Elephant
(Though all of them were blind),
That each by observation
Might satisfy his mind.

The *First* approached the Elephant,
And happening to fall
Against his broad and sturdy side,
At once began to bawl:
"God bless me! but the Elephant
Is very like a WALL!"

The *Second*, feeling of the tusk,
Cried, "Ho, what have we here,
So very round and smooth and sharp?
To me 'tis mighty clear
This wonder of an Elephant
Is very like a SPEAR!"

The *Third* approached the animal,
And happening to take
The squirming trunk within his hands,
Thus boldly up and spake
"I see," quoth he, "the Elephant
Is very like a SNAKE!"

The *Fourth* reached out an eager hand,
And felt about the knee
"What most this wondrous beast is like
Is mighty plain" quoth he:
"'Tis clear enough the Elephant
Is very like a TREE!"

The *Fifth*, who chanced to touch the ear,
Said: "E'en the blindest man
Can tell what this resembles most;
Deny the fact who can,
This marvel of an Elephant
Is very like a FAN!"

The *Sixth* no sooner had begun
About the beast to grope,
Than seizing on the swinging tail
That fell within his scope,
"I see," quoth he, "the Elephant
Is very like a ROPE!"

And so these men of Indostan
Disputed loud and long,
Each in his own opinion
Exceeding stiff and strong,
Though each was partly in the right,
And all were in the wrong!

The Joy of Critical Thinking

20. How does Christianity affirm what is good and true in these philosophies?

    Materialism:

    Rationalism:

    Empiricism:

    Romanticism:

The Good, the True, and the Pagan

21. "Paul was making the astounding claim that Christianity provides the context of meaning for the Greeks to understand *their own* culture." Explain what that means. Choose one example from our own day, and explain how the same principle can be applied.

PRINCIPLE #2

· · · · ·

How Nietzsche Wins

Principle #2: *Identify the Idol's Reductionism*

1. The text argues that an idol-centered worldview is always dehumanizing. Explain why. In your answer, include an explanation of this sentence: "Every concept of humanity is created in the image of *some* god."

Dehumanize Thy Neighbor

2. Reductionism is not just a philosophical concept. Think of ways your own tendency to live for idols has led you to use others for your own needs and goals. Discuss, if you feel comfortable doing so.

The Science of Cheating

3. Read endnote 4 to learn about another study that was similar to the one reported in *Scientific American*. How did these findings support Romans 1? Read endnote 5. How do these studies implicitly affirm the reality of free will?

The Psychology of Suppression

4. Explain how reductionism functions as a strategy for suppression. Why do people suppress whatever does not fit into their worldview box?

5. Why does an idol-centered worldview always produce a dualism or dichotomy in people's thinking?

6. The text says we will identify the dehumanizing impact of two worldviews (materialism and postmodernism), in two religions, and in two political theories. As you read the chapter, make a diagram like the one presented here. On the top horizontal line, write the name of the worldview or religion being discussed. Under the line, answer two questions: What is its idol? What is its form of reductionism?

NAME						
IDOL						
REDUCTIONISM						

Crick: "Nothing but a Pack of Neurons"

7. Define eliminative materialism. What reasoning does it use to reach its conclusions? How does it refute itself?

"Deepest Irrationality"

8. Galen Strawson writes that eliminative materialism shows "that the capacity of human minds to be gripped by theory, by faith, is truly unbounded." It reveals "the deepest irrationality of the human mind." Unpack what he means. Describe Thomas Reid's response. What do you think of Reid's view?

Revenge of the Romantics

9. Dialogue: What did Schopenhauer mean when he said, "Materialism is the philosophy of the subject who forgets to take account of himself"? Some Christian apologists have adapted this argument to support a biblical worldview. Try your hand at using the argument in an imagined dialogue with a materialist.

Emerson's Over-Soul

10. Define neo-Platonism. Why does it qualify as an idol-belief? Read endnote 26 and explain what Paul means when he writes about the "fullness" of divinity. How is he taking the term from the early Gnostics and claiming it for Christianity?

The Great Chain of Being in Shakespeare's day: Note that it has been Christianized so that the One is identified with the biblical God, and the spiritual entities are identified as angels. Christian neo-Platonism was widely held in the Middle Ages and the Renaissance.

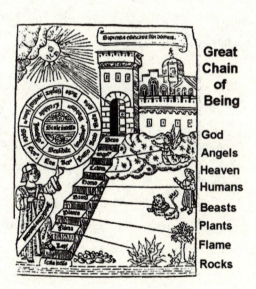

Great Chain of Being

God
Angels
Heaven
Humans
Beasts
Plants
Flame
Rocks

Hegel's Evolutionary Deity

11. Explain how Hegel altered the Great Chain of Being. Why did Nietzsche say that "without Hegel, there would have been no Darwin"?

12. Define historicism. How does historicism undercut itself? In what way did Hegel make a tacit exception for himself? How did that create a new problem?

Triumvirate of Race, Class, Gender

13. Explain the logical link leading from Hegel to postmodernism. What is the idol in postmodernism?

Roots of Political Correctness

14. Dialogue: Engage with a postmodernist to show where you agree and where you disagree. Make a case that postmodernism is reductionistic, that it reduces individuals to products of society, race, class, gender, etc.

The Fall of Postmodernism

15. Dialogue: Based on the text, explain to a postmodern Christian the reasons for not accepting a postmodern interpretation of Christianity.

Pantheism versus You

16. Dialogue: Many people who embrace pantheism claim that it gives greater meaning to life by causing us to see ourselves as part of an interconnected whole. In a conversation with a New Age friend, explain why pantheism is reductionistic and dehumanizing, and why

it does not give people the dignity and meaning that your friend is looking for.

Islam versus Human Dignity
17. Dialogue: Practice explaining to a Muslim where Christianity and Islam agree and where they differ, and why the difference is crucial.

From Secular Idols to Death Camps / From Liberators to Despots
18. Describe the secular idols that led to Nazism and Communism, and their political consequences. In your view, what are today's political idols?

More Than Is Dreamed of in Your Philosophy
19. What biblical meaning is most often associated with the phrase "put to shame"? How does that change our understanding of Romans 1:16?

20. Turn back to this diagram on page 113.

Western philosophy divides into two philosophical "families"

ROMANTICISM
The Box of Mind

ENLIGHTENMENT
The Box of Things

(A) Review Principles #1 and #2. Make a diagram like the one presented here. Under ENLIGHTENMENT fill in all the isms we have discussed that belong to the Enlightenment category (the analytic tradition). Under ROMANTICISM fill in all the isms we have discussed that belong in the Romantic category (the continental tradition). As you read through the rest of the book, for every ism you encounter, decide which tradition it belongs to and write it in.

ROMANTICISM (continental tradition)

ENLIGHTENMENT (analytic tradition)

By mastering these two basic categories, you will find it much easier to make sense of the diversity of modern Western worldviews. Worldviews are not a scattershot of disconnected ideas to memorize, master, and slot into a grid. They form ongoing traditions that move along the same path, in the same basic direction, following the same map—either the Enlightenment map or the Romantic map. Or you can think of them as two genealogical lines connected by family resemblances. To make sense of any particular worldview, the first step is to identify the family lineage it belongs to and the common themes it shares.

(B) What are those common themes? To get you started, here is a segment from the text: "The analytic tradition traces its roots to the Enlightenment and tends to highlight science, reason, and facts. The continental tradition traces its roots to the Romantic movement and seeks to defend mind, meaning, and morality."

Make a second diagram. As you review Principles #1 and #2, look for common themes or family resemblances within each of the two traditions and write them in:

Connecting themes in the continental tradition

Connecting themes in the analytic tradition

PRINCIPLE #3
·····
Secular Leaps of Faith

1. Endnote 2 says the argument from evil fails logically. Explain why.

The Gravity of Fact

2. The text says that when we apply the practical test, "we can be confident that all idol-centered worldviews *will* be falsified." Explain why. Use the CNN article as an example.

I, Robot—We, Machines

3. Should Christians argue in favor of free will? Some Calvinists are not so sure. Read endnote 6. What do you think? Explain the difference between predestination and determinism.

Principle #3: *Test the Idol: Does It Contradict What We Know about the World?*

4. Why is free will such an enduring question in philosophy? Which distinctively human abilities depend on free will? Can you think of any additional abilities that depend on free will beyond those mentioned in the text?

Why Secularists Can't Live with Secularism

5. What are some phrases showing that a worldview has bumped up against a reality it cannot explain? How does that serve to falsify the worldview?

Double-Minded Secularists / Losing Total Truth

6. Why does every idol-centered worldview lead to a mental dichotomy or dualism? How is dualism a signal that evidence from general revelation is being suppressed?

A Leap of Doubt

7. We have come far enough to detect important patterns. As you read through the rest of this chapter, make a diagram like the one presented here. Go back to the sections titled "Why Secularists Can't Live with Secularism" and "Double-Minded Secularists," so you can include Strawson and Slingerland in your diagram.

    A. List the name of each thinker discussed in the text.

    B. List the ism that each thinker embraces.

    C. List the phrases he uses that are clues to general revelation—the ideas that bubble up inescapably and irresistibly no matter which worldview he holds. I'll give you the first one: Galen Strawson says he "can't really live with" his own philosophy. The key phrase is what humans "can't live with." A worldview is supposed to be a guide to living in the world. When people cannot live on the basis of their worldview, that means they have bumped against the hard edge of a reality that does not fit their professed system of thought.

D. List the phrases he uses showing that evidence from general revelation is being suppressed. For example, Marvin Minsky says, "We're virtually forced to maintain that belief, even though we know it's false." He is suppressing a truth that he is "forced to maintain" by reducing it to the status of a necessary falsehood—by putting it in the upper story.

Name	ism	Clues to general revelation (phrases)	Clues to suppression (phrases)

When you have finished filling in your diagram, answer this question: Why do secular thinkers suppress the evidence from general revelation?

Atheism versus Civilization

8. Smilansky acknowledges that his deterministic worldview is socially destructive. Explain why determinism has socially harmful consequences. How does Smilansky propose to get around those negative consequences? What do you think about his proposal?

Dawkins's "Intolerable" Worldview

9. How does Dawkins show that he has bumped up against the hard edge of a reality that does not fit his worldview? Why would the consequences of his worldview be "intolerable"?

Einstein's Dilemma

10. What does the phrase "as if" signal? Why did Kant propose the phrase? Read endnote 24 and explain why even Einstein's scientific work depends on free will.

Secular Mysticism

11. Why did Francis Schaeffer claim that any worldview that contains an epistemological dualism leads to "mysticism"? Explain how the examples in the text support Schaeffer's claim.

Darwinian Psychopaths

12. The text says, "We can picture worldviews falling along a continuum: The more consistently people work out the logic of their worldview, the more reductionistic the result will be, the wider the gap, and the further its leap into irrational mysticism." How does Edward Slingerland exemplify this ever-widening gap?

13. How do the Greek terms for "futile" and "foolish" throw new light on how Romans 1:21 can be applied to today's secular worldviews? How can Paul's statement that those who worship idols are "without excuse" be applied to secular worldviews?

MIT Prof: My Children Are Machines

14. Brooks's worldview contradicts his own lived experience so sharply that he says he "maintains two sets of inconsistent beliefs." The text calls this "the tragedy of the postmodern age." Why is it a tragedy?

Chesterton: Christianity "Too Good to Be True"

15. How does a biblical view of humanity lead to a unified, logically consistent worldview? Explain why Chesterton says secularists reject Christianity not because it is a bad theory but because it seems "too good to be true."

Walking Off the Postmodern Map

16. Dialogue: Imagine talking with a postmodernist. Based on the text, how could you argue against his or her anti-realism?

Don't Impose Your Facts

17. How do most people apply postmodernism selectively? How does that lead to a dualism or dichotomy in the way people think and act? (If you've read *Total Truth*, how does this dichotomy represent the fact/value split?)

A Harvard Professor's Admission

18. The text quotes two philosophers (Parfit and Harries) who admit outright that they hold inconsistent beliefs. Summarize what they say. Then make the case that Christianity offers a unified view of truth. Keep in mind that, as the introduction says, you should use the study guide answers to practice doing apologetics with real people.

19. Explain the religious motivations that drove Francis Crick and James Watson in their search for reductionist theories.

Secularism Is Too Small for Secularists

20. Dialogue: The text says, "We should begin by expressing solidarity with their deepest longings for meaning and significance—and then show that in a biblical worldview, those longings are not merely illusions or useful fictions." Write out a conversation modeling what this would look like.

PRINCIPLE #4

·····

Why Worldviews Commit Suicide

1. Explain reverse engineering. How do biologists use it? How does it provide evidence of design?

2. How is Michael Ruse's thinking an example of cognitive dissonance?

It's Not Brain Surgery ... Oh Wait, Yes It Is

3. Explain how Freud's notion that religion is wish fulfillment can be turned against his own theory.

Tests for Truth

4. Explain self-referential absurdity. Explain *why* idol-based worldviews commit suicide.

Principle #4: *Test the Idol: Does It Contradict Itself?*

5. Define logical positivism. How was it discredited? Do you still hear emotivist views expressed today? Give an example.

6. As you read through this chapter, make a diagram like the one presented here. For each school of thought that commits suicide: List the ism. Describe its form of reductionism. Explain why it refutes itself. Start with logical positivism.

Name the ism	Describe Its Reductionism	How Does It Undercut Itself?

Hitting the Marx

7. Dialogue: Choose one of the theories discussed in this section. Create a realistic dialogue with someone who holds that theory. Help the person to see how the theory undercuts itself.

Debunking the Debunkers

8. How do reductionist worldviews try to avoid committing suicide? How does that "solution" create yet another problem?

9. The text says "all worldviews have to borrow a Christian epistemology.... They have to function *as if* Christianity is true, even as they reject it." Summarize the biblical basis for epistemology, and then explain why other worldviews have to borrow it.

C. S. Lewis Unmasks Materialism

10. Dialogue: Imagine a conversation with a materialist. Help him or her see that the position commits suicide and is therefore untenable.

Evolution Cannot Survive Itself

11. Dialogue: Imagine a conversation with an avid supporter of evolutionary epistemology. Craft a realistic dialogue in which you explain how it undercuts the very basis for rationality—and therefore undercuts itself.

Darwin's Selective Skepticism

12. The passage by Darwin about his "horrid doubt" is typically misinterpreted to mean he himself realized that his theory committed suicide. Explain how Darwin applied his doubt selectively. Then explain why Darwinism undercuts not only itself but also the entire scientific enterprise.

Why Science Is a "Miracle"

13. Dialogue: You are talking to a secular person who insists that Christianity has always stood in the way of science and progress. Explain how Christianity provided the philosophical underpinnings for the rise of modern science. Then explain why even today, anyone who wants to pursue science has to adopt an epistemology derived from a Christian worldview—at least in practice.

Postmodern Prison

14. Dialogue: Argue in a polite and respectful manner with your university literature professor who is a postmodernist, showing that the theory commits suicide. In your explanation, include the concept of "performative contradiction."

Barthes Busted

15. Explain what "deconstructionism" means, the logic behind it, and how it contains a fatal internal contradiction. How do deconstructionists try to avoid that contradiction? Does it work?

Postmodernism and Terror

16. Where did many postmodernists get their opposition to metanarratives? What did they propose as a solution? What is the problem with that solution? Why does postmodernism lead to complicity with evil and injustice?

The Tyranny of Diversity

17. Explain how postmodernism became imperialistic and coercive. Describe any examples that you have encountered.

Losing Your Self

18. Explain the difference between a modernist (Enlightenment) and a postmodernist view of the self. How does a postmodern view refute itself?

The Trinity for Postmoderns

19. Practice explaining how the Christian concept of the Trinity offers a better answer than either modernism or postmodernism to the balance of individual and community.

Escape from Reductionism

20. Dialogue: Choose one example from this section and imagine a conversation in which you make the positive case that Christianity offers better answers than any competing worldview.

PRINCIPLE #5

Free-Loading Atheists

Principle #5: *Replace the Idol: Make the Case for Christianity*

1. Dialogue: Imagine a conversation with someone who holds moral relativism or skepticism or some other position that you think of yourself. Create a realistic dialogue in which you show such persons that their behavior contradicts their own worldview, and that in practice they "borrow" from a biblical worldview.

The Confession of Richard Rorty

2. Why does Richard Rorty call himself a "free-loading atheist"? Do you agree that Christianity is the only source of universal rights? Why or why not? (Read endnote 8 for more background.)

3. As you read through the chapter, make a list of the truths that free-loading atheists borrow from Christianity. (Go back to the beginning of the chapter and include any examples you find up to this point.) When you are finished reading to the end of the chapter, take one of those truths as an example and make a persuasive case that Christianity provides its only adequate philosophical basis.

4. Dialogue: The text says, "Atheists often denounce Christianity as harsh and negative. But in reality it offers a much more positive view of the human person than any competing religion or worldview. It

is so appealing that adherents of other worldviews keep free-loading the parts they like best." Drawing on the text, how could you make a positive case for Christianity?

What Makes Science Possible?

5. Dialogue: Write a dialogue making the case that (in the words of Paul Davies) "science can proceed only if the scientist adopts an essentially theological world view."

An Atheist Decries Humanism

6. Dialogue: Imagine having a conversation with someone who is a "humanist" in John Gray's definition of the term. Make a persuasive case that his or her high view of human dignity derives from Christianity and is a case of free-loading. (Read endnote 13 for more detail from Gray.)

Nagel: Darwin "Almost Certainly False"

7. Explain the reasons Thomas Nagel gives for "why the materialist neo-Darwinian conception of nature is almost certainly false."

8. What reasons does Nagel give for rejecting theism? Explain how he is free-loading.

Problems of a "Proud Atheist"

9. Raymond Tallis says that "something rather important about us is left unexplained by evolutionary theory"—or rather, several things.

Choose two things and in your own words tell why they are "left unexplained by evolutionary theory."

10. Choose an example of "neuro-evolutionary reductionism" (in art, literature, legal theory, philosophy, economics, politics, theology, or any other field), research it, and write a description of its claims. How would you critique those claims?

11. Why does Tallis reject neurotheology as applied to Christianity? Do you think his objection is a good one?

Gimme That Old-Time Philosophy

12. The text describes several examples of atheists who seek to hijack the spiritual and emotional benefits of religion. Choose one, research it in greater depth, and describe how it seeks to make secular ideas fulfill spiritual aspirations.

A Mass for Charles Darwin

13. Define scientism. Explain how it goes beyond anything that science could possibly establish.

14. How does evolution itself sometimes function as a religion? Listen to a segment from "Missa Charles Darwin." This is the kyrie eleison ("Lord have mercy") with words from Darwin substituted: www.gregorywbrown.com/missa-charles-darwin/.

Evolutionary Religion

15. What is Stuart Kauffman's definition of "God," and why does he retain the word at all?

16. Summarize Jeremy Rifkin's spiritualist view of evolution. In what way do religious views of evolution give a clue to general revelation?

Losing Faith, Finding God / Bertrand Russell

17. Make two lists, side by side. Based on my personal story, list the consequences of giving up Christianity. On the left, summarize Christian teaching. On the right, summarize the secular view that results when Christianity is given up.

Think of additional consequences of giving up Christianity beyond those mentioned in the text, and add them to your list.

18. Dialogue: Imagine a conversation with someone like I was as a teenager, ready to give up Christianity. Choose some of the consequences described in the text and paraphrase them in your own words. Gently help this person recognize that the consequences of abandoning Christianity are far-reaching, and encourage him or her to think twice about it—as no one did for me!

What Is *Your* Answer?

19. The text says, "When people raise questions about Christianity, often the best response is not to shut them down, but precisely the opposite." Explain why, then choose an example and illustrate what that approach might look like.

Lesson from *To Kill a Mockingbird*

20. The text says that learning other people's worldviews should be motivated by love for them. Readers of *Finding Truth* have told me they had not connected apologetics with love before. Practice explaining to another person why the two are connected.

PART THREE

How Critical Thinking Saves Faith

1. Chesterton wrote that ideas are actually *more* dangerous to the person who has never studied them—that a new idea will "fly to his head like wine to the head of a teetotaler." Do you agree? Why or why not?

Churched but Not Prepared

2. Summarize in your own words the five strategic principles described in *Finding Truth*.

>   Principle #1
>
>   Principle #2
>
>   Principle #3
>
>   Principle #4
>
>   Principle #5

Stealth Secularism

3. Choose one movement in art or literature, research it, and describe in greater detail the worldview that motivates it. (You can use *Saving Leonardo* for your research.)

What Wags Your Theology?

4. Make a diagram like the one presented here. On the left side, list the names of the theological schools discussed in the text and summarize each one's basic tenets. On the right side, write the philosophy each one was influenced by. Do you know any additional examples of theologies that were influenced by some school of philosophy? If so, explain.

Theological School	Which philosophy helped shape it?

5. Choose one form of liberal theology, research it, and describe in greater detail the philosophy that motivates it.

Critique and Create

6. The text says, "Christians often have a habit of defining themselves by what they are against. Yet to oppose what is wrong, it is most effective to offer something better." Choose an example from the text, or one that you think of yourself, and suggest principles for being a redemptive force in that area of life.

A Total Book for Total Truth

7. All systems of thought are structurally the same: they start with certain foundational assumptions that color everything else. How does that common structure help make sense of Scripture's claim that *all* truth—not just spiritual truth—begins with God?

Crazy Crae: How Do We Break Free?

8. Do you recognize a sacred/secular split in your own thinking?

9. Where did the sacred/secular split come from?

10. What did you appreciate most in the section about Lecrae?

SAMPLE TEST

Total Possible Points: 100

Name: _____

Write short paragraph answers to the following questions.

1. What is Principle #1? (Points: 15)

First state what the principle is. Then explicate it in greater detail. In your answer, be sure to cover these questions:

- What is an idol, according to Romans 1?
- Give at least one verse from Romans 1 supporting your definition of an idol.
- Give at least 3 examples of worldviews and their idols.
- Use the poem of the blind men and the elephant to illustrate what an idol is.
- Write anything else you think is important for applying Principle #1. (This is where you have a chance to show everything you know beyond what was covered in the questions.)

2. What is Principle #2? (Points: 20)

First state what the principle is. Then explicate it in greater detail. In your answer, be sure to cover these questions:

- What does the term *reductionism* mean?
- Why do idol-based worldviews lead to reductionism?

- Give a passage from Romans 1 that explains why idols lead to a lower, less humane view of humanity.
- How does the process of reductionism explain why idols lead to treating people badly (the long list of destructive behaviors at the end of Romans 1)?
- Give at least 3 examples of reductionism. In each case, explain what the idol is, and how it leads to reductionism.
- Write anything else you think is important for applying Principle #2.

3. What is Principle #3? (Points: 35)

First state what the principle is. Then explicate it in greater detail. In your answer, be sure to cover these questions:

- What is general revelation?
- How can we use general revelation to test worldviews?
- Why do idol-based worldviews typically get some things right?
- Why do they always get some things wrong? (Use the concept of reductionism in your answer.)
- What do they do with the things they cannot explain?
- How do they lead to dualism—holding two inconsistent and contradictory views?
- Which concept from Romans 1 explains the motivation for creating a dualism?
- Give at least 3 examples of thinkers whose philosophy leads to dualism.

- Write anything else you think is important for applying Principle #3.

4. What is Principle #4? (Points: 20)

First state what the principle is. Then explicate it in greater detail. In your answer, be sure to cover these questions:

- What does it mean for a worldview to be self-refuting (it is self-referentially absurd, it commits suicide)?
- Why are idol-based worldviews self-refuting?
- Give at least 3 examples of worldviews that are self-refuting. In each case, explain why.
- How do people try to avoid the problem of self-refuting worldviews? Why doesn't that strategy work?
- Write anything else you think is important for applying Principle #4.

5. What is Principle #5? (Points: 10)

First state what the principle is. Then explicate it in greater detail. In your answer, be sure to cover these questions:

- Why do so many non-Christians reach over and borrow from Christianity?
- Give at least 3 examples of free-loading.
- How does free-loading suggest a strategic starting point in making a case for Christianity?
- One way to highlight the attractive features of Christianity is to show where secularists borrow from it. Another way is to ask

what you lose when you give it up. Choose at least 2 elements of a Christian worldview and explain the consequences of giving them up.

• Write anything else you think is important for applying Principle #5.

INDEX

A

Abbott, Lyman, 266
Absolute Spirit, Hegel, 115–18, 240, 266
Absolute, Neo-Platonic, 114
absolutize, 45, 60–61, 80–81, 85, 99, 113, 118, 122, 129, 135–38, 167, 199, 203–5
  false absolute, 61, 85, 135, 138, 203
abstract art, 263–64
Ackley, Alfred, 13
altruistic behavior, 100–101
analytic tradition, 113
Anaximenes, 68
Anomaly (musical album), 272
Anselm, 215–16
The Antichrist (Nietzsche), 17
anti-humanism, 122
anti-realism, 119, 169
Aping Mankind (Tallis), 232
apologetics
  Greek word for, 163, 251
  necessity of, 247–52, 254
  postmodern theology's rejection of, 267–68
  Romans as training for, 24–26
Apostles' Creed, 214
Aquinas, Thomas, 215–16
arché (source or first cause), 68–70

architects and architecture, 262–63
Aristotle, 66, 69–70, 77, 86
artistic expressions of philosophy. *See* visual arts
art, as religion substitute 83–84
ashamed, biblical meaning of, 139
  "not ashamed" of the gospel (Romans 1:16), 51, 139, 234, 255, 275
"as if" concept, 159–60, 173, 179–80, 190, 199, 222–23, 239
The Astonishing Hypothesis (Crick), 193
atheists and atheism
  atheistic religions, 64
  children of, 31
  church for, 236
  New Atheists, 43, 60, 70, 157
  science undermined by, 196
  as a substitute religion, 235–41
  as wish fulfillment, 180–81
Augustine, 66
Avatar (movie), 65

B

Bacon, Francis, 78–80
Barbour, Ian, 112
Barna, George, 220
Barrett, Justin, 31
Barthes, Roland, 200–202

Baum, Eric, 160
Bedau, Mark, 109–10
Berlin, Isaiah, 136
"The Blind Men and the Elephant" (poem), 85
Bloom, Allan, 271
Bloom, Paul, 31
Botton, Alain de, 236
brain, as a computer, 107–8, 153–54
A Brief History of Thought (Luc), 235–36
Brooks, Rodney, 164–65
Buddhism, 64, 66, 126, 127–28

C

Call of the Wild (London), 259
Calvin, John, 31, 38, 145
Cézanne, 262
cheating experiment, 102
Chesterton, G. K., 137, 165–67, 254–55
children
  innate knowledge of God, 31
Christians and Christianity
  apologetics, necessity of, 247–52
  creativity and, 269–70
  incarnation, 213
  not logically contradictory, 181–82, 183
  not reductionistic, 41, 45, 48, 86, 136, 138, 183, 188–90, 210
  resurrection, 214

science, origins in
Christianity, 95,
197–99, 215,
226–28
Scripture, 125–26,
244–45
Secular conseqences
of giving it up,
241–46
as total truth, 139,
152–53, 155,
166–67, 170–72,
181, 216, 270–71,
272, 273–74
Trinity, 130–31, 209–12
Cicero, 28
The Closing of the American Mind (Bloom), 271
Clouser, Roy, 44, 66
cognitive dissonance, 39, 47, 48, 149, 162, 164, 166, 179–80, 231, 232
Cohen, Richard, 197
Coleridge, Samuel, 84
common grace, 30–31
Communism, 133–35
Confucianism, 64
consciousness
denial of, 45, 106–11, 144, 148, 150, 160–61, 166, 173, 174, 194, 229, 230
continental tradition, 113, 117, 167
"contrary to nature" (Romans 1:26–27), 41
Copernicus, 82
Cosmos (television series), 71
Coyne, Jerry, 71
Craig, William Lane, 22, 170, 185
Crick, Francis, 107, 173–74, 193
critical thinking, 253–55

Critiques (Kant), 122
cubism, 262–63
Culture and the Death of God (Eagleton), 61

D

Darwin, Charles, 96, 238, 259
his horrid doubt, 194–95
his selective skeptism, 194–97
Darwinism
evolution, 108–11, 124, 150–51, 160–65, 177–81, 192–94, 219, 225–26, 229
Hegel as precursor, 115
Nagel on, 230–31
Tallis on, 232–34
Davies, Paul, 26–27, 228
Dawkins, Richard, 13, 157–58, 243
de Botton, Alain, 236
de Tocqueville, Alexis, 225
debased, Greek word for, 40
Declaration of Independence, 226
deconstructionism, 200–202, 265
moral claims, impact on, 204
imperialistic, 205–7
self-referential absurdity of, 201–2, 204
Democritus, 77
denial, psychology of, 31–33
Derrida, Jacques, 201
Descartes, René, 78–81
The Descent of Man (Darwin), 238
design and intelligent design theory, 25–28,
31, 178–80, 213, 214, 215, 219, 223, 230–31, 233, 243
determinism and determined, 19, 45, 47, 72, 102, 142, 144–50, 158–65, 191, 206, 259
dialegomai Greek word for reasoned, 90
diversity, 204–7, 209–12
divine and divinity, concept at core of every religion and philosophy, 43, 66–68, 69, 71, 77, 80, 83, 98, 115–16, 127–29, 131, 137, 174, 216, 270–71
DNA, 27
Dooyeweerd, Herman, 85, 118, 143
double truth theory, 173
doublethink, 152, 154
Douglas, Mary, 65
Druidism, 67
dualism and dual consciousness, 104–5, 113, 151–65, 168–73
Dupré, Louis, 171–72
"Dylan's" story, 55–57

E

Eagleton, Terry, 61, 114–15, 204, 235
Edwards, Jonathan, 25
Egnor, Michael, 177–81
Einstein, Albert, 43, 158–59
eliminative materialism, 106–8,
as self-refuting, 106
Ellis, Albert, 51
emergentism, 108–10

Emerson, Ralph Waldo,
114–15
emotivism, 184
empiricism
Bacon and, 78, 80
Christian response to,
87–88, 214–15
as idol, 72–74
impressionist art and,
260–62
logical positivism,
184–85
practical test and,
261–62
mentalism and, 75–77
rationalism and, 77
The End of Apologetics
(Penner), 267–68
Enlightenment, 61, 79,
85, 88, 112, 113,
117, 119, 120, 126,
133–34, 167, 168,
207, 208, 210, 268
Epicurus, 77
epistemology, biblical,
49, 125–26, 169–70,
188–90, 192, 197–99,
214–16, 223
epistemological sin, 34–35
equality and human rights,
224–26
Erickson, John, 93–96
evolution, 115–18, 208,
238–41. *See also*
Darwinism
evolutionary epistemology,
192–97, 230
evolutionary psychology,
100–101
evolutionary religion,
239–41
"exchanged" the glory of
God (Romans 1:23,
25), 35, 41, 44, 98,
256

existentialism, impact on
theology, 266
Ezekiel, idols of the heart, 61

F

Fales, Evan, 109
Fawlty Towers (British
television show),
157–58
feminist theology, 267
Ferry, Luc, 225, 235–36
fine-tuning problem,
25–26
Fiorenza, Elisabeth
Schüssler, 267
Flesh and Machines
(Brooks), 164
Fletcher, Joseph, 94
foolish, Greek word for,
163
forms, Platonic, 69–70
Foucault, Michel, 208
free will and freedom,
45, 46–48, 49, 89,
102, 104, 107,
142, 144–50, 152,
154, 156, 158–61,
165, 166, 173, 176,
194, 225, 229, 246,
259–60
predestination and,
145–46
"free-loading" from
Christianity, 49, 50,
190, 192, 220–41,
257
free-will defense, 141
Freud, Sigmund, 51, 55,
180, 186
Fromm, Erich, 51
futile, Greek word for, 163

G

Galileo, 262
Garcia, Robert, 266, 268

Gellner, Ernest, 171
general revelation "what
can be known about
God is plain to them
… in the things that
have been made"
(Romans 1:19, 20),
24–25, 28, 30, 31–32,
38–39, 134, 170, 172,
180
known by undeniable
experience, 46–47,
110–11, 142–43,
146, 149–69,
172–73, 176, 181,
208–9, 224
as source of philosophies,
79–81
as test for truth claims,
46–48, 51, 103–4,
142–44, 148–69,
173, 189–90, 209,
222–24, 230–31,
241, 256–57
genetic information, 26–27
Gilson, Étienne, 29, 135
Gnosticism, 213
The God That Failed
(Koestler), 136
The God Who Is There
(Schaeffer), 161
God "gave them up"
(Romans 1:24, 26,
28), 39, 96–97, 99,
135–36, 161, 164
God's-eye view, 80, 86,
119, 125
Goldilocks dilemma, 26
Gould, Stephen Jay,
195–96
Gray, John, 135, 193, 229,
237
Greek polytheism, 65–67
Greenstein, George, 26
Gutiérrez, Gustavo,
267–68

H

Habakkuk, prophet, 37, 252
Hadot, Pierre, 236
Hall, A. R., 227
Hamlet, 138
Hank the Cowdog (Erickson), 96
Harries, Karsten, 173
heart (*kardia*),
  Greek word for, 62,
  biblical meaning of, 62
Heathenry, 67
Hegel, G. W. F., and Hegelian evolutionary worldview, 115–18, 124, 208, 240, 266
Heidegger, Martin, 235
Heraclitus, 68
Herder, Johann Gottfried, 84
hermeneutics of suspicion, 186–87, 216
Hesse, Hermann, 65
Hinduism, 64, 127
historicism, 116, 124–25, 208
  as self-refuting, 116
homosexual behavior, 41
Horgan, John, 47
"horrid doubt," Darwin's, 194–95
human rights, 95, 101, 136, 224–26, 249
humanism, 229–34
Hume, David, 73, 76, 223
Humphrey, Nicholas, 106
Huxley, Aldous, 135

I

idealism, philosophy of,
  definition of, 82–83, 167
  Hegelian, 115–17
  Kantian, 81–83
  neo-Platonic, 114–15, 130, 213
  Romantic, 112–15
identity politics, 117
idols and idolatry
  community, idol of, 117–23, 209–12
  definition of, 42–43, 85–86, 256
  as deification of something in creation, 35, 42–44, 61, 82–83, 83–85, 113, 115–16, 135, 137, 150, 187, 256
  as God substitutes, 35–37, 61–62, 79–81
  good gifts of God as, 37–38
  of the heart, 61–62
  as human inventions, 124
  identifying, 42–44, 60–63
  imagination, idol of, 83–85
  matter, idol of, 43, 45, 46–48, 70–72, 104–5, 109–11, 165–67, 190–92
  mind, idol of, 81–83
  personhood and, 29
  reason, idol of, 43–44, 61
  reductionism, as consequence of, 44–45, 98–101
  self-referential absurdity of, 48–49
  senses, idol of, 72–74
  testing of, 46–49
  unmasking of, 135–36
The Illusion of Conscious Will (Wegner), 107
image of God and image of an idol, 30, 44–45, 49, 51, 57–58, 89, 98, 101, 105, 138, 165, 187, 189, 197–98, 202, 209, 215, 222, 223, 224, 225, 256
imagination, idol of, 83–85
impressionism, 260–62
Islam, 129–33

J

Jacobs, Alan, 84, 201, 204
Jeremiah, prophet, 29
John, the Baptist, 15–16
Johnson, Thomas K., 34, 138, 150, 224
Joshua, 35
just-war doctrine, 95

K

Kaiser, Christopher, 197
Kandinsky, Wassily, 263
Kant, Immanuel, 81–83, 118, 122, 159–60
Kant's Copernican revolution, 82
kardia, Greek word for heart, 62
Kauffman, Stuart, 239
Keller, Timothy, 61
Kenny, Anthony, 83
kin altruism, 101
Kinnaman, David, 58
Kline, Morris, 198
knowledge, moral responsibility for, 33–34
Koran (that which is recited), 132
Koukl, Greg, 182

L

L'Abri ministry, Switzerland, 23, 56–57, 146–47, 247
language games, 199–200
Latour, Bruno, 206
"The Law of Life" (London), 259
leap of faith, secular, 155
Lennox, John, 196
Lentricchia, Frank, 205–6
Letham, Robert, 131–32
Lewis, C. S., 22, 32–33, 131, 191, 241, 246, 269
Li Po, 127
liar's paradox, 193
liberation theology, 267–68
literary criticism, postmodern, 205–6
literary naturalism, 259–60
The Little Book of Atheist Spirituality (Comte-Sponville), 236
logical positivism, 184–85
London, Jack, 259
love
  Christian view of, 243
  reductionist view of, 100
Luther, Martin, 37, 145–46
Lynn, Barry, 253
Lyotard, Jean-François, 199–200, 203

M

Mach, Ernst, 76
Malik, Kenan, 196
Mars Hill, Paul's speech, 90–91
Marx, Karl, 96
Marxism, 72, 185–86, 205
Maslow, Abraham, 55
materialists and materialism
  abstract art and, 263–64
  Christian response to, 87, 213–14
  definition of, 70–72
  eliminative materialism, 106–8
  as idol, 43, 45–49, 70–72, 104–5, 108, 165–66
  pantheism and, 128–29
  as philosophical family, 51–52
  physicalism and, 70–71
  reductionism and, 104–5, 122, 146
  as religion or faith, 71
  self-referential absurdity of, 190–92
mathematical order in nature, 198
The Matrix (movie), 76
matter, idol of, 43, 45–49, 70–72, 104–5, 108, 165–66
maya (illusion), 127
McGinn, Colin, 109, 160–61
mechanistic worldview (world as machine), 45, 46, 47, 107, 112, 142, 144, 146, 157, 159, 162, 164–65, 243, 260, 263
meditation, Eastern, 127
metanoia, Greek word for repentance, 40
Middelmann, Udo, 132
Midgley, Mary, 227
Mill, John Stuart, 75–76
Miłosz, Czesław, 181
mind (*nous*), Greek word for, 39–40
mind, idol of, 81–83, 113, 167
Mind and Cosmos (Nagel), 230
Minsky, Marvin, 153–54
"Missa Charles Darwin" (Brown), 238
missionary training, apologetics as, 250
Mitchell, Deborah, 141–42
modernism, 79, 124, 210
Monet, Claude, 261
monotheism, 130
Moore, Lecrae, 272–75
morality, 64–66, 100–101, 184
  emotivism, 184–85
  relativism, moral, 19, 221–22
  religions without morality, 64–66
  skepticism, moral, 100–101
Moreland, J. P., 141
multiculturalism, 117
mysticism, secular, 160–61

N

Nagel, Thomas, 194, 229–31
Nasr, Seyyed Hossein, 130
Native American religions, 67
naturalism and naturalistic, 26, 71, 156, 158, 192, 228, 259–60
nature
  as idol, 68
  laws of, 95, 227–28
  mathematical order in, 198
Nazism, 133–35
neo-orthodoxy, 266
neo-Platonism, 114–15, 130, 213

neuroscience, reductionism and, 47, 100, 107–8, 111, 146, 183, 233–34
New Atheists, 43, 60, 70, 157
Nietzsche, Friedrich, 17, 94–96, 119–20, 186, 199, 225
nirvana (to become extinguished), 127
noetic effects of sin, 121
nous, Greek word for mind, 39–40

O

objective truth, 168, 170
the one and the many, 210–12
ontology, 212
origin of life, 26–28, 174
Origin of Species (Darwin), 238
origin of the universe, 25–26
organic worldview, Romanticism, 112
Orwell, George, 152, 154

P

paganism, 65, 67–68
pantheism, 64, 65, 112, 126–29
Parfit, Derek, 172–73
Passmore, John, 116
Pavlov, Ivan, 51
Penner, Myron, 267
Percy, Walker, 113
performative contradiction, 200
personal, as philosophical term, definition of, 29–30, 144
personal beings and personhood, as evidence for a personal God, 28–30, 129, 131–32
personal God, as explanation for personal beings, 29–30, 32–33, 48, 64, 103, 144, 154, 166
non-personal causes inadequate to explain personal beings, 29–30, 64, 115, 128–29
Peter, Apostle, 244, 251
Philosophical Counseling, 235
Philosophy as a Way of Life (Hadot), 236
physicalism, 70–72
Pilgrim's Regress (Lewis), 246
Pinker, Steven, 193
Plantinga, Alvin, 22, 82, 189, 215
Plato, 69–70, 77, 114, 215
Plato, Not Prozac! (Lou), 235
"Plunder the Egyptians," 90
political correctness, 117, 120–23, 206–7
polytheism, 36, 67, 68
Popper, Karl, 79
The Postmodern Condition (Lyotard), 203
postmodern theology, 267–68
postmodernism
 artistic expressions of, 264–65
 Christian response to, 120, 123–26, 169–71, 175, 203, 207, 209–12, 216–17
 coercive consequences, 204–7
 death of God and, 202
 "death of the author," 201
 diversity, 204–7
 dualism of, 170–72
 evolution and, 124, 208
 historical development of, 112, 117–20
 idol of community, 117–23, 126, 199, 200, 209–12
 imperialistic, 205–7
 individuality, denial of, 126–29, 199, 201–2
 language games, 199–200
 political correctness and, 120–23, 206–7
 "prison house of language," 199–200, 268
 reductionism and, 117–20, 121, 122, 123–24
 science, view of, 119–20
 self, dissolution of, 119, 208–9
 as self-contradictory, 123–24, 168–69, 200, 201–2, 208
 self-referential absurdity of, 199–200, 203–4
 theology, postmodern, 124, 267–68
 totalitarianism, as response to, 202–4
Trinity, as answer to, 209–12
truth as a social construction, 119, 121, 123–24, 168, 169

Powlison, David, 37
predestination, 145–46
"prison house of language," 199–200, 268
process theology, 267
Provine, William, 246
Pythagoras, 68–69

R

Randall, John Herman, 80, 112, 116
rationalism
 Christian response to, 49, 87, 215–16
 cubism as expression of, 262–63
 Descartes and, 78, 80–81
 history of, 77–81
 as idol (of reason), 43–44, 61
Rauschenberg, Robert, 265
Reach Records, 272, 275
reasoned, (*dialegomai*)
 Greek word for, 90
reciprocal altruism, 100
reductionism
 behavioral effect of, 101–3
 Chesterton on, 137
 Darwinian evolution as source of, 229–34
 definition of, 44–45, 98–100
 dehumanizing impact of, 99–101, 121–22, 135, 138, 142, 164–65, 166, 175, 256
 idolatry as source of 98–99
 illusory status given to mind, will, self, consciousness, 73, 104, 106–8, 110, 127–28, 150–52, 156, 160, 176, 194
 Islam and, 129–33
 materialism and, 104–5, 122, 146, 190–92
 Nagel on, 230–31
 "nothing but," 100–101
 pantheism and, 126–29
 political correctness as consequence, 120–23
 postmodernism and, 117–20, 121, 122, 123–24
 self-referential absurdity as consequence, 48–49, 183, 185–88
 as suppression of evidence from general revelation, 32–33, 103–5, 128, 129, 134, 139, 149–50, 152, 157, 161, 173, 209, 222, 224, 256
 Tallis on, 232–34
Reid, Thomas, 110
relativists and relativism, 19, 49, 221–22, 243–44
religion
 atheist forms of, 64
 amoral forms of, 64–66
 Eastern religions, 64, 114, 126–29, 263
 generic meaning of, 63–64, 66–68
 ritualless forms of, 66
 secular forms of, 71, 235–38
Religion for Atheists (de Botton), 236
repentance (*metanoia*), Greek word for, 40
reverse engineering, 178–79
Rifkin, Jeremy, 239–40
robots, humans reduced to, 142, 146, 150–52, 157, 162, 164, 166
Roman gods, 65–66
Romantics and Romanticism, 83–85, 88–89, 112–15, 117, 167
Rorty, Richard, 101, 124, 125, 170, 225–26
Rothko, Mark, 264
Ruse, Michael, 179, 238
Russell, Bertrand, 237, 245–46

S

sacred/secular divide, 273–74
Sagan, Carl, 71
Sartre, Jean-Paul, 208, 235, 244
Saving Leonardo (Pearcey), 253
Schaeffer, Edith, 247
Schaeffer, Francis, 22, 57, 105, 126
 The God Who Is There, 161
 L'Abri ministry, 23, 56–57, 146–47, 247
 love as the "final apologetic," 212
 mysticism with nobody there, 264
Schopenhauer, Arthur, 112, 126, 167
Schweder, Richard, 133–34
science, Christian origin of, 95, 197–99, 215, 226–28

scientism, 237–38
Scripture, as
  communication from
  God, 125–26, 244–45
Searle, John, 47, 71
secular mysticism, 160–61
secular religion, 63–64, 71,
  235–37
self or sense of personal
  identity, 80–81,
  107–8, 119, 207–9
self-organization theory,
  239
self-referential absurdity
  ("commits suicide")
  Christianity and, 49,
    183
  definition of, 48–49,
    182–85, 257
  evolutionary
    epistemology and,
    192–97
  evolution, 192–94
  Freudianism and, 186
  idols and, 48–49
  Marxism and, 185–86
  materialism and,
    190–92
  Nietzsche and, 186
  postmodernism and,
    199–200, 204
  reductionism, as source
    of, 48–49, 183,
    185–88
  Skinner and, 186
  tacit exemption for own
    views, 116, 188,
    190, 191–92, 197,
    202, 257
Sellars, Wilfrid, 237
senses, idol of, 72–74
Shamanism, 67
Siddhartha, 65
Situation Ethics (Fletcher),
  94
skeptical crisis, 77

skepticism, 194–97,
  222–24, 245
Skinner, B. F., 51, 55, 186
Slingerland, Edward,
  150–51, 162
Smilansky, Saul, 156
sodium chloride, 144, 146
solipsism, 83, 245
sophism, 100
special grace, 30
special revelation, 24
speech codes, 117, 207
spirit of the age (Zeitgeist),
  118, 122, 123
Star Trek (television series),
  73–74, 260
Strawson, Galen, 110,
  148–49
sunyata (Buddhist mystical
  state), 264
"suppress the truth"
  (Romans 1:18), 32
suppressing the evidence
  for God from general
  revelation, 32–33,
  38–39, 48, 53, 103–5,
  111, 128–29, 134,
  137, 139, 149–50,
  152, 157, 161, 173,
  209, 222, 224, 256
studies: why people reject
  Christianity, 58,
  247–48
suffering, as context for
  apologetics, 252
Symons, Arthur, 38

T

tacit exception, as strategy
  for avoiding self-
  referential absurdity,
  116, 188, 190,
  191–92, 197, 202,
  257
Tallis, Raymond, 232–34

Taoism, 64
Taylor, Mark C., 202
Ten Commandments,
  15, 36
Thales, 68
theological liberalism,
  266–69
Thompson, W. R., 238
To Kill a Mockingbird
  (Lee), 250
Tocqueville, Alexis de, 225
Total Truth, 152–53,
  270–71, 272, 273–74
totalitarianism, 136, 203
transcendental ego, Kant,
  82, 112
trigger warnings, 122
Trinity, 130–31, 209–12
truth
  divided concept of,
    104–5, 113,
    151–65, 168–73
  Enlightenment view of,
    78–81, 119, 120,
    126, 133, 207, 210,
    268
  postmodern view of,
    119, 121, 123–24,
    168, 169
  unified concept of,
    139, 152–53, 155,
    166–67, 170–72,
    181, 216, 271
Twain, Mark, 18
Tyson, Neil deGrasse, 71
Tysonism, 71

U

Unashamed movement,
  275
unity of truth, 139,
  152–53, 155, 166–67,
  170–72, 181, 216,
  271
universe, origin of, 25–26

"The Unreasonable Effectiveness of Mathematics in the Natural Sciences" (Wigner), 198

V

visual arts
   abstract art, 263–64
   cubism, 262–63
   impressionism, 260–62
   postmodernism 264–65

W

Watson, James, 174
Wegner, Daniel, 107
What Is Thought? (Baum), 160
What Science Offers the Humanities (Slingerland), 150
Wicca, 67–68
Wichterman, Bill, 21–22
Wieseltier, Leon, 194
Wigner, Eugene, 198
Willard, Dallas, 71, 122, 168, 270
willful blindness, 33–35
Wilson, E. O., 70
"without excuse" (Romans 1:20, 2:1), 53, 172
   Greek meaning of, 163
Wolters, Albert, 58
Wordsworth, William, 84
"wrath of God" (Romans 1:18), 137
"written on their hearts" (Romans 2:15), 221–22

X

Xenophanes, 65–66

Y

Yeats, William Butler, 84
You Lost Me (Kinnaman), 58

Z

Zacharias, Ravi, 250, 265
Zeitgeist, 118, 122
Zizek, Slavoj, 211